KENJIRO HATA

VOLUME 10

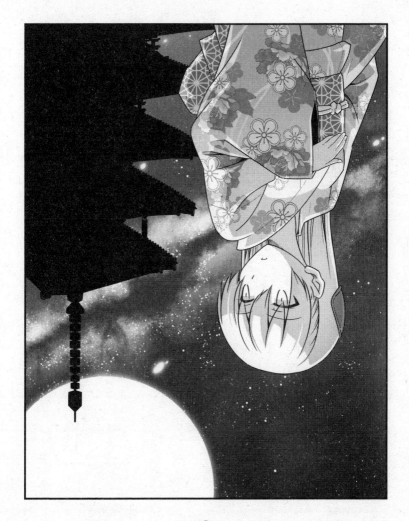

FLY ME TO THE MOON

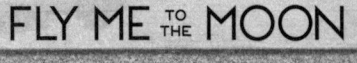

FLY ME TO THE MOON

Contents

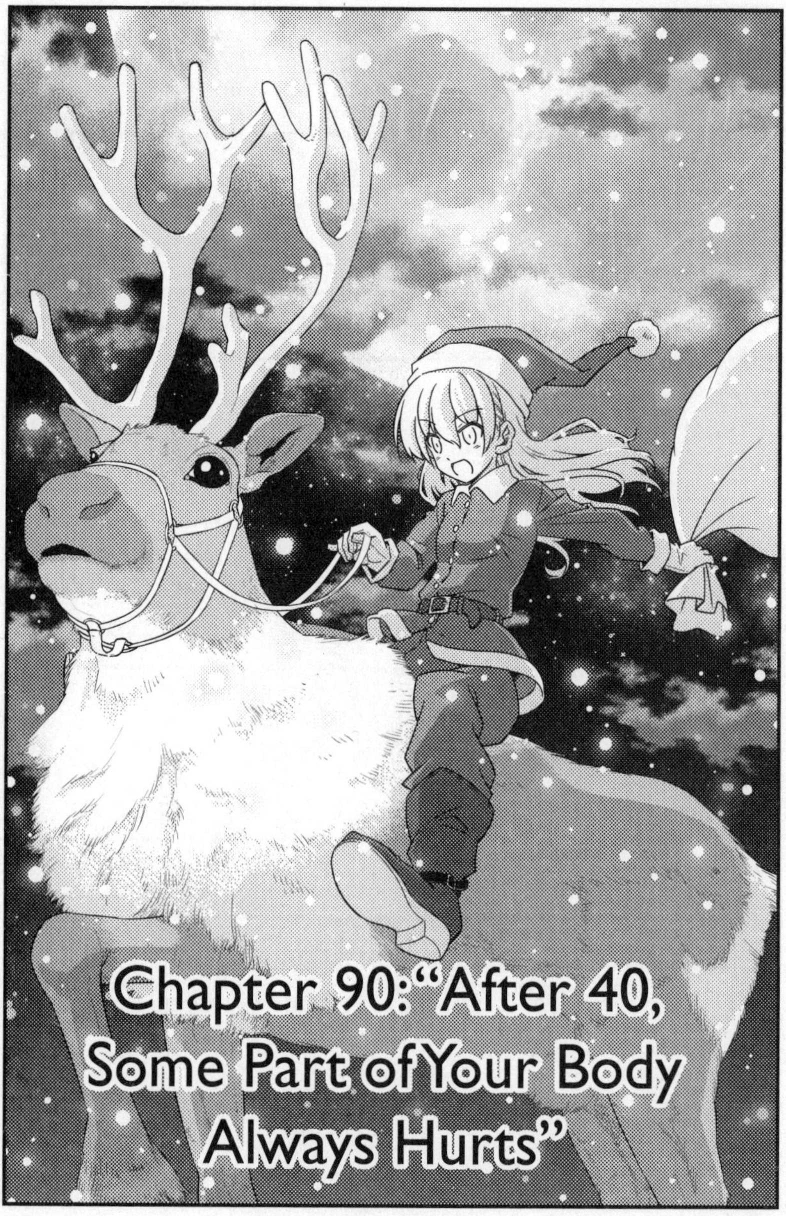
Chapter 90: "After 40, Some Part of Your Body Always Hurts"

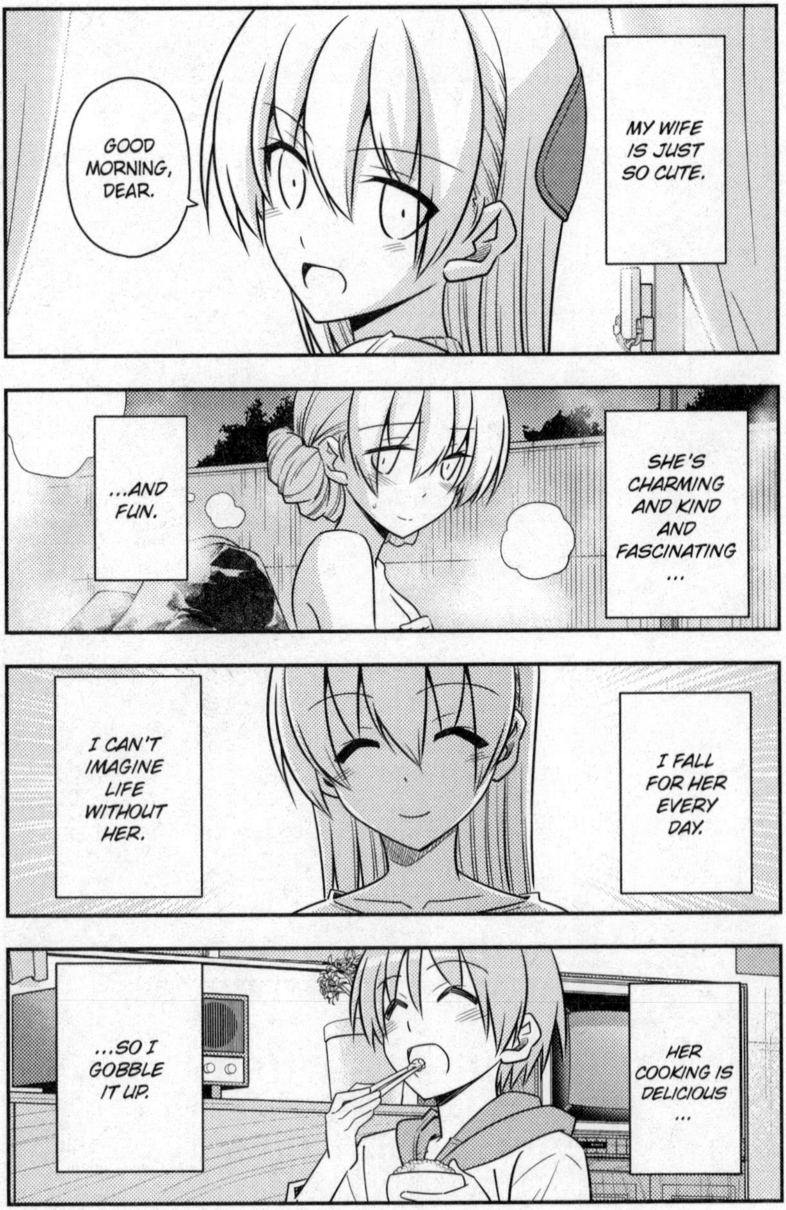
MY WIFE IS JUST SO CUTE.
GOOD MORNING, DEAR.
SHE'S CHARMING AND KIND AND FASCINATING ...
...AND FUN.
I FALL FOR HER EVERY DAY.
I CAN'T IMAGINE LIFE WITHOUT HER.
HER COOKING IS DELICIOUS ...
...SO I GOBBLE IT UP.

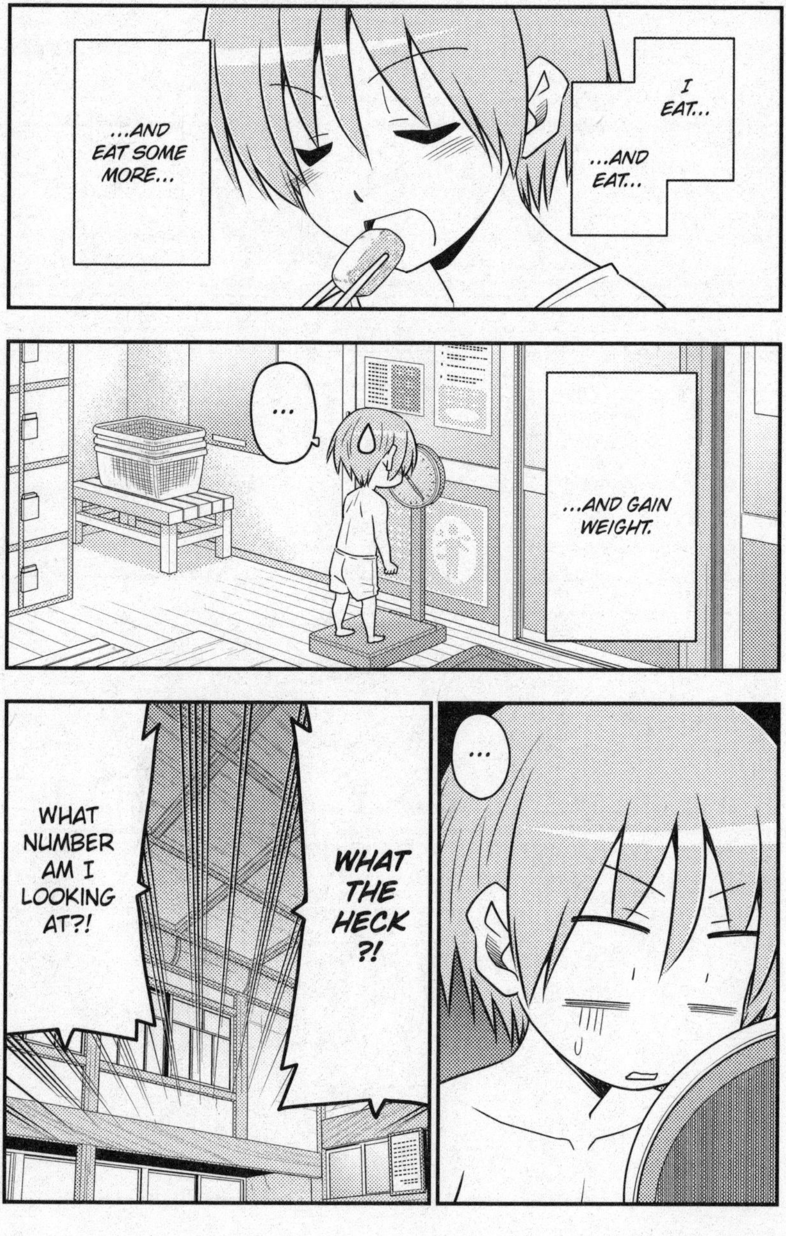
I EAT...
...AND EAT...
...AND EAT SOME MORE...
...AND GAIN WEIGHT.
...
...
WHAT THE HECK ?!
WHAT NUMBER AM I LOOKING AT?!

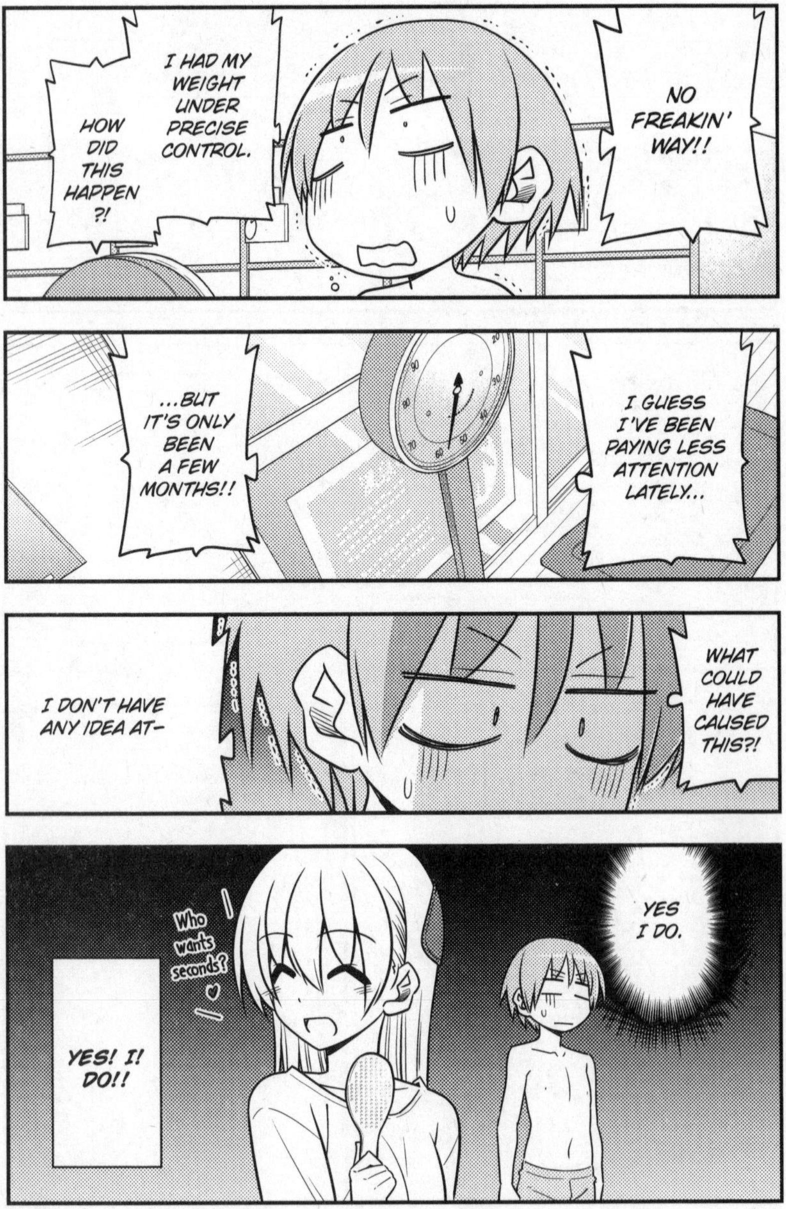
NO FREAKIN' WAY!!
I HAD MY WEIGHT UNDER PRECISE CONTROL.
HOW DID THIS HAPPEN?!
I GUESS I'VE BEEN PAYING LESS ATTENTION LATELY...
...BUT IT'S ONLY BEEN A FEW MONTHS!!
WHAT COULD HAVE CAUSED THIS?!
I DON'T HAVE ANY IDEA AT-
YES I DO.
Who wants seconds? ♥
YES! I! DO!!

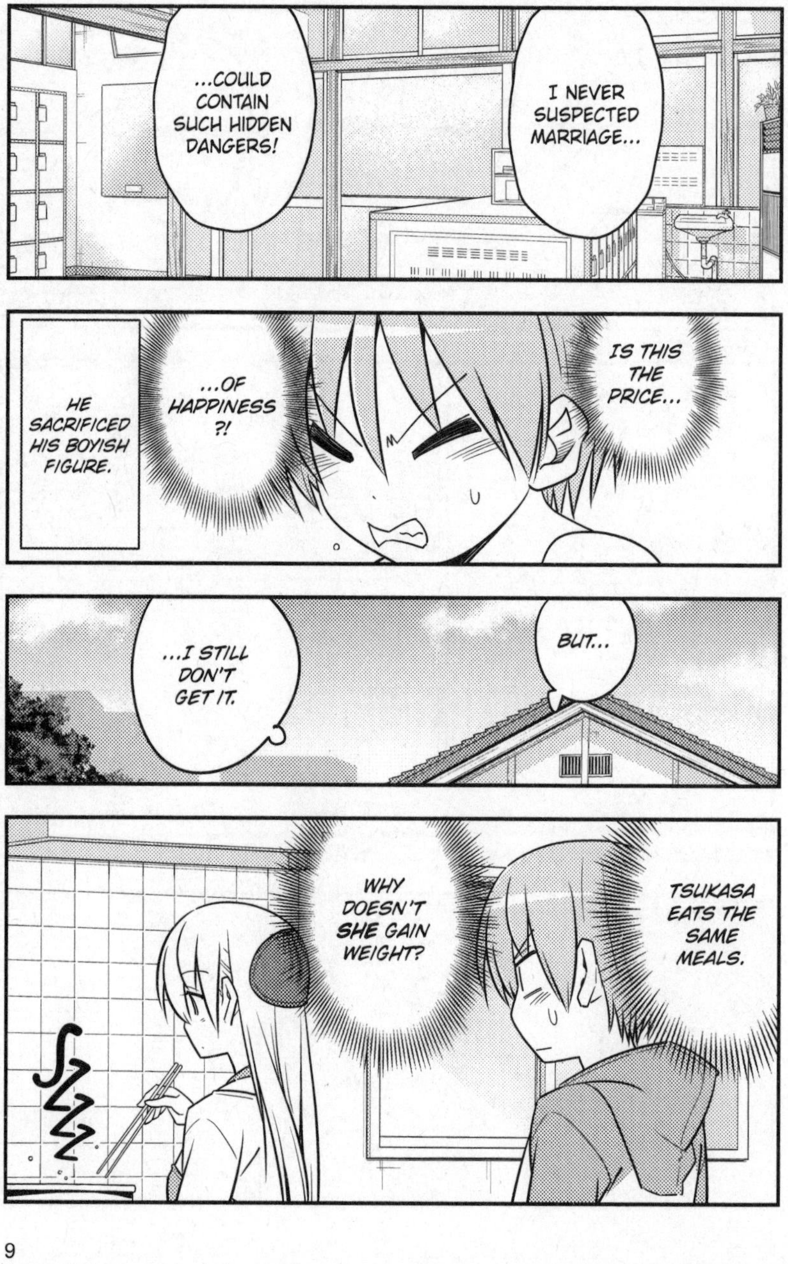
I NEVER SUSPECTED MARRIAGE...
...COULD CONTAIN SUCH HIDDEN DANGERS!
IS THIS THE PRICE...
...OF HAPPINESS ?!
HE SACRIFICED HIS BOYISH FIGURE.
BUT...
...I STILL DON'T GET IT.
TSUKASA EATS THE SAME MEALS.
WHY DOESN'T SHE GAIN WEIGHT?
SIZZ

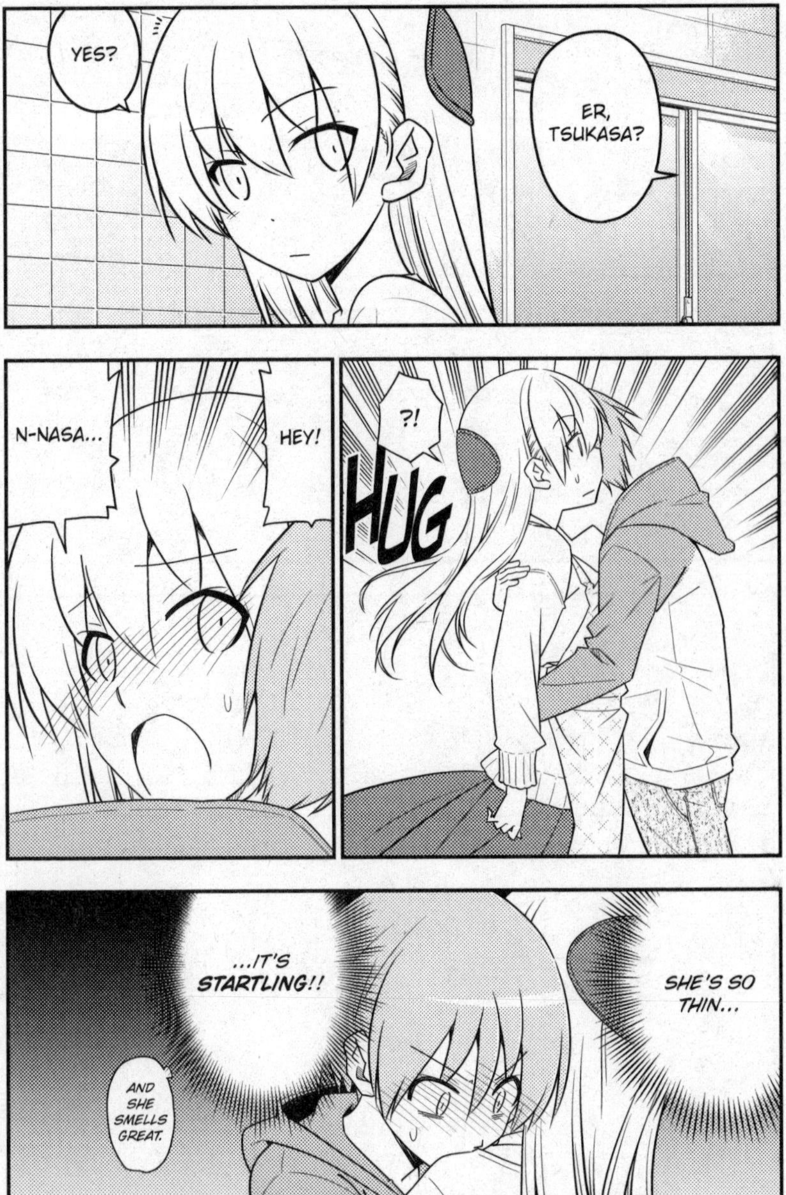
ER, TSUKASA?
YES?
?!
HUG
HEY!
N-NASA...
SHE'S SO THIN...
...IT'S STARTLING!!
AND SHE SMELLS GREAT.

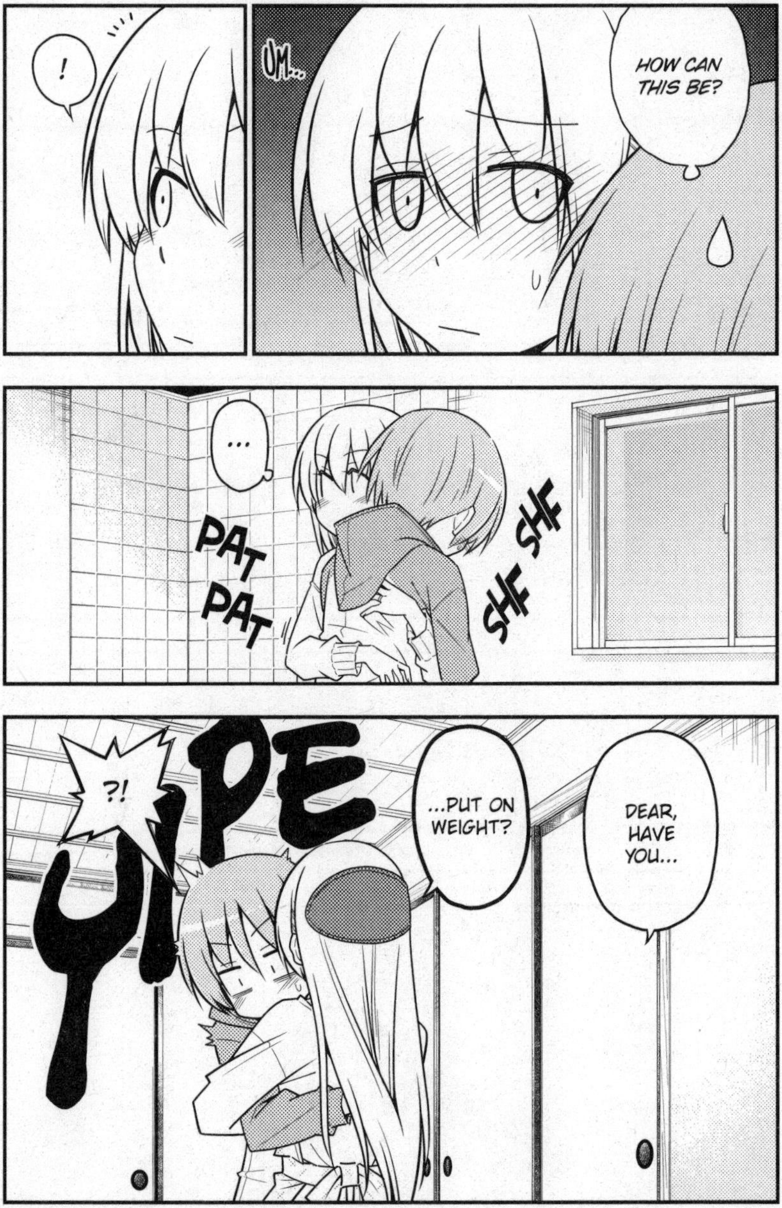
HOW CAN THIS BE?
UM...
!
...
SHF SHF
PAT PAT
DEAR, HAVE YOU...
...PUT ON WEIGHT?
YIPE
?!

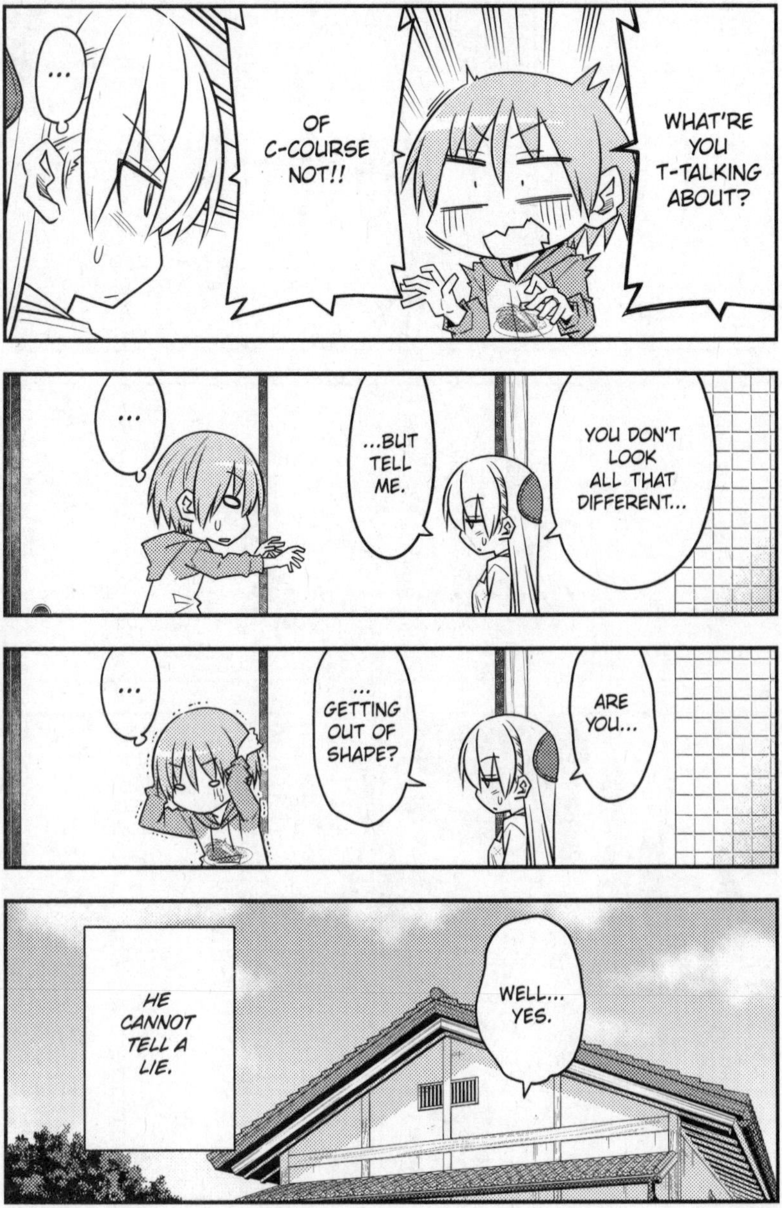
WHAT'RE YOU T-TALKING ABOUT?
OF C-COURSE NOT!!
...
YOU DON'T LOOK ALL THAT DIFFERENT...
...BUT TELL ME.
...
ARE YOU...
... GETTING OUT OF SHAPE?
...
WELL... YES.
HE CANNOT TELL A LIE.

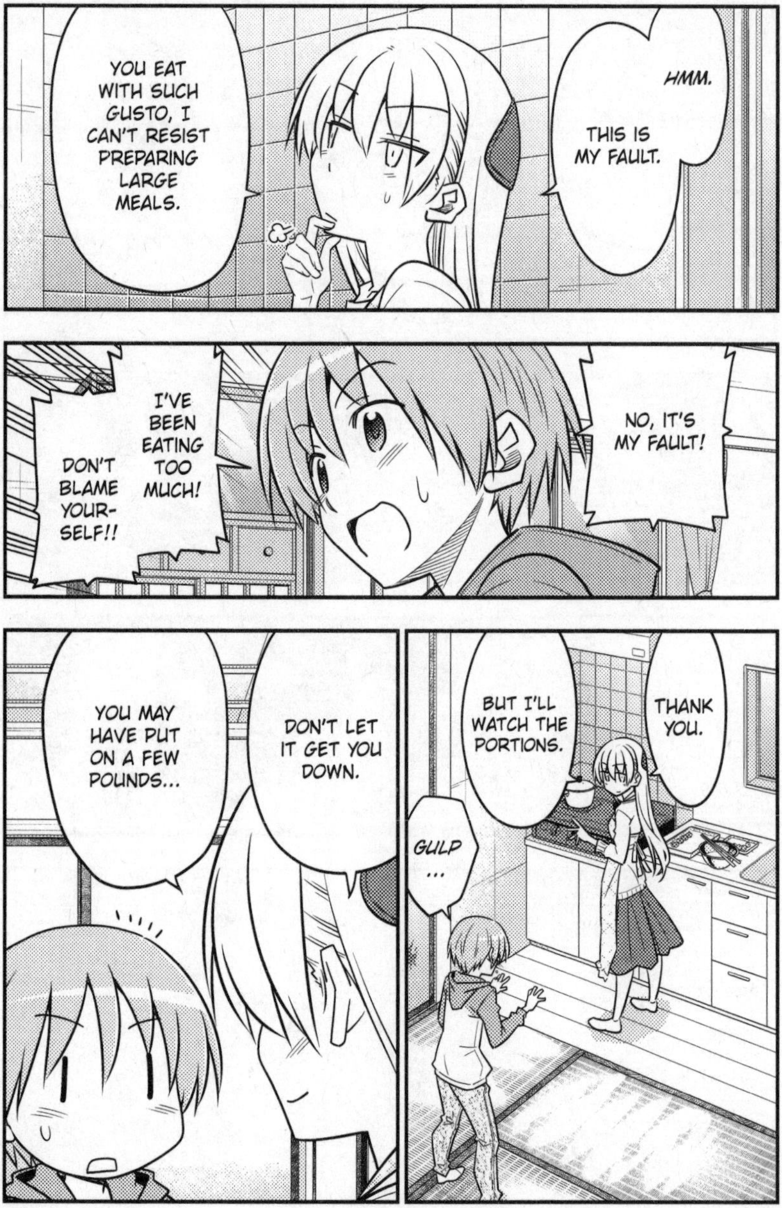
HMM.
THIS IS MY FAULT.
YOU EAT WITH SUCH GUSTO, I CAN'T RESIST PREPARING LARGE MEALS.
NO, IT'S MY FAULT!
I'VE BEEN EATING TOO MUCH!
DON'T BLAME YOURSELF!!
THANK YOU.
BUT I'LL WATCH THE PORTIONS.
GULP ...
DON'T LET IT GET YOU DOWN.
YOU MAY HAVE PUT ON A FEW POUNDS...

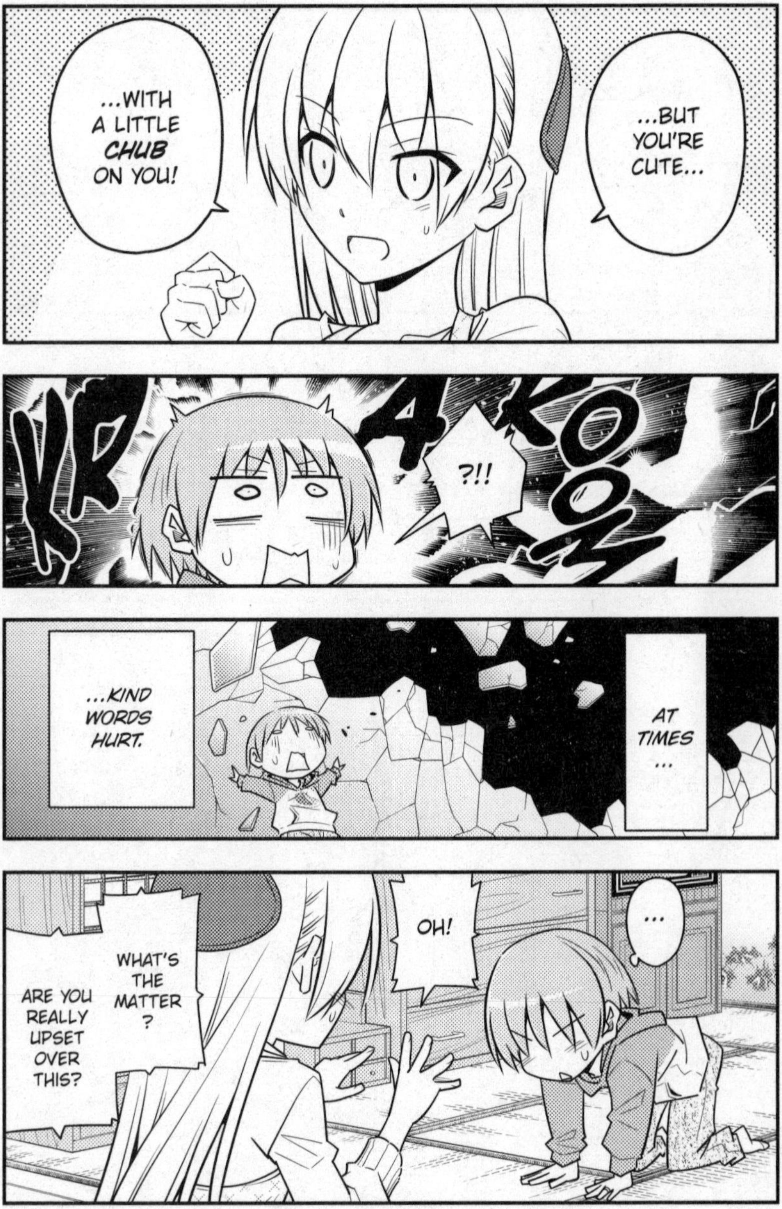
...BUT YOU'RE CUTE...
...WITH A LITTLE CHUB ON YOU!
KRAKOOM
?!!
AT TIMES ...
...KIND WORDS HURT.
...
OH!
WHAT'S THE MATTER ?
ARE YOU REALLY UPSET OVER THIS?

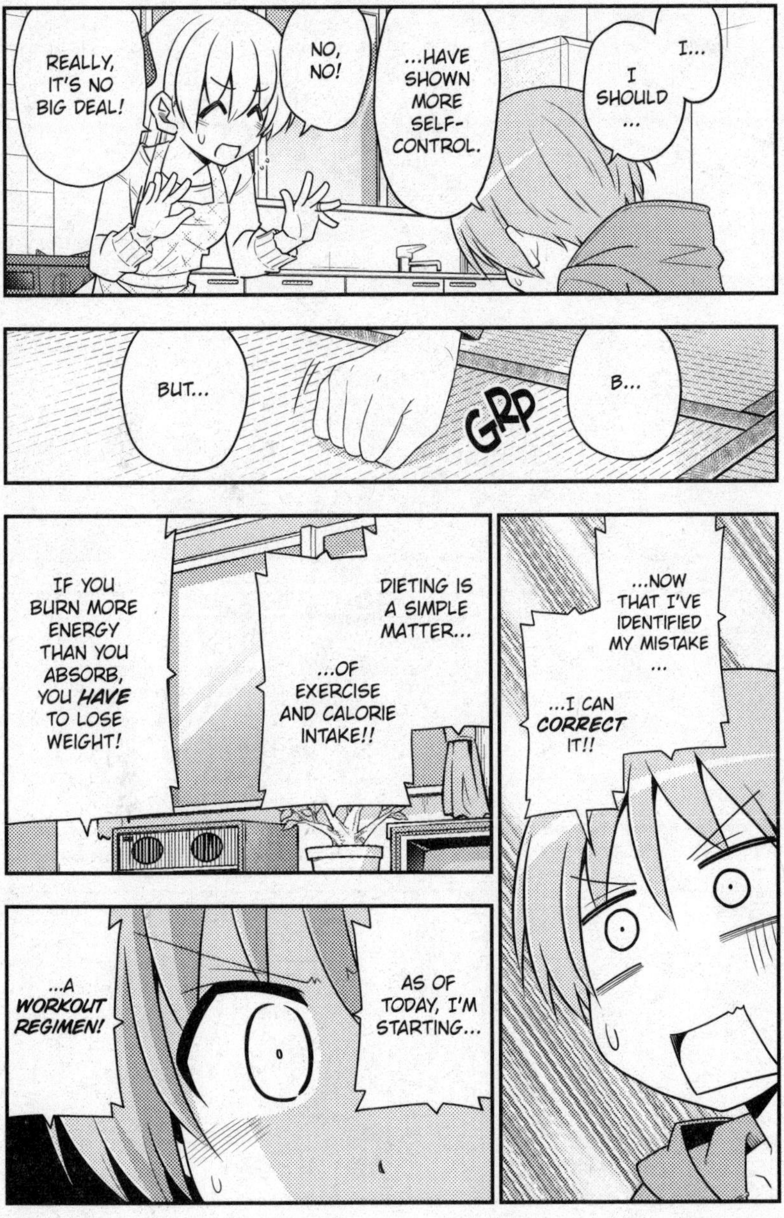
I...
I SHOULD ...
...HAVE SHOWN MORE SELF-CONTROL.
NO, NO!
REALLY, IT'S NO BIG DEAL!
B...
GRP
BUT...
...NOW THAT I'VE IDENTIFIED MY MISTAKE ...
...I CAN *CORRECT* IT!!
DIETING IS A SIMPLE MATTER...
...OF EXERCISE AND CALORIE INTAKE!!
IF YOU BURN MORE ENERGY THAN YOU ABSORB, YOU *HAVE* TO LOSE WEIGHT!
AS OF TODAY, I'M STARTING...
...A *WORKOUT REGIMEN!*

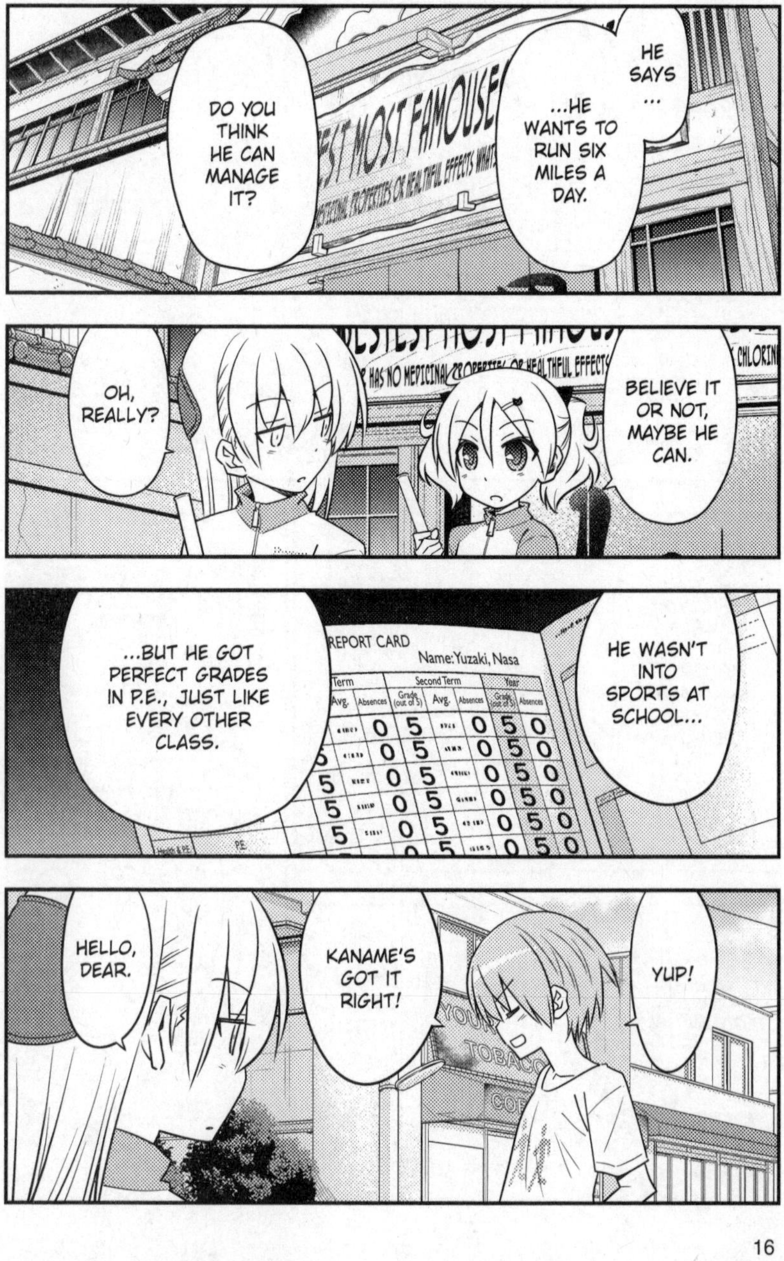
HE SAYS ...
...HE WANTS TO RUN SIX MILES A DAY.
DO YOU THINK HE CAN MANAGE IT?
BELIEVE IT OR NOT, MAYBE HE CAN.
HAS NO MEDICINAL PROPERTIES OR HEALTHFUL EFFECTS
OH, REALLY?
HE WASN'T INTO SPORTS AT SCHOOL...
REPORT CARD
Name: Yuzaki, Nasa
...BUT HE GOT PERFECT GRADES IN P.E., JUST LIKE EVERY OTHER CLASS.
YUP!
KANAME'S GOT IT RIGHT!
HELLO, DEAR.

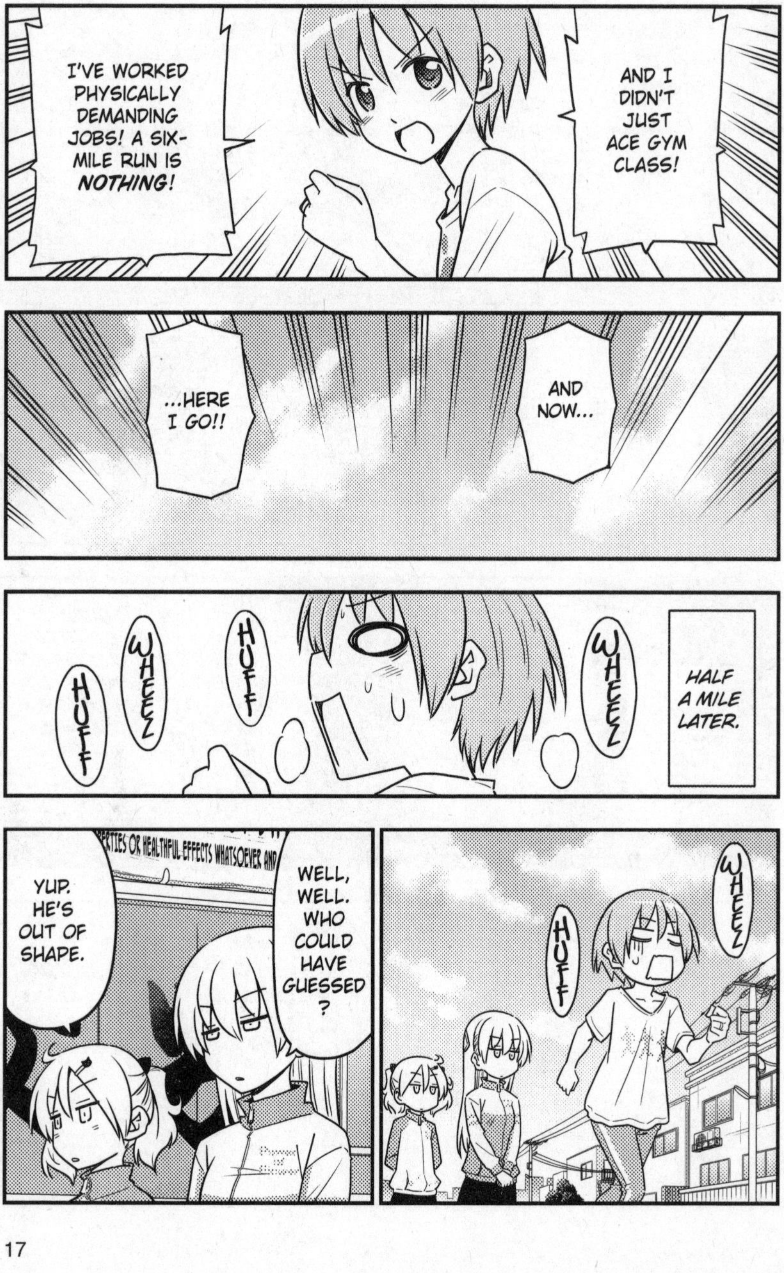
AND I DIDN'T JUST ACE GYM CLASS!
I'VE WORKED PHYSICALLY DEMANDING JOBS! A SIX-MILE RUN IS **NOTHING**!
AND NOW...
...HERE I GO!!
HALF A MILE LATER.
WHEEZ
HUFF
WHEEZ
HUFF
WHEEZ
HUFF
...ERTIES OR HEALTHFUL EFFECTS WHATSOEVER AND...
WELL, WELL. WHO COULD HAVE GUESSED?
YUP. HE'S OUT OF SHAPE.

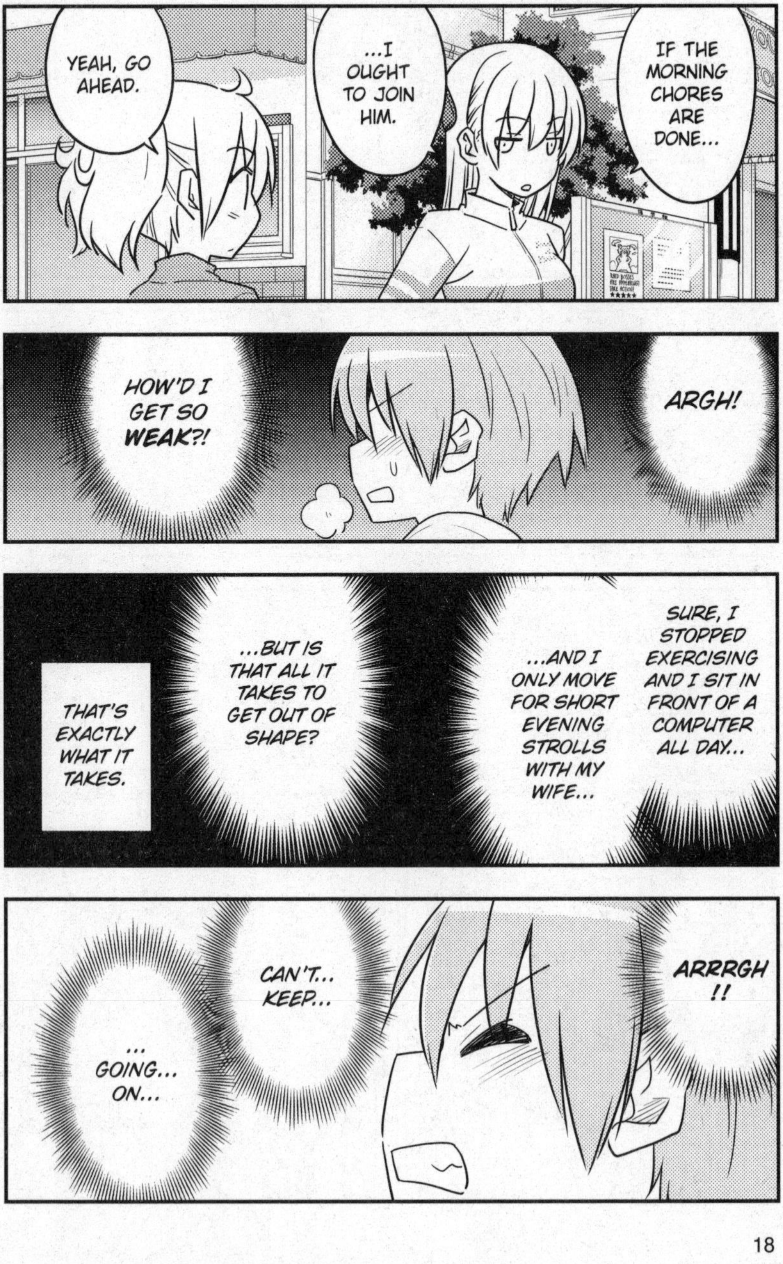
IF THE MORNING CHORES ARE DONE...
...I OUGHT TO JOIN HIM.
YEAH, GO AHEAD.
ARGH!
HOW'D I GET SO WEAK?!
SURE, I STOPPED EXERCISING AND I SIT IN FRONT OF A COMPUTER ALL DAY...
...AND I ONLY MOVE FOR SHORT EVENING STROLLS WITH MY WIFE...
...BUT IS THAT ALL IT TAKES TO GET OUT OF SHAPE?
THAT'S EXACTLY WHAT IT TAKES.
ARRRGH!!
CAN'T... KEEP...
... GOING... ON...

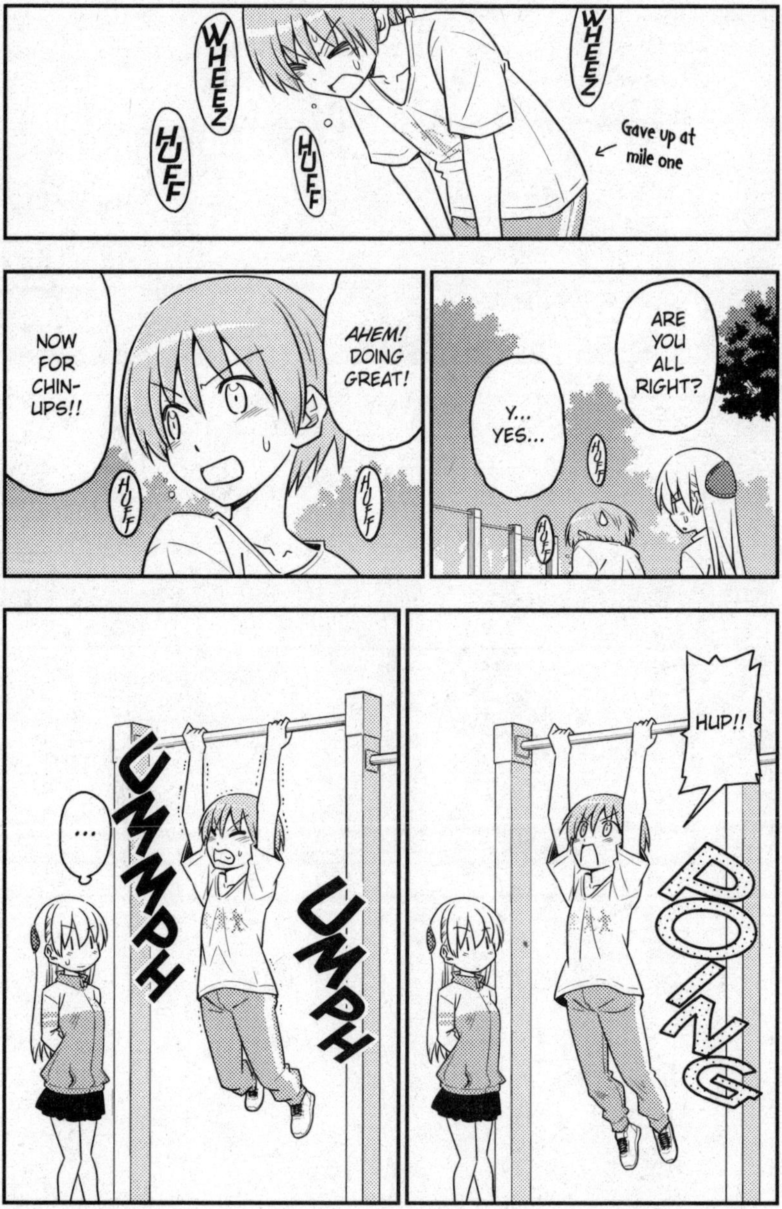
WHEEZ
Gave up at mile one
HUFF
WHEEZ
HUFF
ARE YOU ALL RIGHT?
Y... YES...
HUFF
HUFF
AHEM! DOING GREAT!
HUFF
NOW FOR CHIN-UPS!!
HUP!!
POING
UMPH
UMPH
...

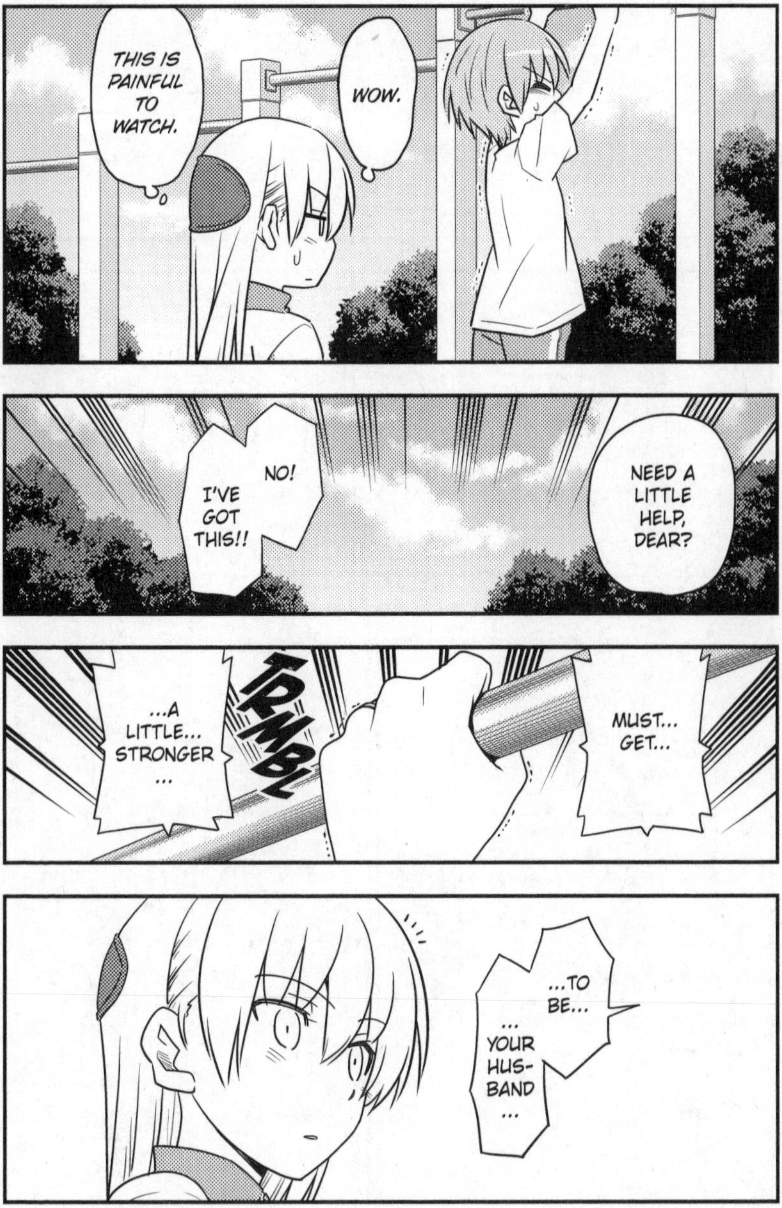
WOW.
THIS IS PAINFUL TO WATCH.
NEED A LITTLE HELP, DEAR?
NO! I'VE GOT THIS!!
MUST... GET...
TRMBL
...A LITTLE... STRONGER ...
...TO BE...
... YOUR HUS-BAND ...

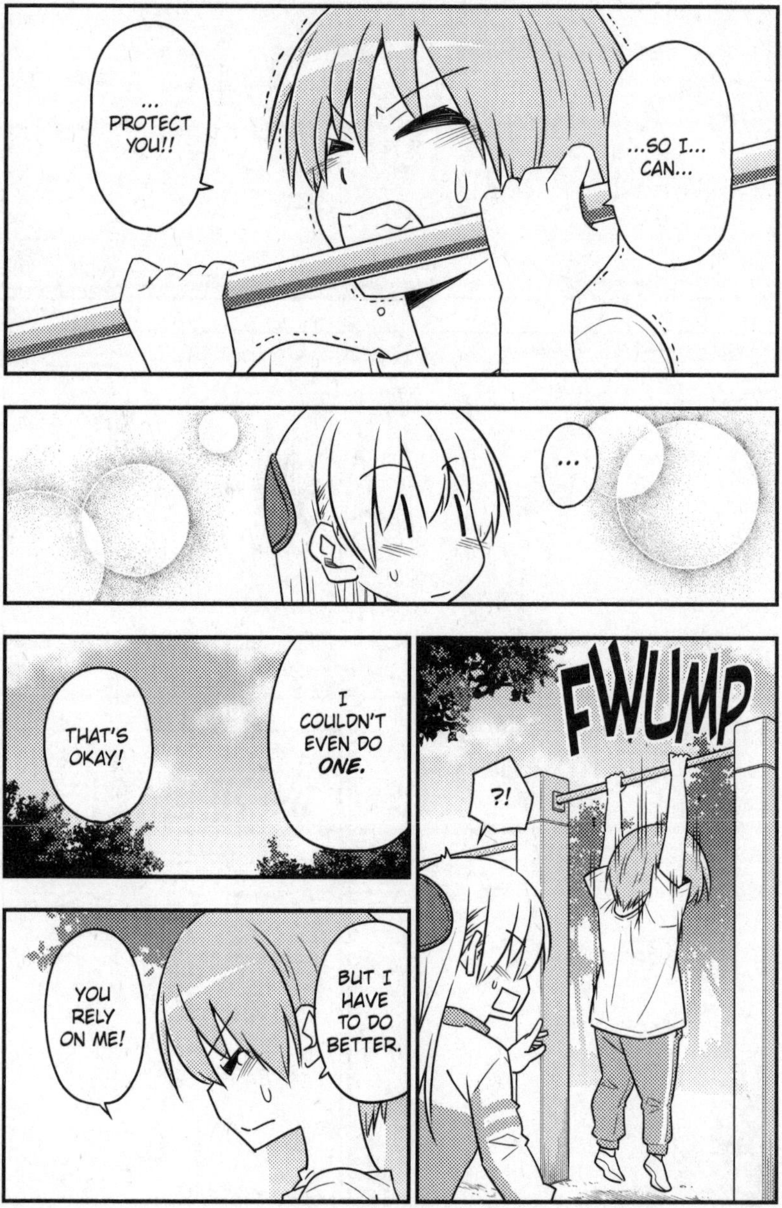
...SO I... CAN...
... PROTECT YOU!!
...
FWUMP
?!
I COULDN'T EVEN DO ONE.
THAT'S OKAY!
BUT I HAVE TO DO BETTER.
YOU RELY ON ME!

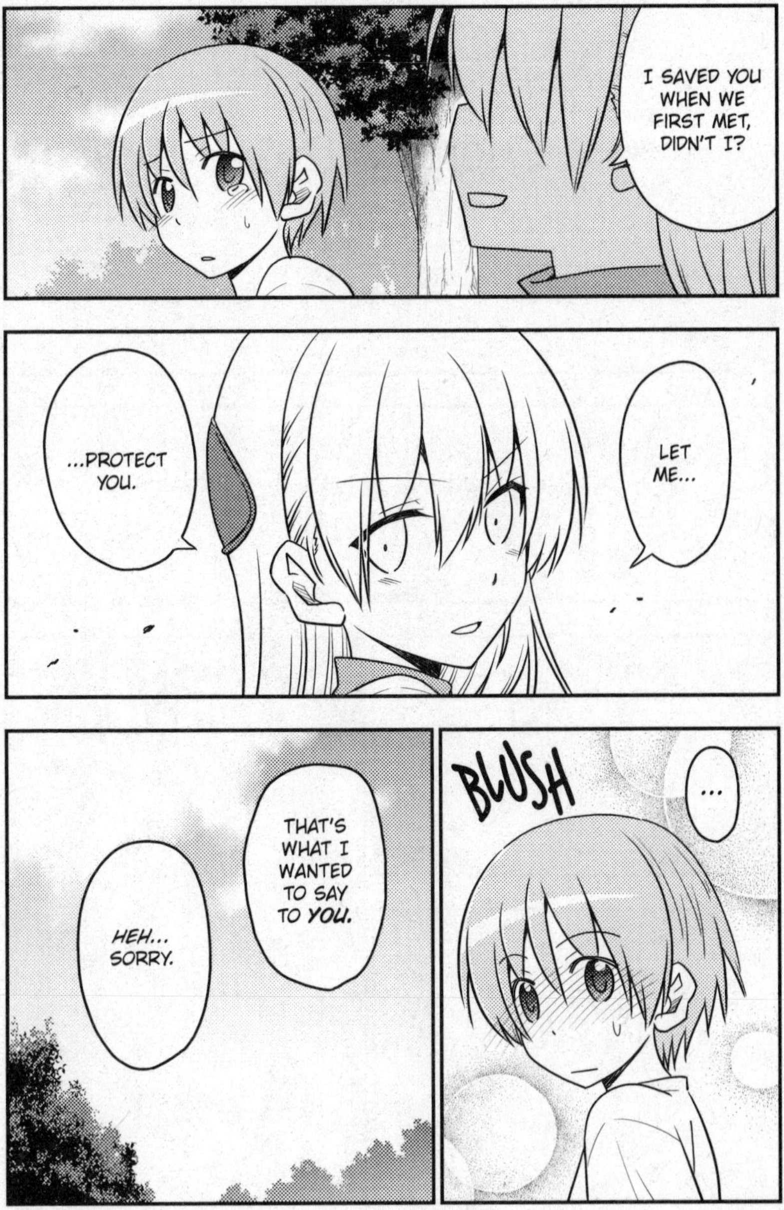
I SAVED YOU WHEN WE FIRST MET, DIDN'T I?
LET ME...
...PROTECT YOU.
BLUSH
...
THAT'S WHAT I WANTED TO SAY TO *YOU.*
HEH... SORRY.

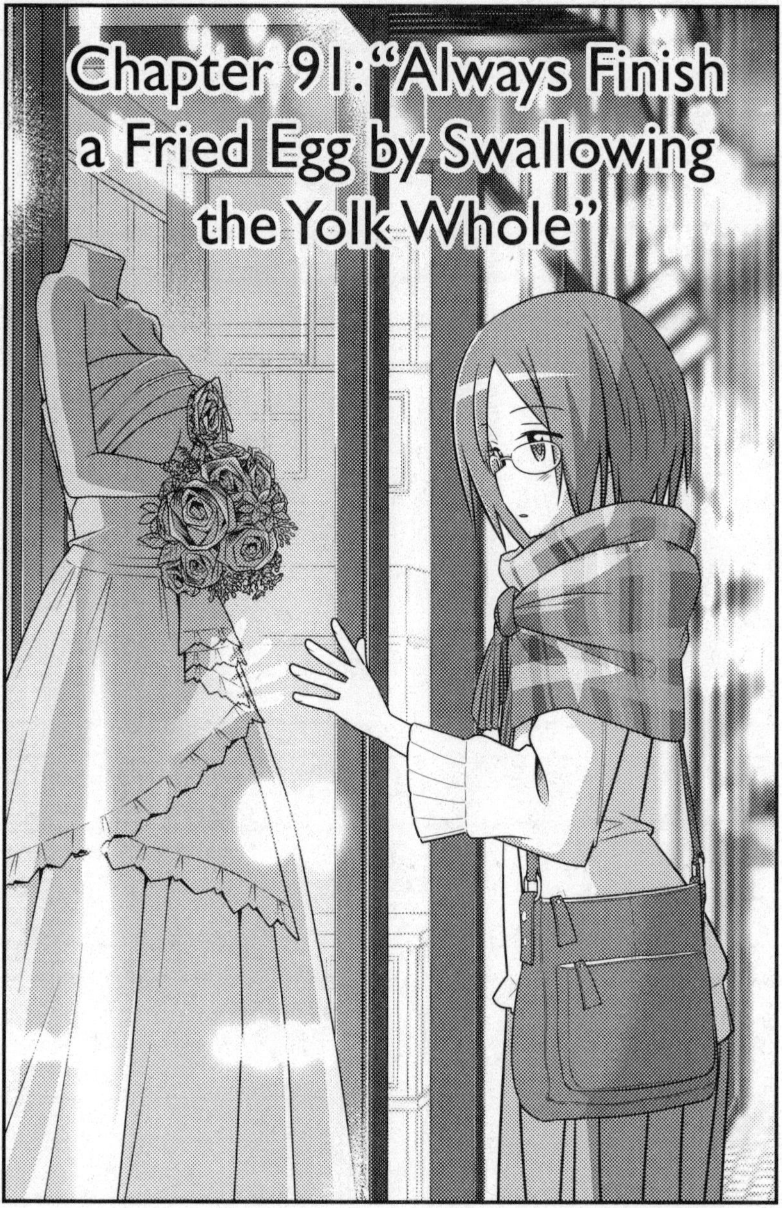
Chapter 91: "Always Finish a Fried Egg by Swallowing the Yolk Whole"

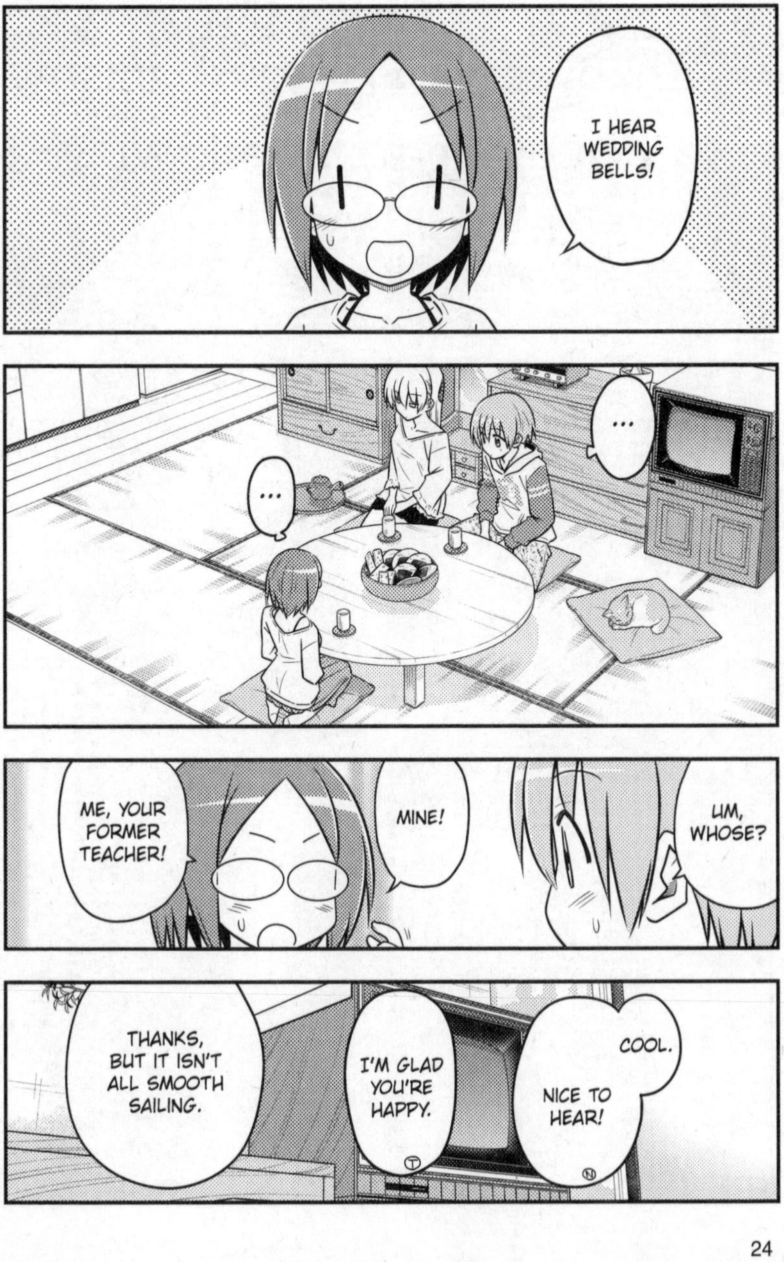
I HEAR WEDDING BELLS!
...
...
UM, WHOSE?
MINE!
ME, YOUR FORMER TEACHER!
COOL.
NICE TO HEAR!
I'M GLAD YOU'RE HAPPY.
THANKS, BUT IT ISN'T ALL SMOOTH SAILING.

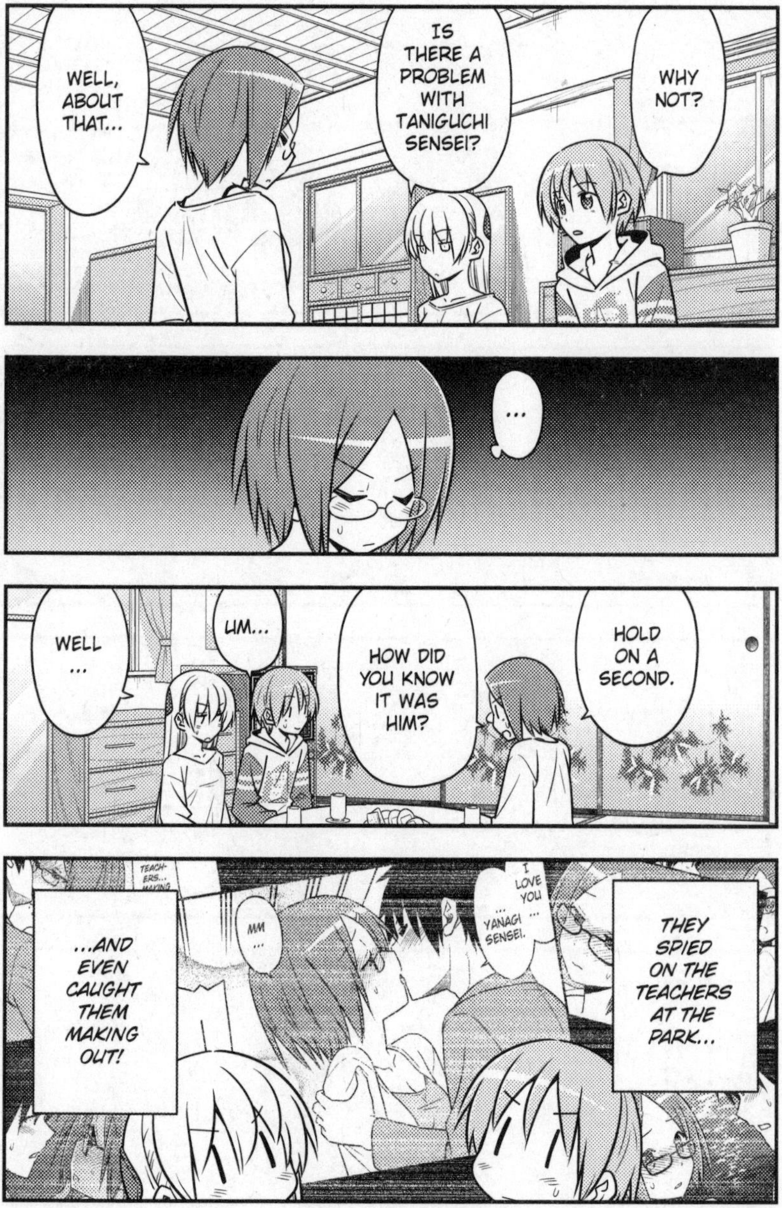
WHY NOT?
IS THERE A PROBLEM WITH TANIGUCHI SENSEI?
WELL, ABOUT THAT...
...
HOLD ON A SECOND.
HOW DID YOU KNOW IT WAS HIM?
UM...
WELL ...
THEY SPIED ON THE TEACHERS AT THE PARK...
I LOVE YOU ... YANAGI SENSEI.
MM ...
TEACHERS... MAKING
...AND EVEN CAUGHT THEM MAKING OUT!

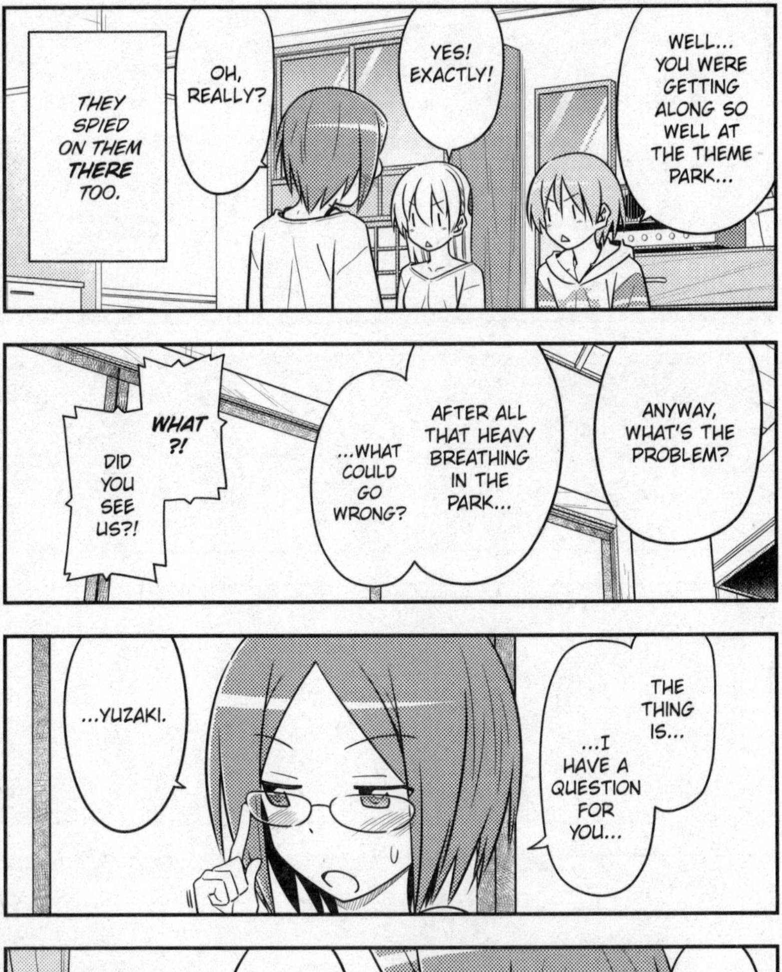
WELL... YOU WERE GETTING ALONG SO WELL AT THE THEME PARK...
YES! EXACTLY!
OH, REALLY?
THEY SPIED ON THEM **THERE** TOO.
ANYWAY, WHAT'S THE PROBLEM?
AFTER ALL THAT HEAVY BREATHING IN THE PARK...
...WHAT COULD GO WRONG?
WHAT ?!
DID YOU SEE US?!
THE THING IS...
...I HAVE A QUESTION FOR YOU...
...YUZAKI.
DID YOU HAVE...
...PRE-WEDDING JITTERS?

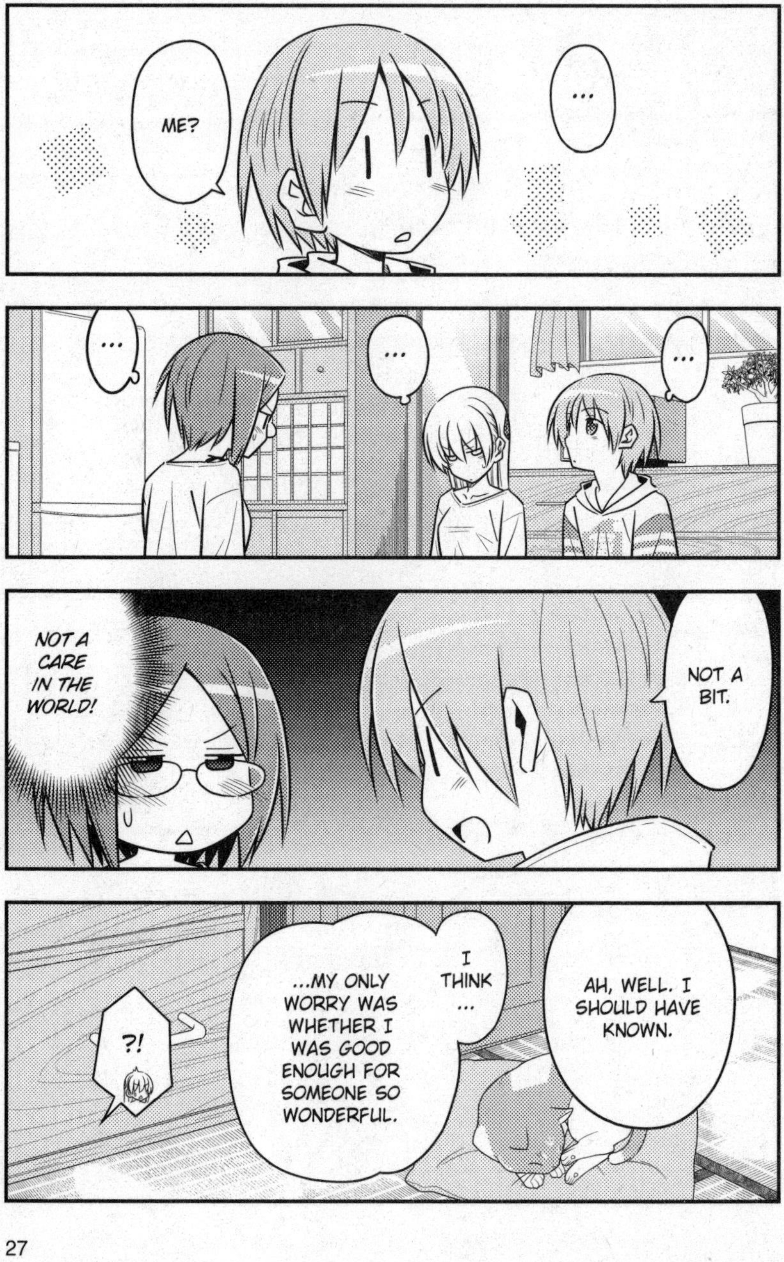
...
ME?
...
...
...
NOT A BIT.
NOT A CARE IN THE WORLD!
AH, WELL. I SHOULD HAVE KNOWN.
I THINK ...
...MY ONLY WORRY WAS WHETHER I WAS GOOD ENOUGH FOR SOMEONE SO WONDERFUL.
?!

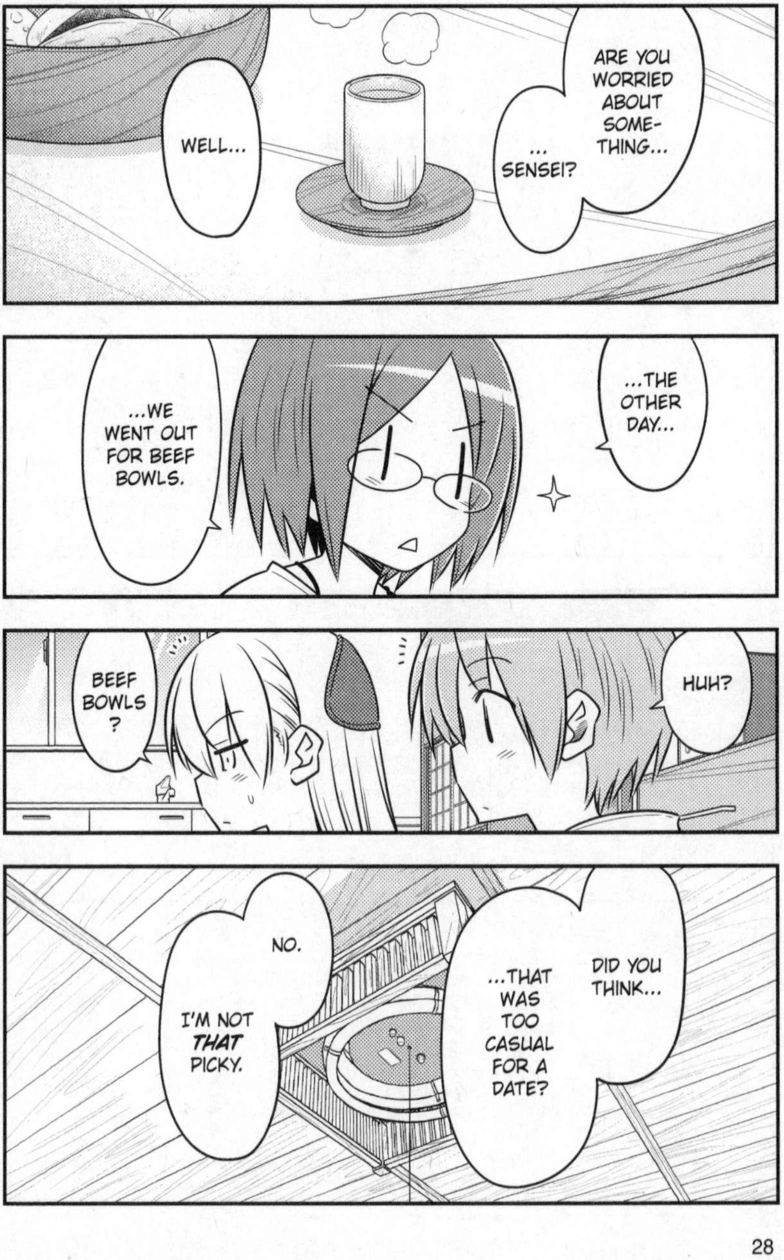
ARE YOU WORRIED ABOUT SOME-THING...
... SENSEI?
WELL...
...THE OTHER DAY...
...WE WENT OUT FOR BEEF BOWLS.
HUH?
BEEF BOWLS?
DID YOU THINK...
...THAT WAS TOO CASUAL FOR A DATE?
NO.
I'M NOT ***THAT*** PICKY.

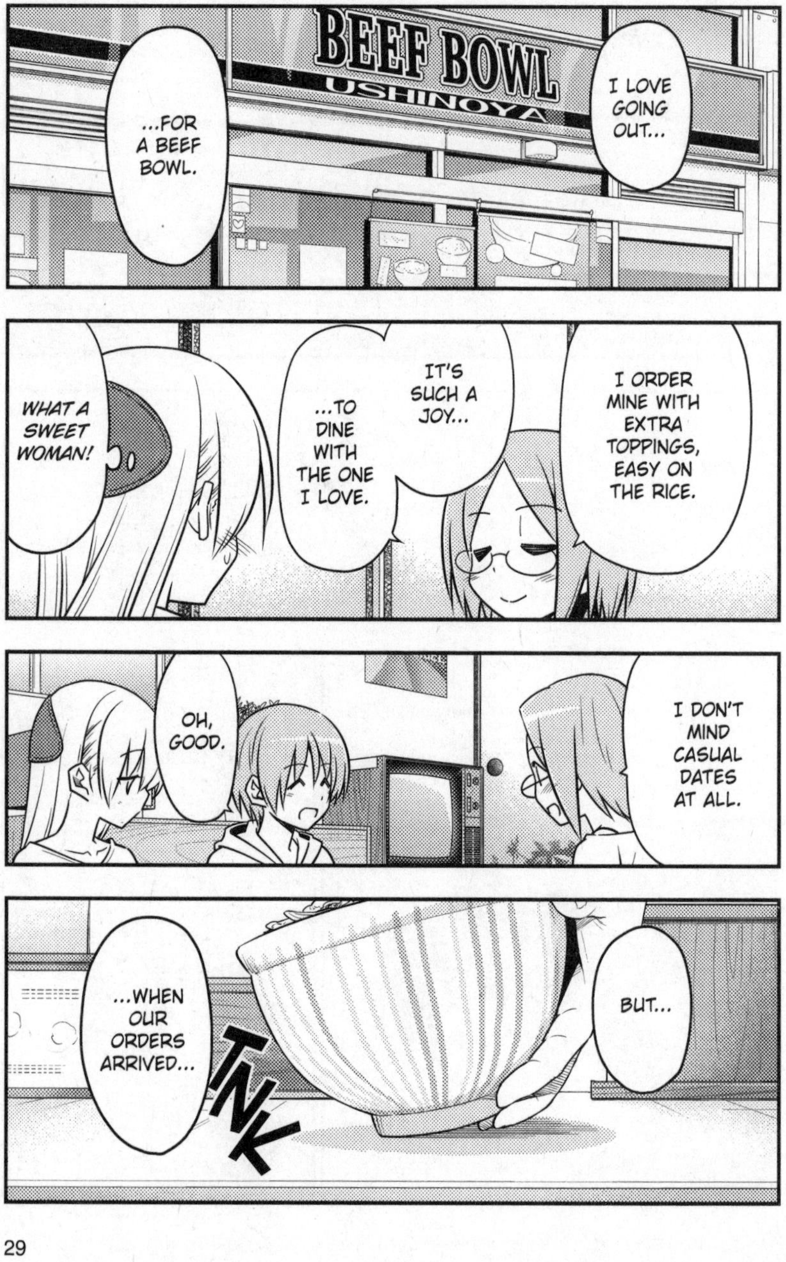
I LOVE GOING OUT...
BEEF BOWL
USHINOYA
...FOR A BEEF BOWL.
I ORDER MINE WITH EXTRA TOPPINGS, EASY ON THE RICE.
IT'S SUCH A JOY...
...TO DINE WITH THE ONE I LOVE.
WHAT A SWEET WOMAN!
I DON'T MIND CASUAL DATES AT ALL.
OH, GOOD.
BUT...
TNK
...WHEN OUR ORDERS ARRIVED...

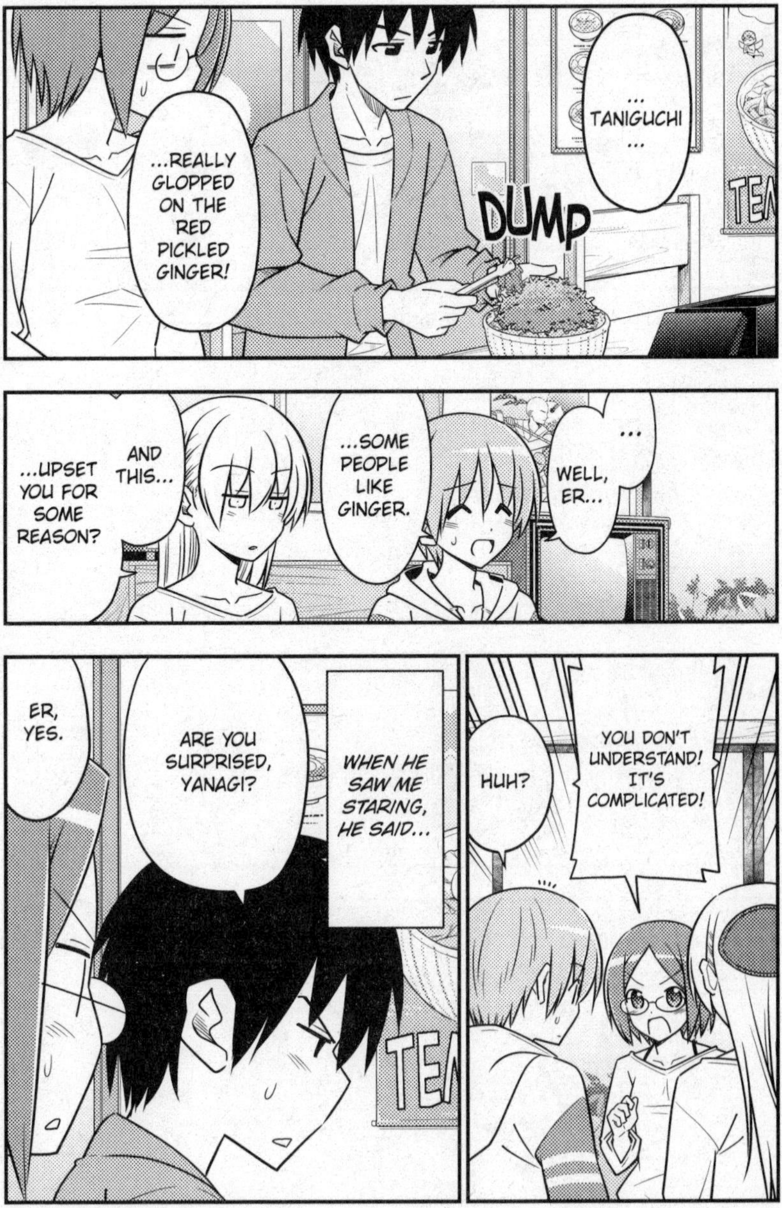

... TANIGUCHI ...
DUMP
...REALLY GLOPPED ON THE RED PICKLED GINGER!
... WELL, ER...
...SOME PEOPLE LIKE GINGER.
AND THIS...
...UPSET YOU FOR SOME REASON?
YOU DON'T UNDERSTAND! IT'S COMPLICATED!
HUH?
WHEN HE SAW ME STARING, HE SAID...
ARE YOU SURPRISED, YANAGI?
ER, YES.

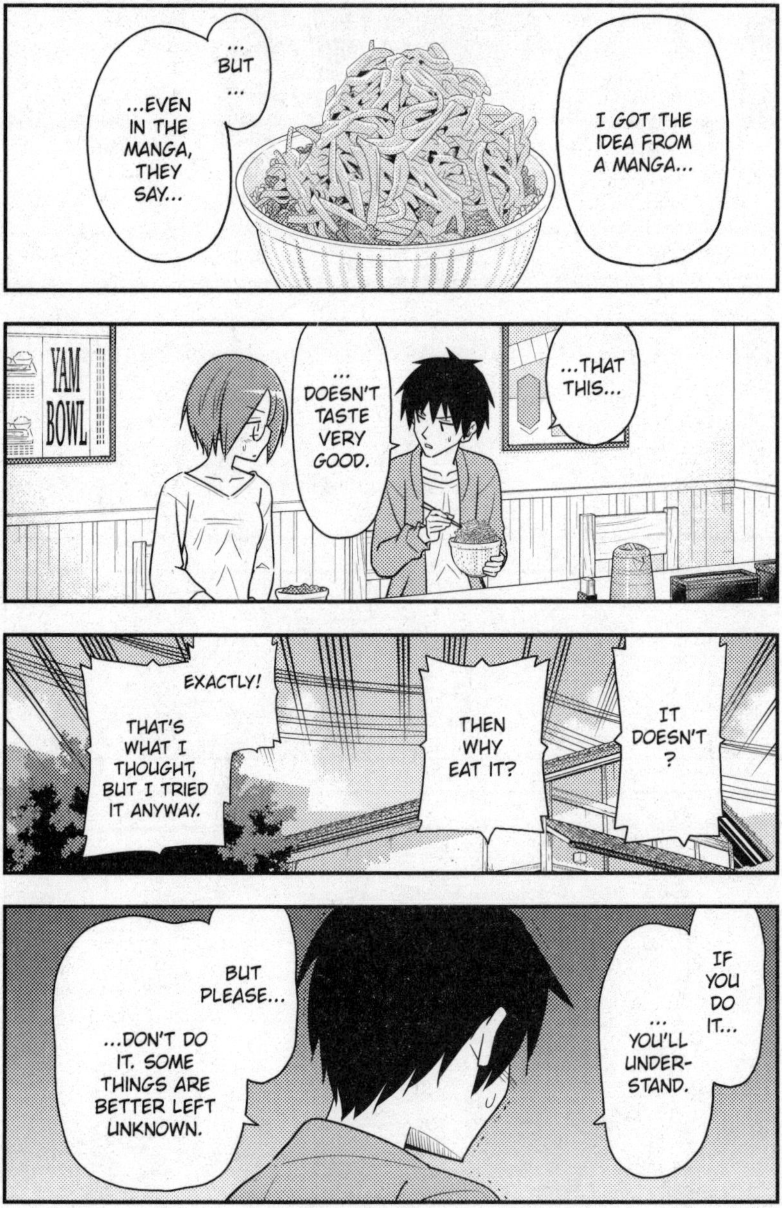
I GOT THE IDEA FROM A MANGA...
... BUT ...
...EVEN IN THE MANGA, THEY SAY...
...THAT THIS...
... DOESN'T TASTE VERY GOOD.
YAM BOWL
IT DOESN'T ?
THEN WHY EAT IT?
EXACTLY!
THAT'S WHAT I THOUGHT, BUT I TRIED IT ANYWAY.
IF YOU DO IT...
... YOU'LL UNDER-STAND.
BUT PLEASE...
...DON'T DO IT. SOME THINGS ARE BETTER LEFT UNKNOWN.

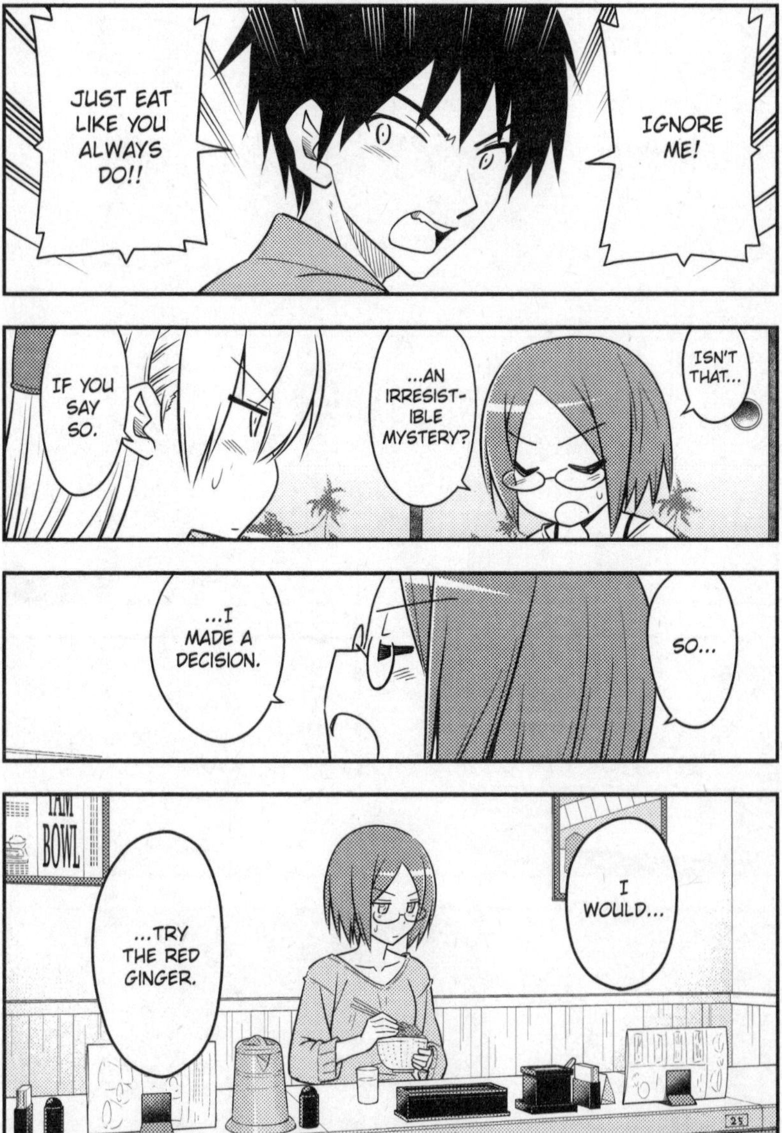
IGNORE ME!
JUST EAT LIKE YOU ALWAYS DO!!
ISN'T THAT...
...AN IRRESIST-IBLE MYSTERY?
IF YOU SAY SO.
SO...
...I MADE A DECISION.
I WOULD...
...TRY THE RED GINGER.
BOWL

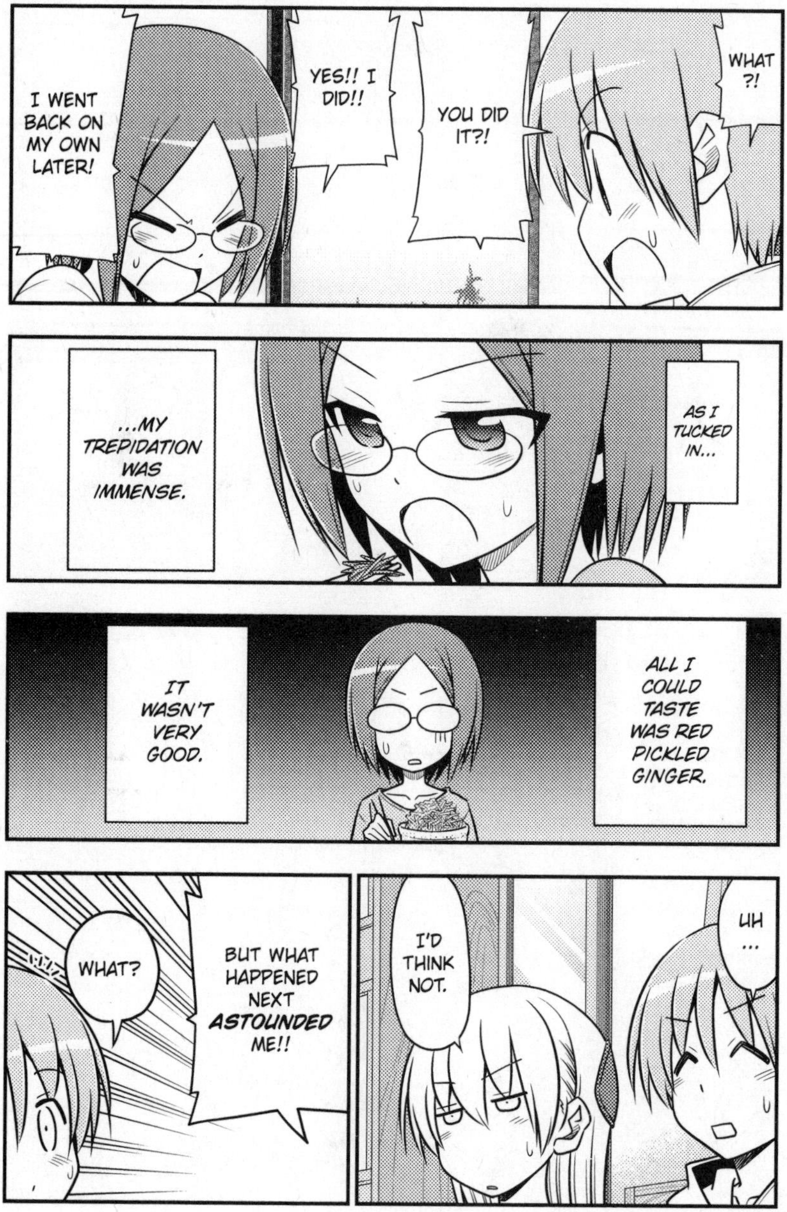
WHAT ?!
YOU DID IT?!
YES!! I DID!!
I WENT BACK ON MY OWN LATER!
AS I TUCKED IN...
...MY TREPIDATION WAS IMMENSE.
ALL I COULD TASTE WAS RED PICKLED GINGER.
IT WASN'T VERY GOOD.
UH ...
I'D THINK NOT.
BUT WHAT HAPPENED NEXT ASTOUNDED ME!!
WHAT?

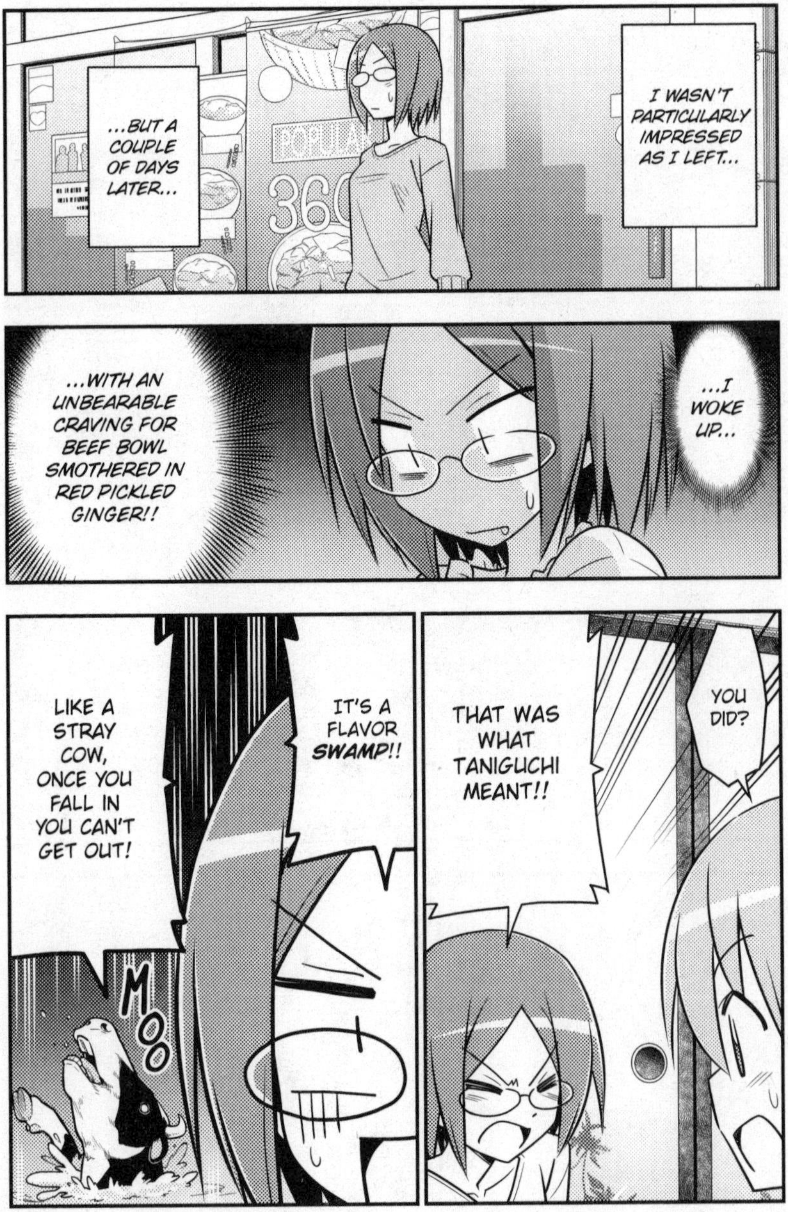
I WASN'T PARTICULARLY IMPRESSED AS I LEFT...
POPULA
360
...BUT A COUPLE OF DAYS LATER...
...I WOKE UP...
...WITH AN UNBEARABLE CRAVING FOR BEEF BOWL SMOTHERED IN RED PICKLED GINGER!!
YOU DID?
THAT WAS WHAT TANIGUCHI MEANT!!
IT'S A FLAVOR **SWAMP**!!
LIKE A STRAY COW, ONCE YOU FALL IN YOU CAN'T GET OUT!
MOO

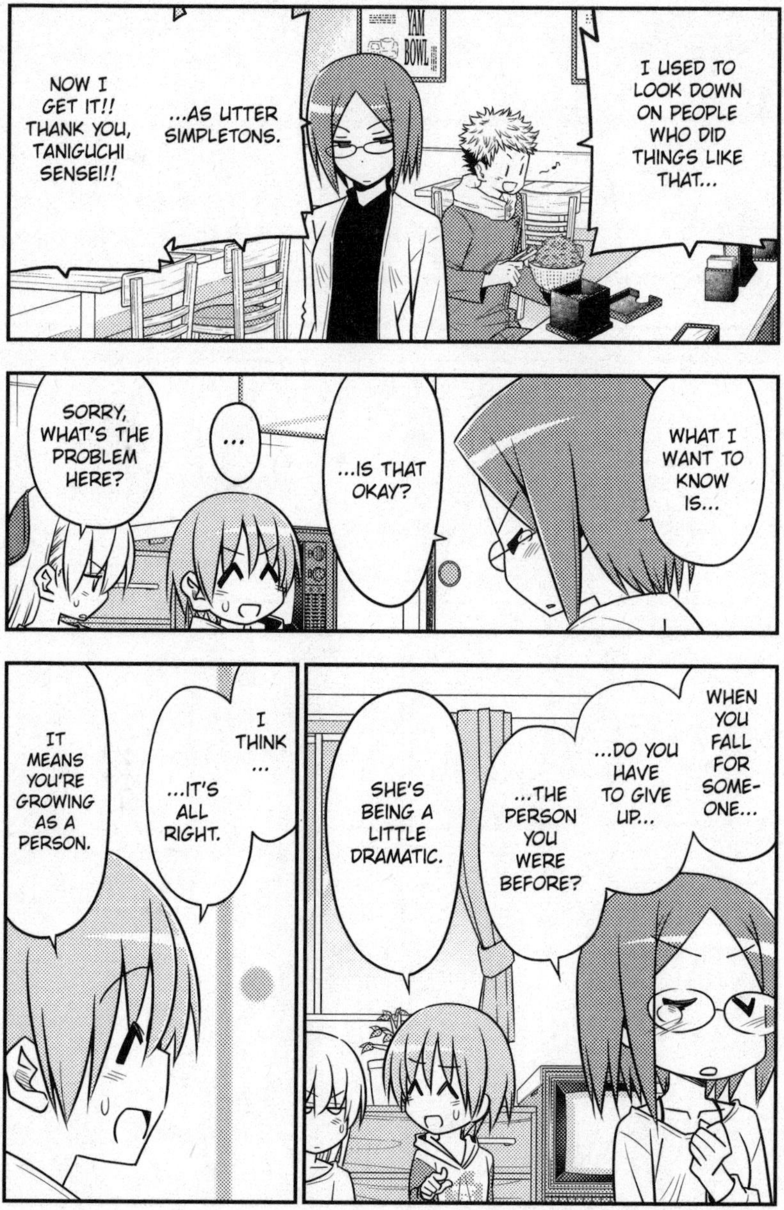
I USED TO LOOK DOWN ON PEOPLE WHO DID THINGS LIKE THAT...
...AS UTTER SIMPLETONS.
NOW I GET IT!! THANK YOU, TANIGUCHI SENSEI!!
WHAT I WANT TO KNOW IS...
...IS THAT OKAY?
...
SORRY, WHAT'S THE PROBLEM HERE?
WHEN YOU FALL FOR SOME-ONE...
...DO YOU HAVE TO GIVE UP...
...THE PERSON YOU WERE BEFORE?
SHE'S BEING A LITTLE DRAMATIC.
I THINK ...
...IT'S ALL RIGHT.
IT MEANS YOU'RE GROWING AS A PERSON.

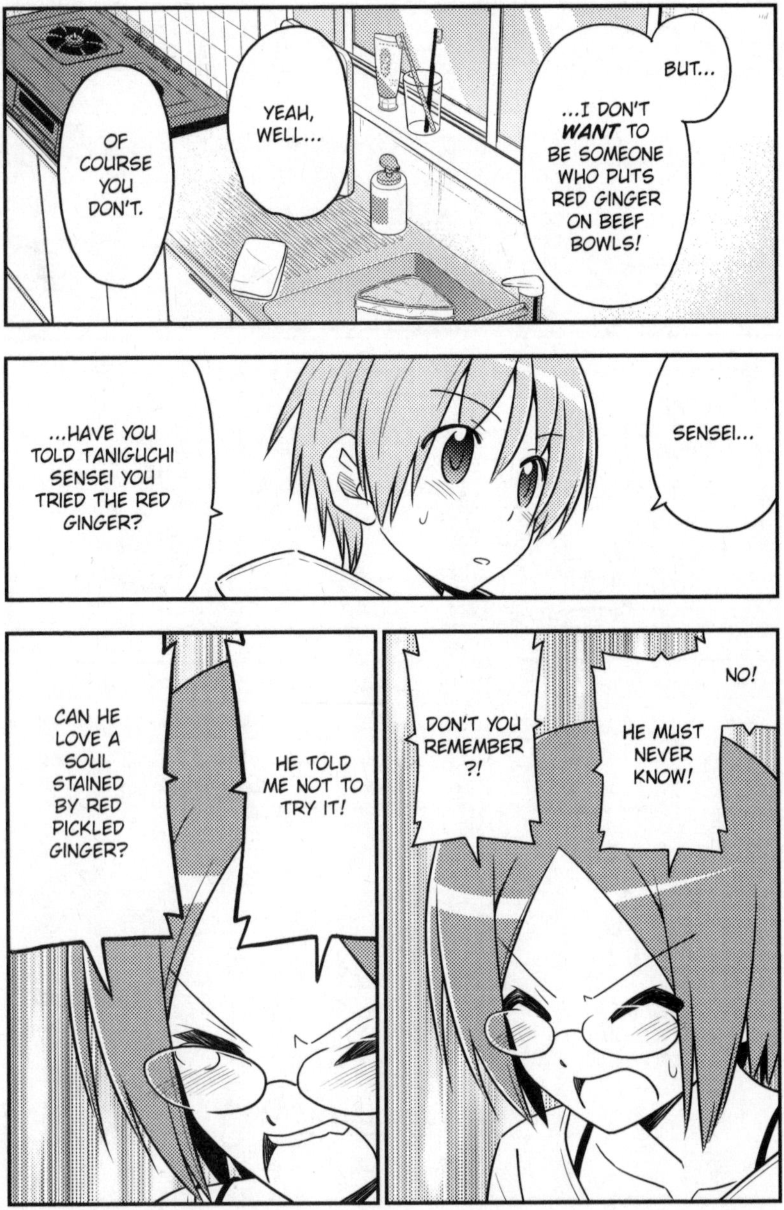
BUT...
...I DON'T **WANT** TO BE SOMEONE WHO PUTS RED GINGER ON BEEF BOWLS!
YEAH, WELL...
OF COURSE YOU DON'T.
SENSEI...
...HAVE YOU TOLD TANIGUCHI SENSEI YOU TRIED THE RED GINGER?
NO!
HE MUST NEVER KNOW!
DON'T YOU REMEMBER ?!
HE TOLD ME NOT TO TRY IT!
CAN HE LOVE A SOUL STAINED BY RED PICKLED GINGER?

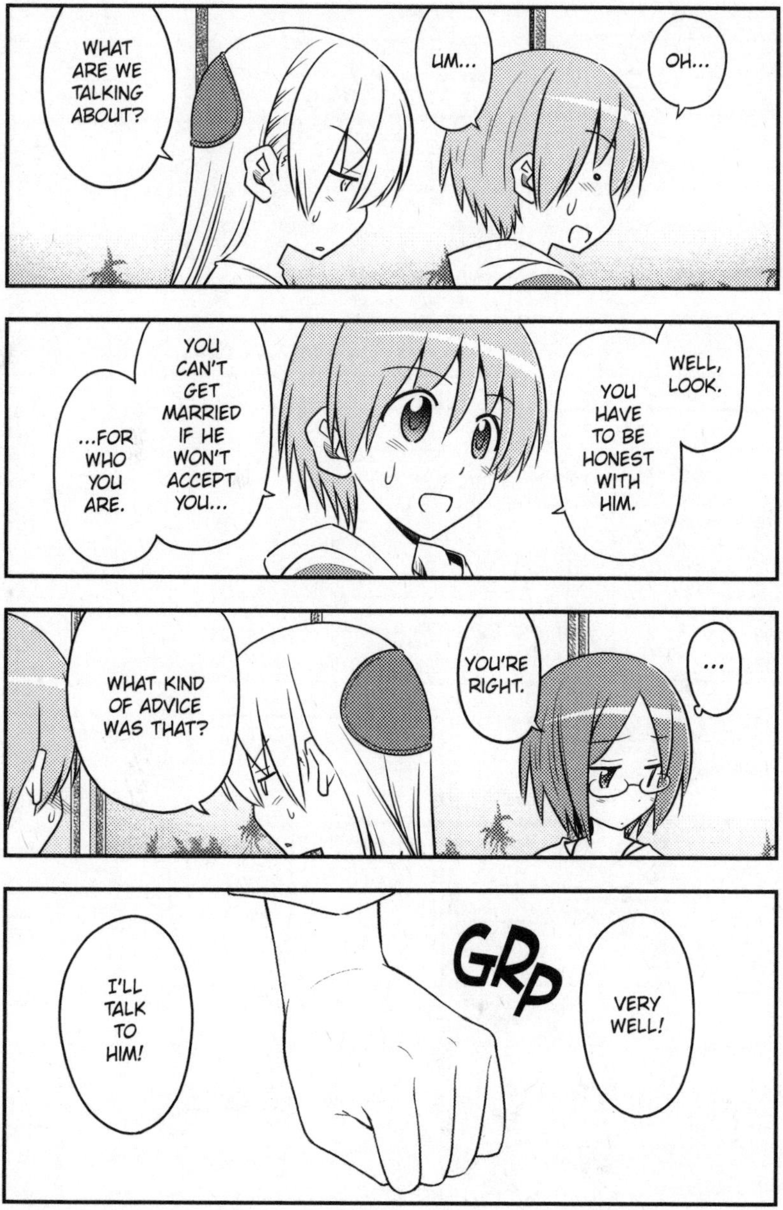
OH...
UM...
WHAT ARE WE TALKING ABOUT?
WELL, LOOK.
YOU HAVE TO BE HONEST WITH HIM.
YOU CAN'T GET MARRIED IF HE WON'T ACCEPT YOU...
...FOR WHO YOU ARE.
...
YOU'RE RIGHT.
WHAT KIND OF ADVICE WAS THAT?
VERY WELL!
GRP
I'LL TALK TO HIM!

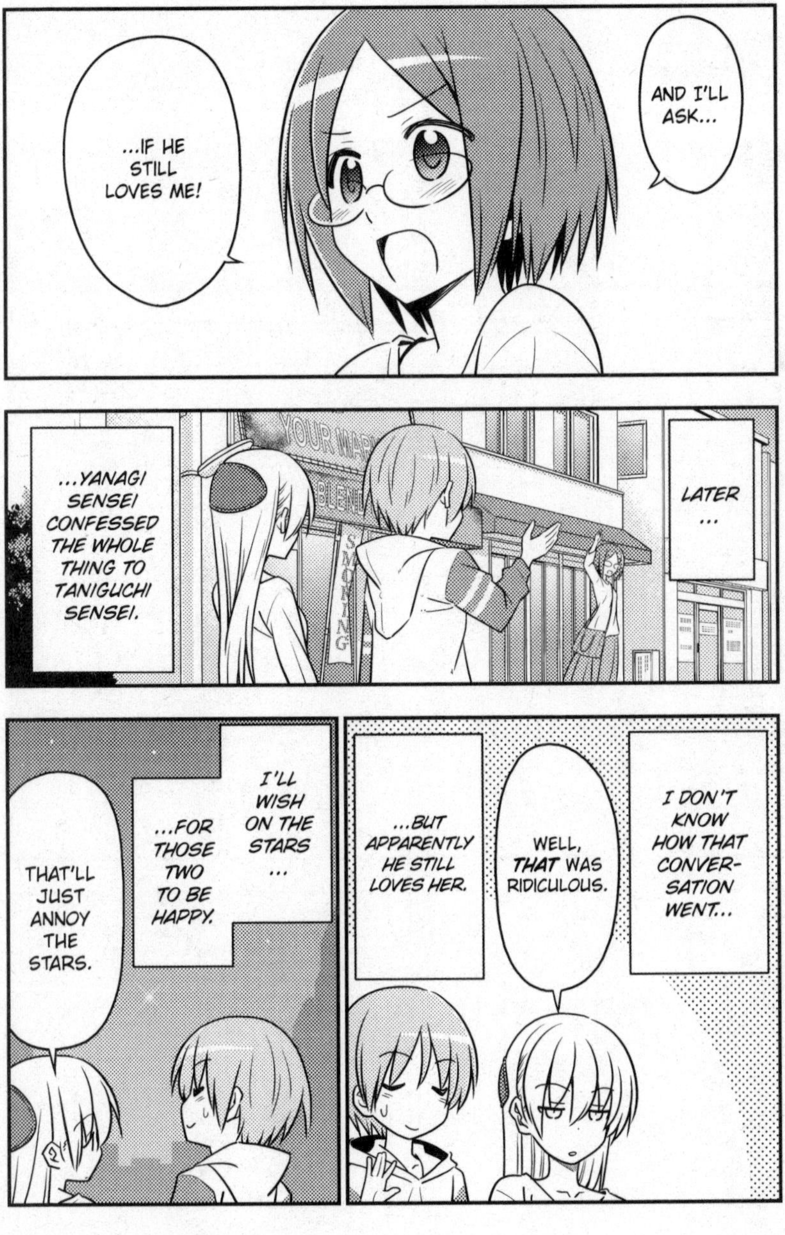
AND I'LL ASK...
...IF HE STILL LOVES ME!
LATER ...
...YANAGI SENSEI CONFESSED THE WHOLE THING TO TANIGUCHI SENSEI.
SMOKING
I DON'T KNOW HOW THAT CONVER-SATION WENT...
WELL, **THAT** WAS RIDICULOUS.
...BUT APPARENTLY HE STILL LOVES HER.
I'LL WISH ON THE STARS ...
...FOR THOSE TWO TO BE HAPPY.
THAT'LL JUST ANNOY THE STARS.

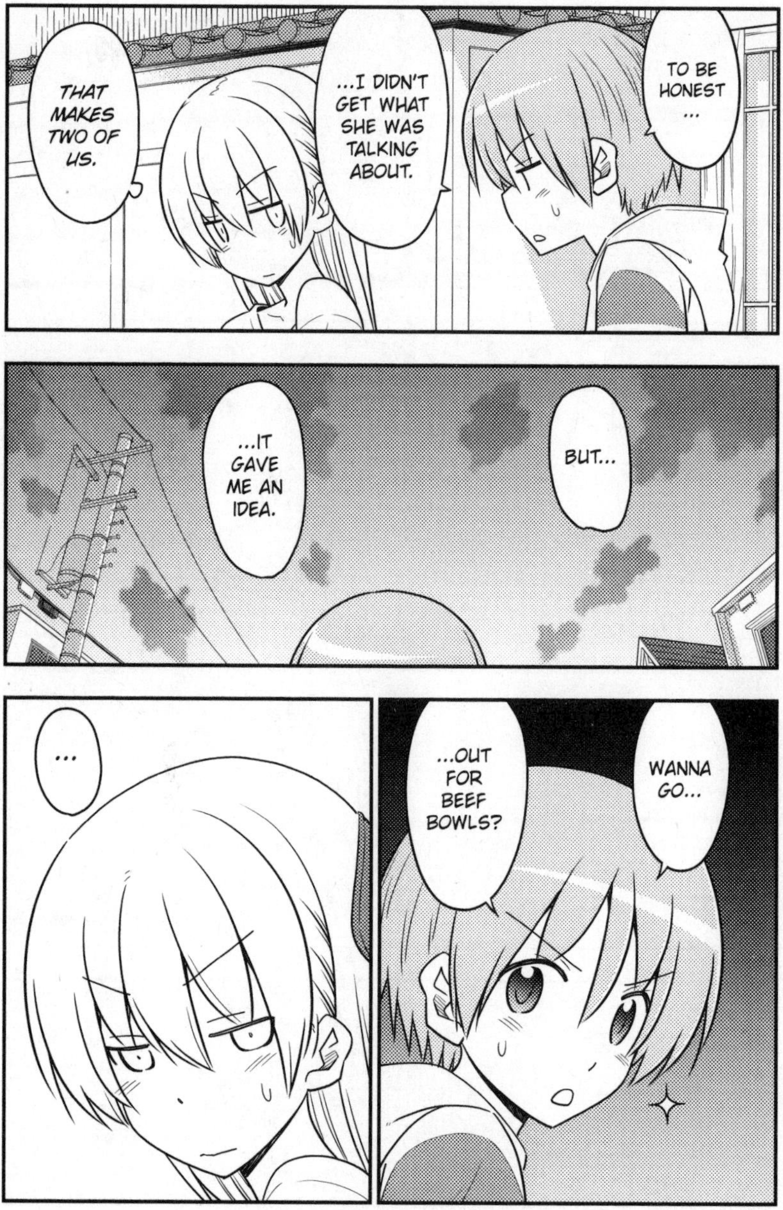
TO BE HONEST ...
...I DIDN'T GET WHAT SHE WAS TALKING ABOUT.
THAT MAKES TWO OF US.
BUT...
...IT GAVE ME AN IDEA.
WANNA GO...
...OUT FOR BEEF BOWLS?
...

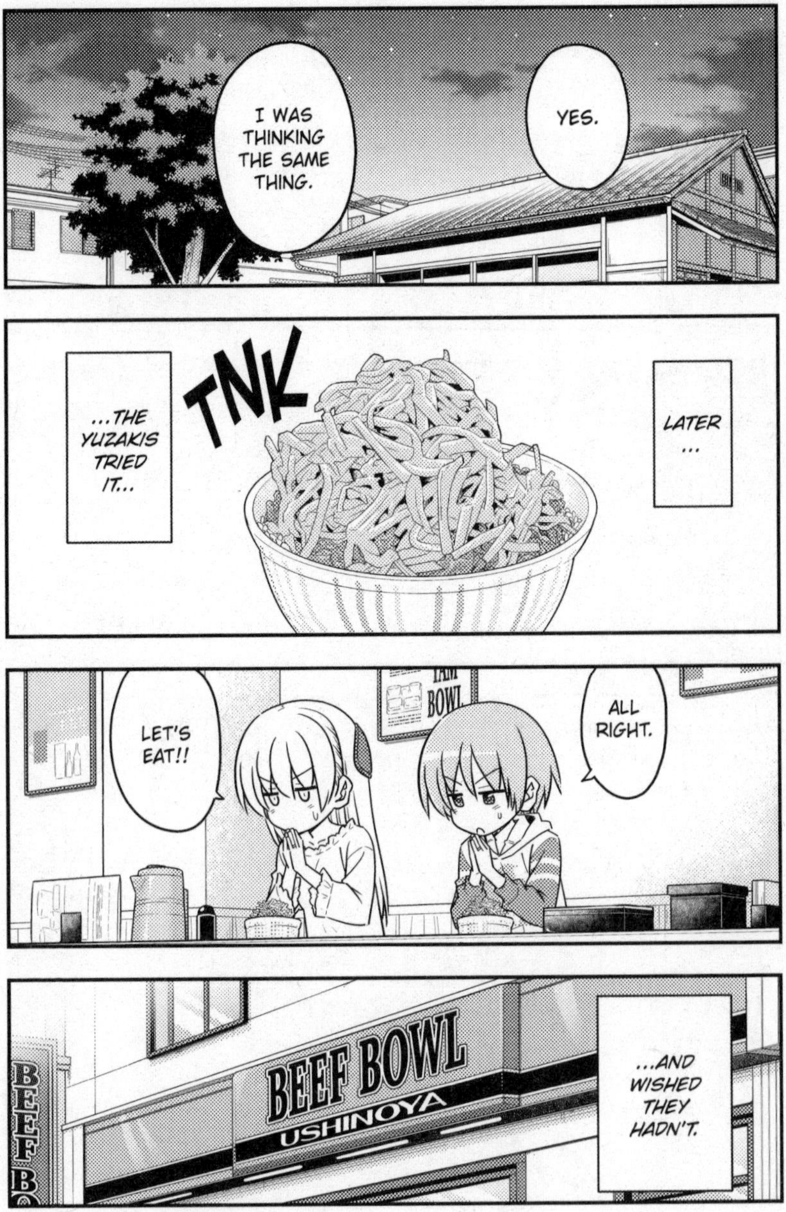
YES.
I WAS THINKING THE SAME THING.
LATER ...
TNK
...THE YUZAKIS TRIED IT...
ALL RIGHT.
LET'S EAT!!
...AND WISHED THEY HADN'T.
BEEF BOWL
USHINOYA

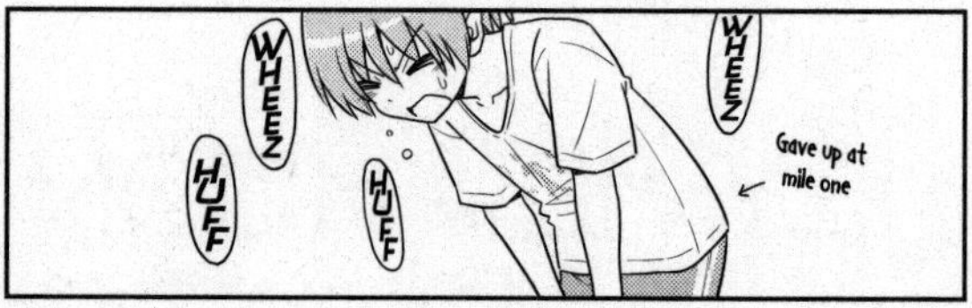
WHEEZ
Gave up at
mile one
WHEEZ
HUFF
HUFF

FLY ME TO THE MOON

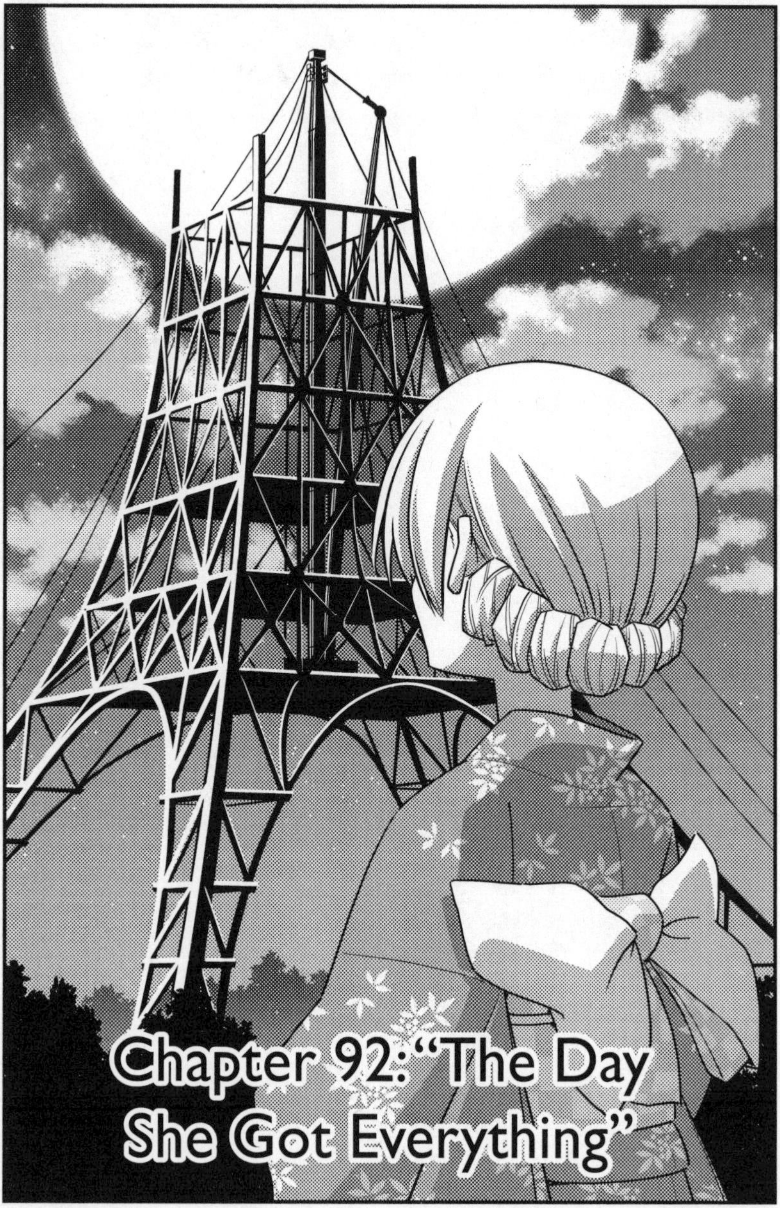
Chapter 92: "The Day She Got Everything"

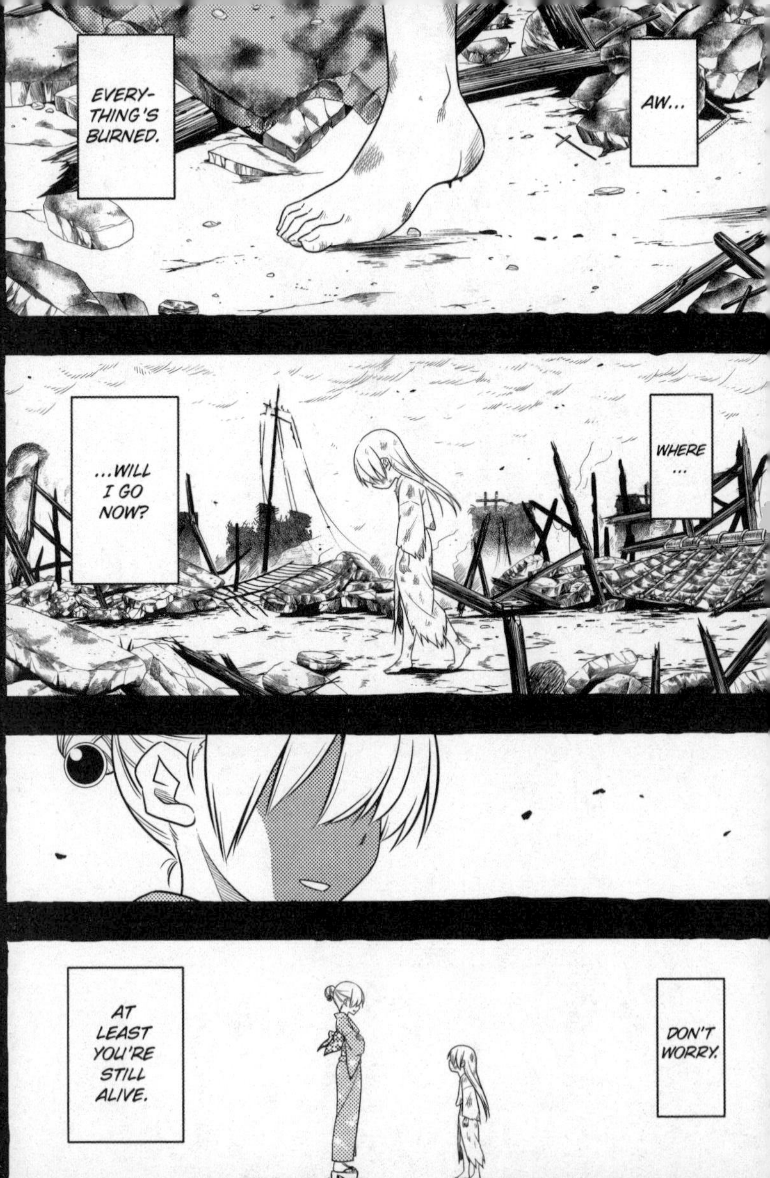
AW...
EVERYTHING'S BURNED.
WHERE ...
...WILL I GO NOW?
DON'T WORRY.
AT LEAST YOU'RE STILL ALIVE.

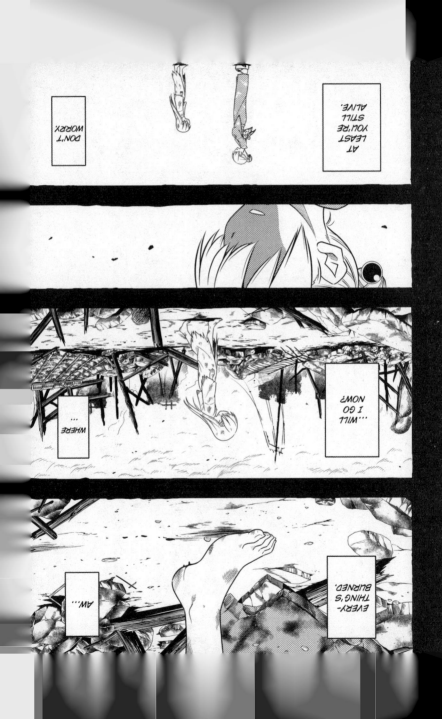

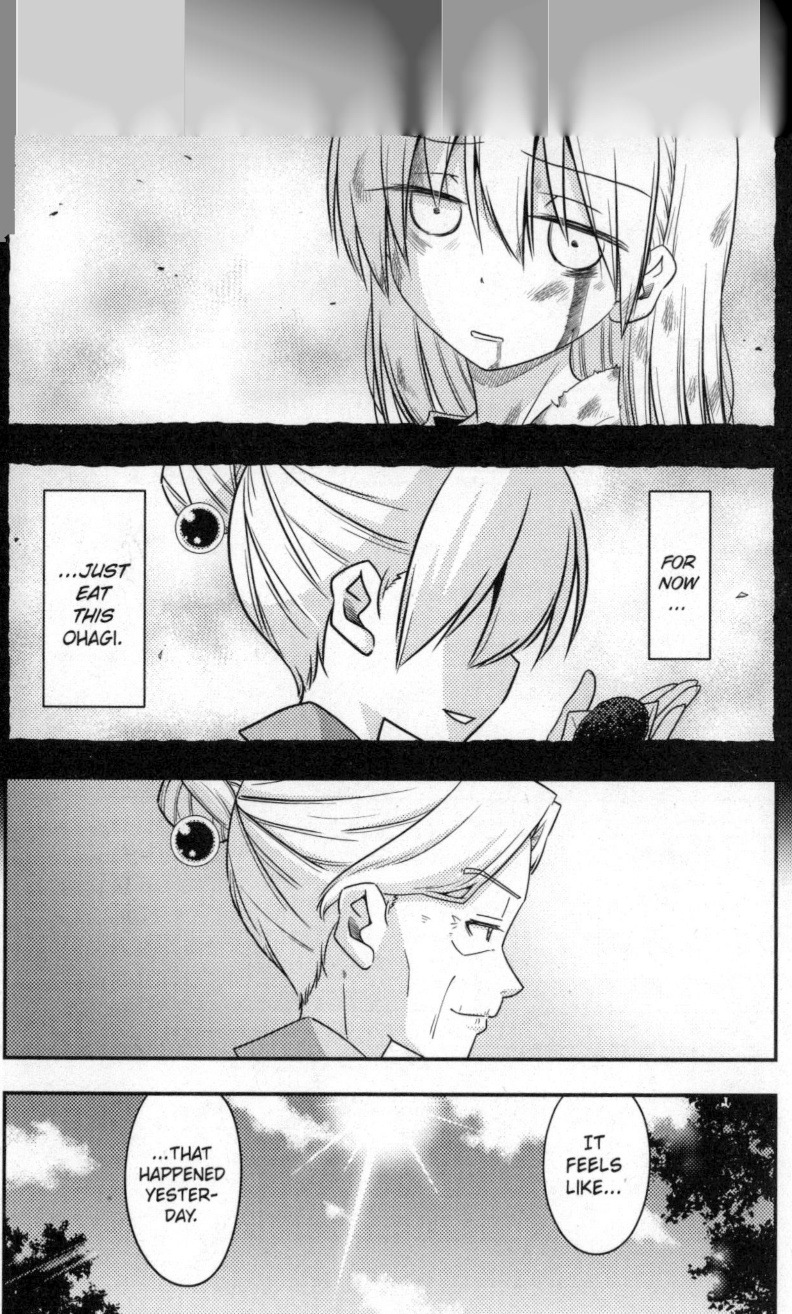
FOR NOW ...
...JUST EAT THIS OHAGI.
IT FEELS LIKE...
...THAT HAPPENED YESTER-DAY.

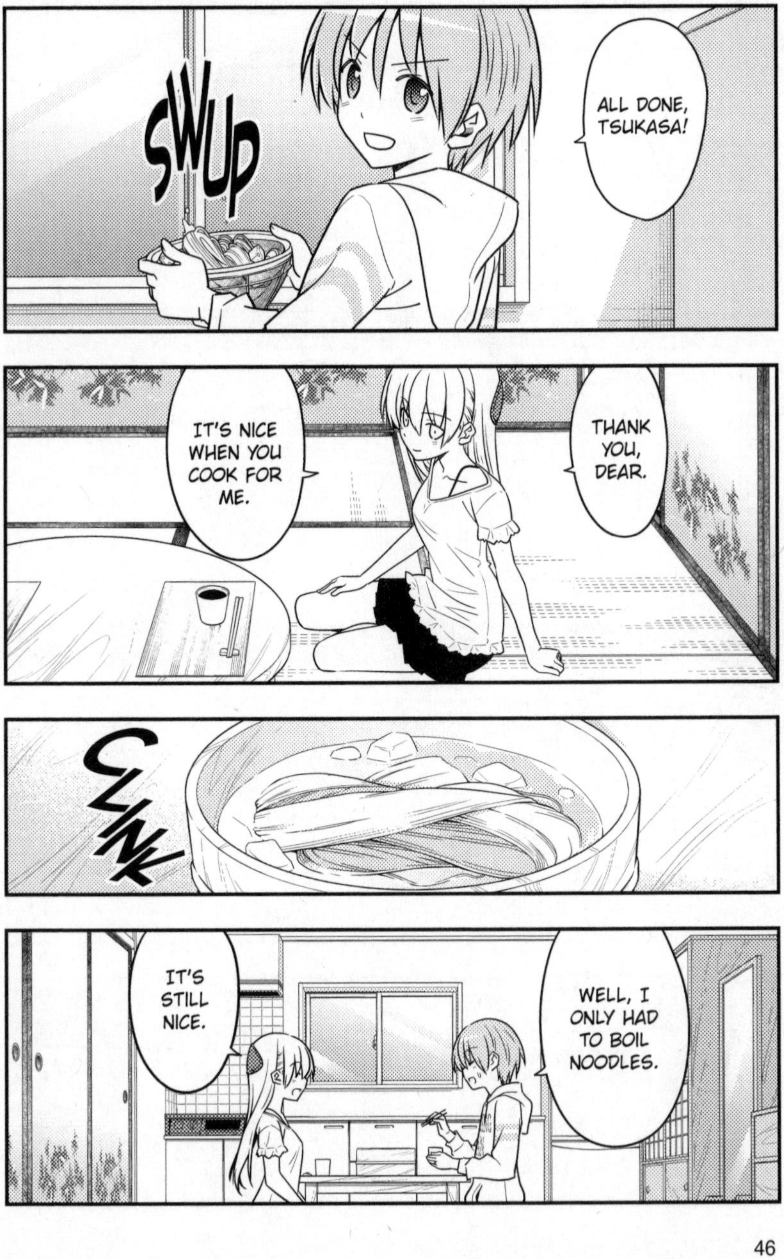
ALL DONE, TSUKASA!
SWUP
THANK YOU, DEAR.
IT'S NICE WHEN YOU COOK FOR ME.
CLINK
WELL, I ONLY HAD TO BOIL NOODLES.
IT'S STILL NICE.

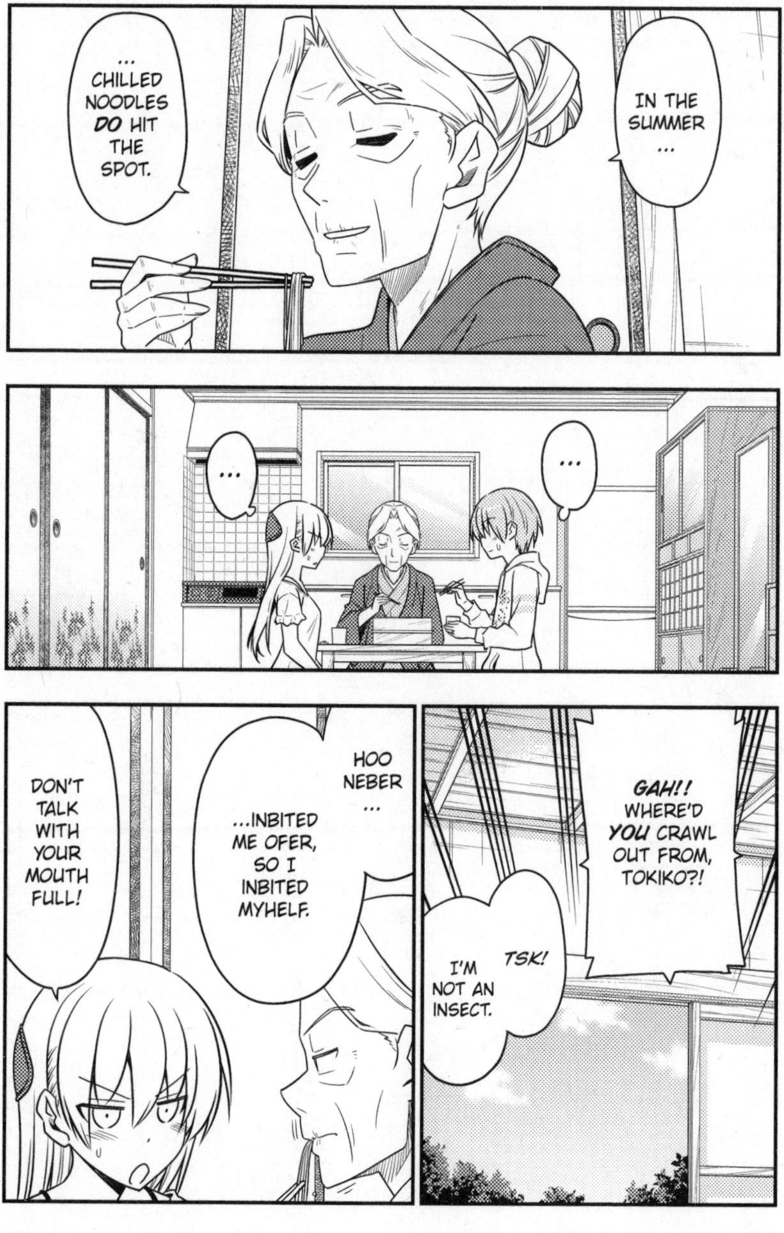
IN THE SUMMER ...
... CHILLED NOODLES **DO** HIT THE SPOT.
...
...
GAH!! WHERE'D ***YOU*** CRAWL OUT FROM, TOKIKO?!
TSK!
I'M NOT AN INSECT.
HOO NEBER ...
...INBITED ME OFER, SO I INBITED MYHELF.
DON'T TALK WITH YOUR MOUTH FULL!

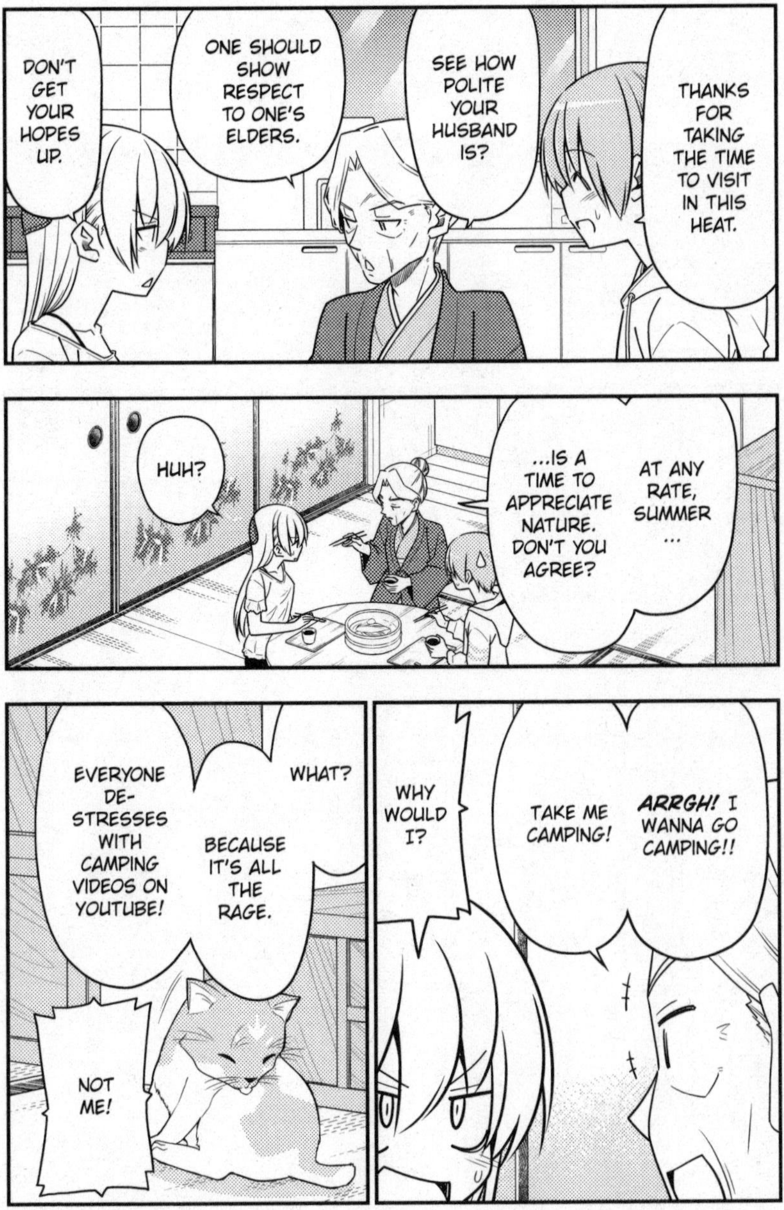
THANKS FOR TAKING THE TIME TO VISIT IN THIS HEAT.
SEE HOW POLITE YOUR HUSBAND IS?
ONE SHOULD SHOW RESPECT TO ONE'S ELDERS.
DON'T GET YOUR HOPES UP.
AT ANY RATE, SUMMER ...
...IS A TIME TO APPRECIATE NATURE. DON'T YOU AGREE?
HUH?
ARRGH! I WANNA GO CAMPING!!
TAKE ME CAMPING!
WHY WOULD I?
WHAT?
BECAUSE IT'S ALL THE RAGE.
EVERYONE DE-STRESSES WITH CAMPING VIDEOS ON YOUTUBE!
NOT ME!

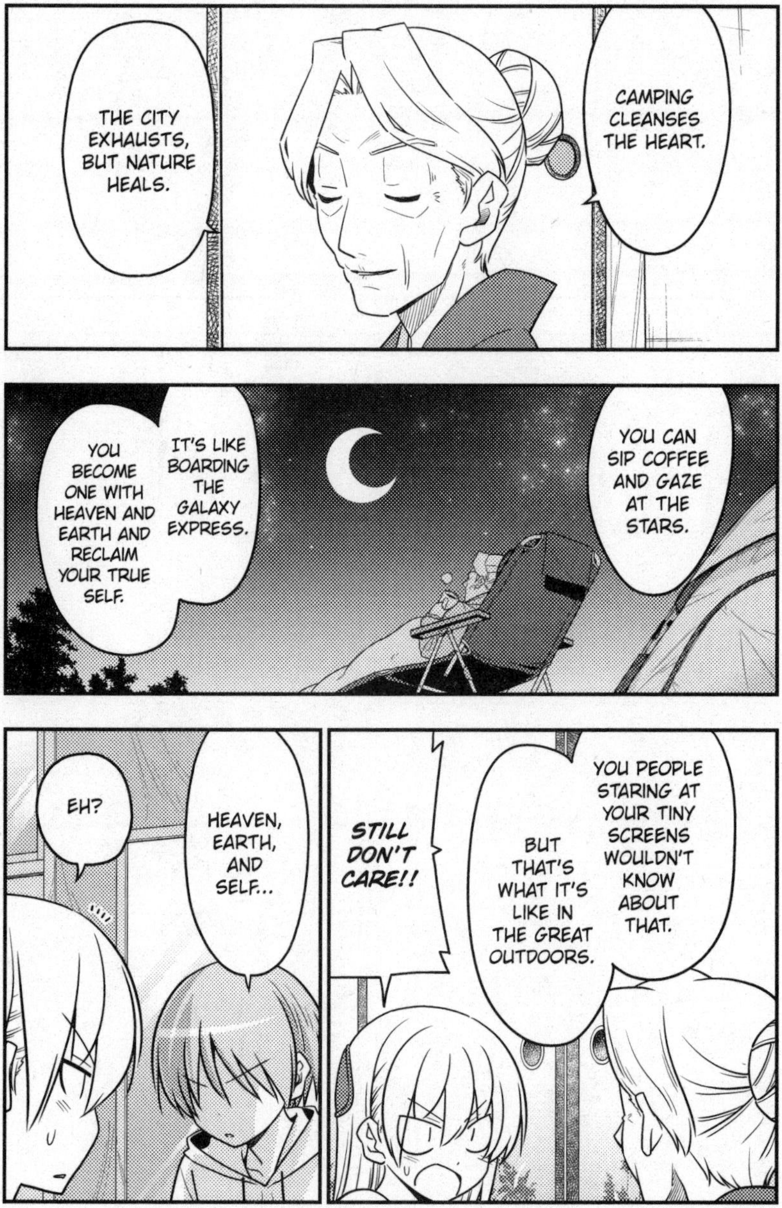
CAMPING CLEANSES THE HEART.
THE CITY EXHAUSTS, BUT NATURE HEALS.
YOU CAN SIP COFFEE AND GAZE AT THE STARS.
IT'S LIKE BOARDING THE GALAXY EXPRESS.
YOU BECOME ONE WITH HEAVEN AND EARTH AND RECLAIM YOUR TRUE SELF.
YOU PEOPLE STARING AT YOUR TINY SCREENS WOULDN'T KNOW ABOUT THAT.
BUT THAT'S WHAT IT'S LIKE IN THE GREAT OUTDOORS.
STILL DON'T CARE!!
HEAVEN, EARTH, AND SELF...
EH?

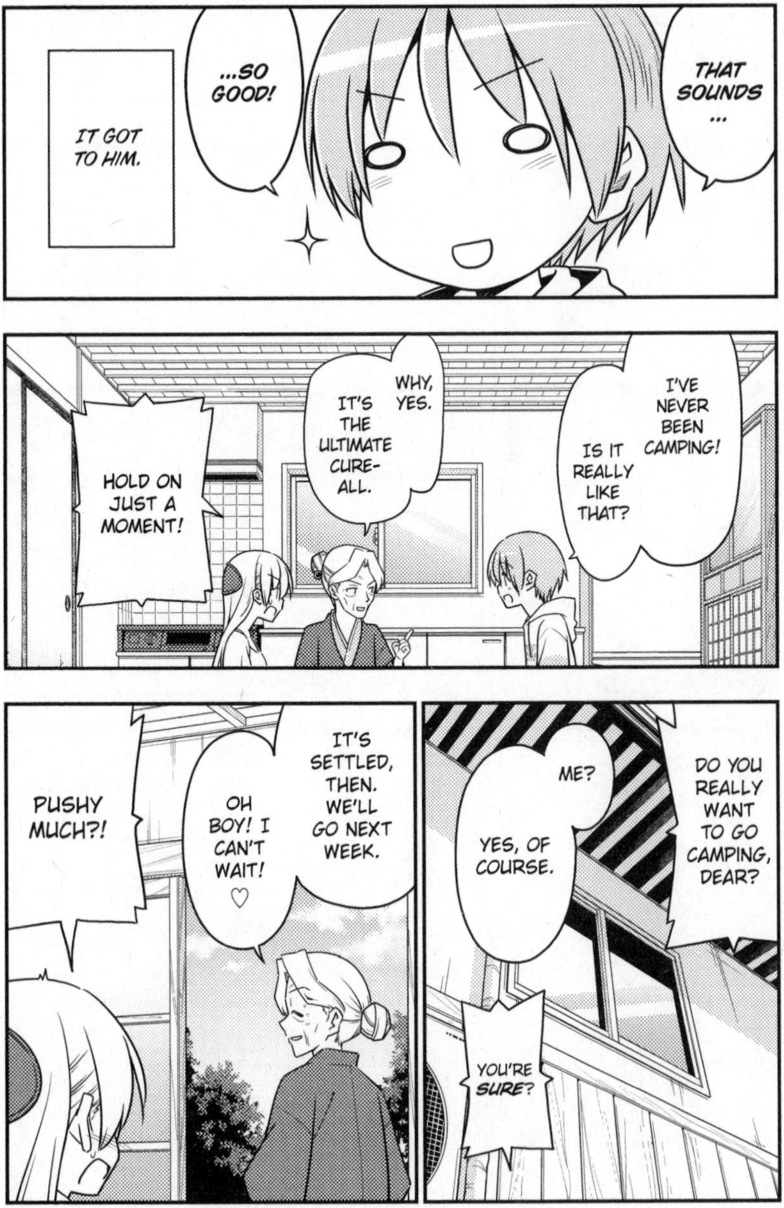
THAT SOUNDS ...
...SO GOOD!
IT GOT TO HIM.
I'VE NEVER BEEN CAMPING!
IS IT REALLY LIKE THAT?
WHY, YES.
IT'S THE ULTIMATE CURE-ALL.
HOLD ON JUST A MOMENT!
DO YOU REALLY WANT TO GO CAMPING, DEAR?
ME?
YES, OF COURSE.
YOU'RE SURE?
IT'S SETTLED, THEN. WE'LL GO NEXT WEEK.
OH BOY! I CAN'T WAIT! ♡
PUSHY MUCH?!

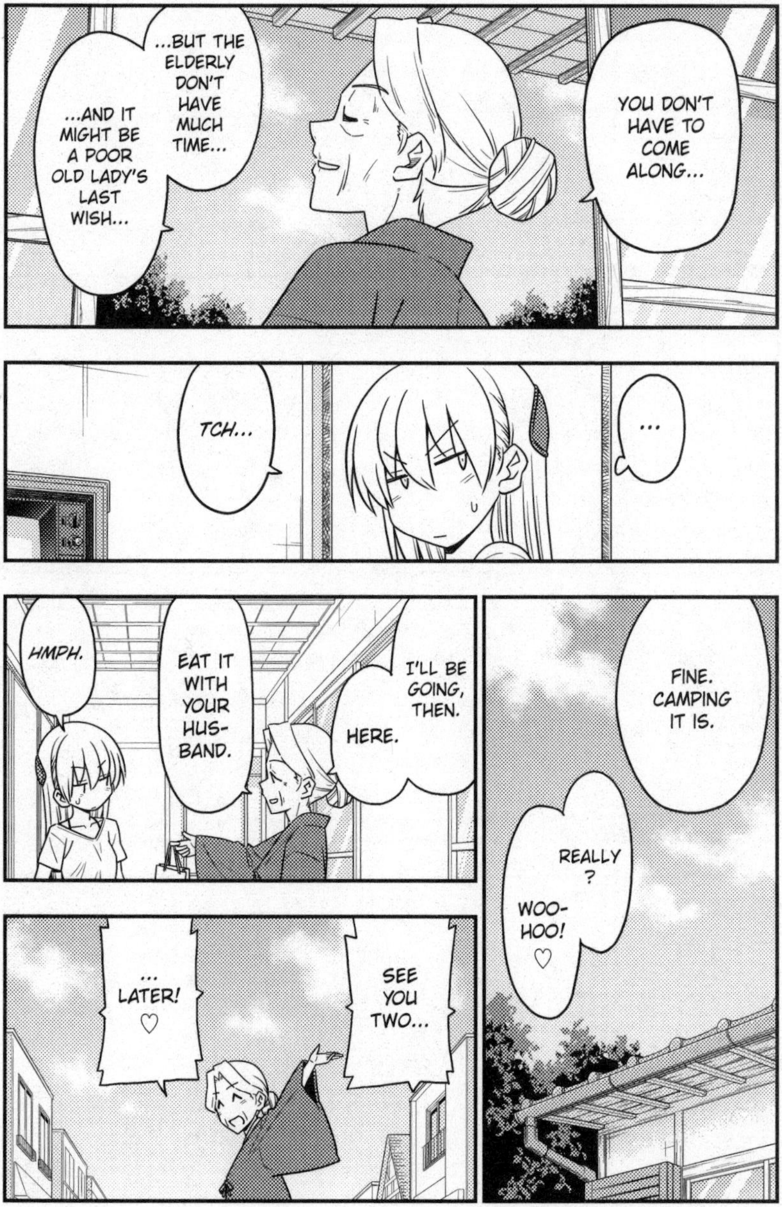
YOU DON'T HAVE TO COME ALONG...
...BUT THE ELDERLY DON'T HAVE MUCH TIME...
...AND IT MIGHT BE A POOR OLD LADY'S LAST WISH...
...
TCH...
FINE. CAMPING IT IS.
REALLY?
WOO-HOO! ♡
I'LL BE GOING, THEN.
HERE.
EAT IT WITH YOUR HUS-BAND.
HMPH.
SEE YOU TWO...
...LATER! ♡

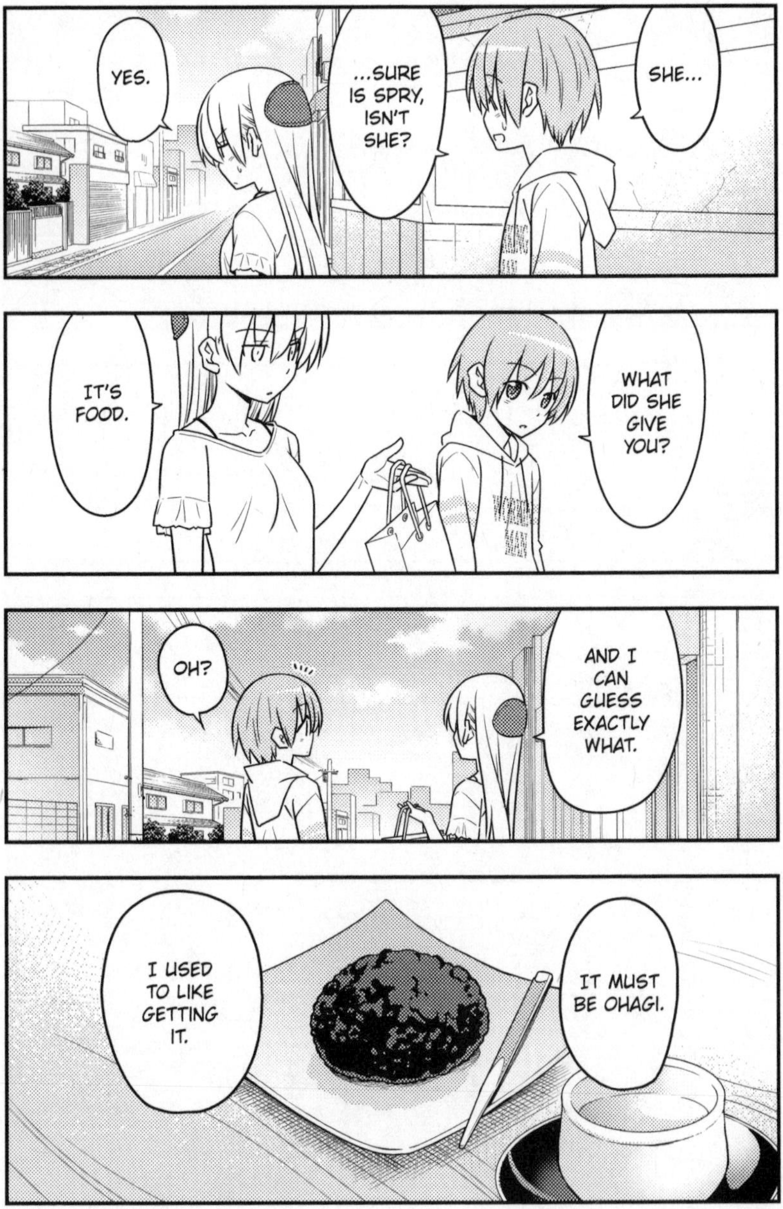
SHE...
...SURE IS SPRY, ISN'T SHE?
YES.
WHAT DID SHE GIVE YOU?
IT'S FOOD.
AND I CAN GUESS EXACTLY WHAT.
OH?
IT MUST BE OHAGI.
I USED TO LIKE GETTING IT.

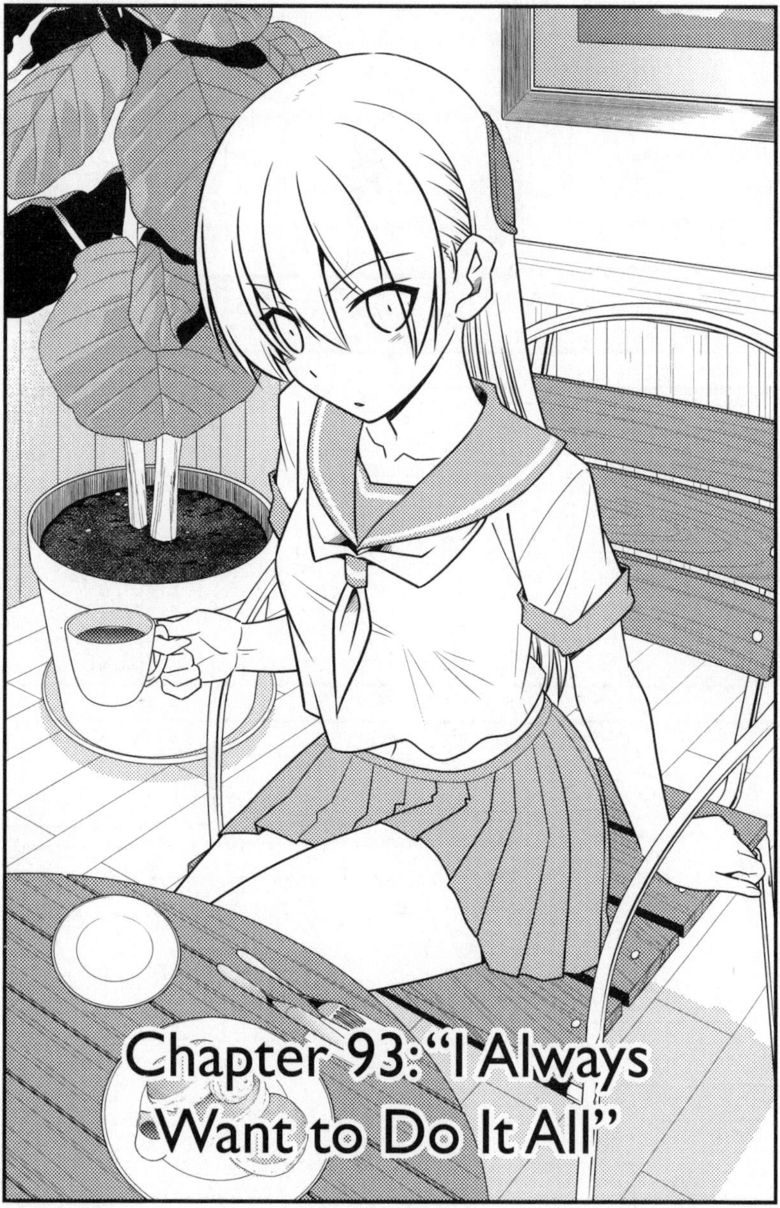
Chapter 93: "I Always Want to Do It All"

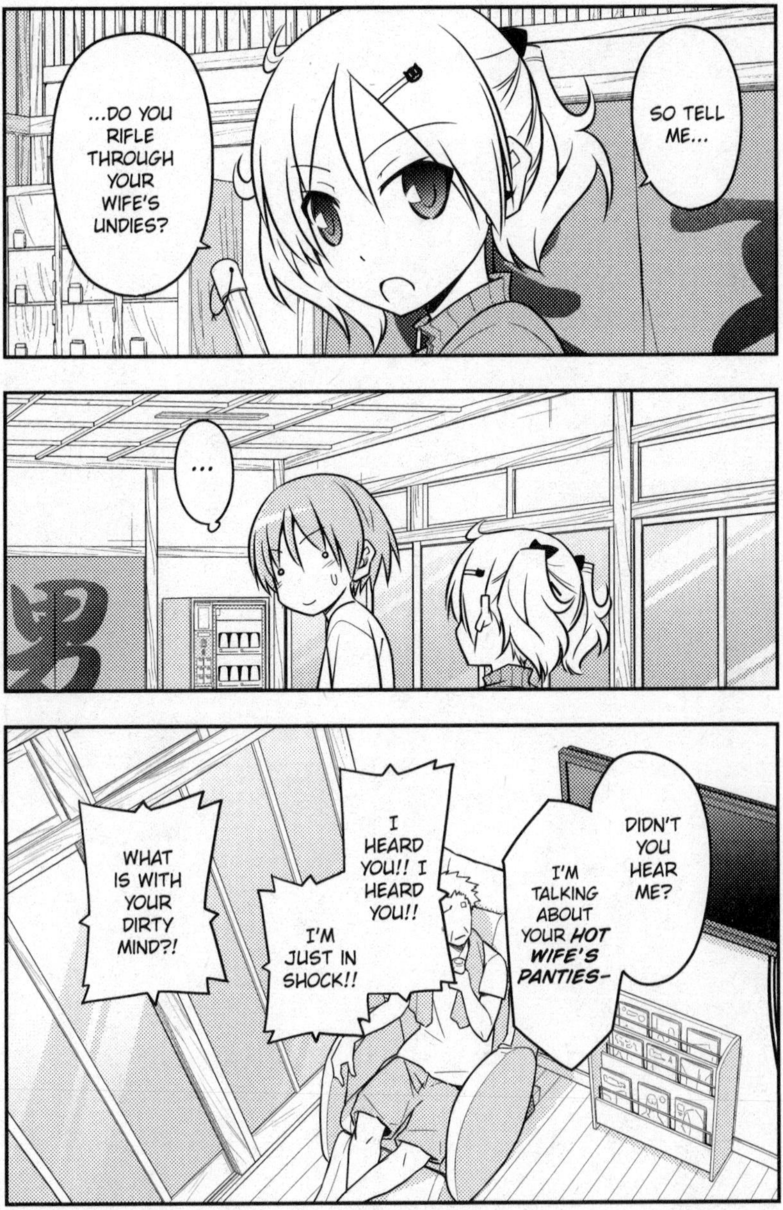
SO TELL ME...
...DO YOU RIFLE THROUGH YOUR WIFE'S UNDIES?
...
DIDN'T YOU HEAR ME?
I'M TALKING ABOUT YOUR *HOT WIFE'S PANTIES*-
I HEARD YOU!! I HEARD YOU!!
I'M JUST IN SHOCK!!
WHAT IS WITH YOUR DIRTY MIND?!

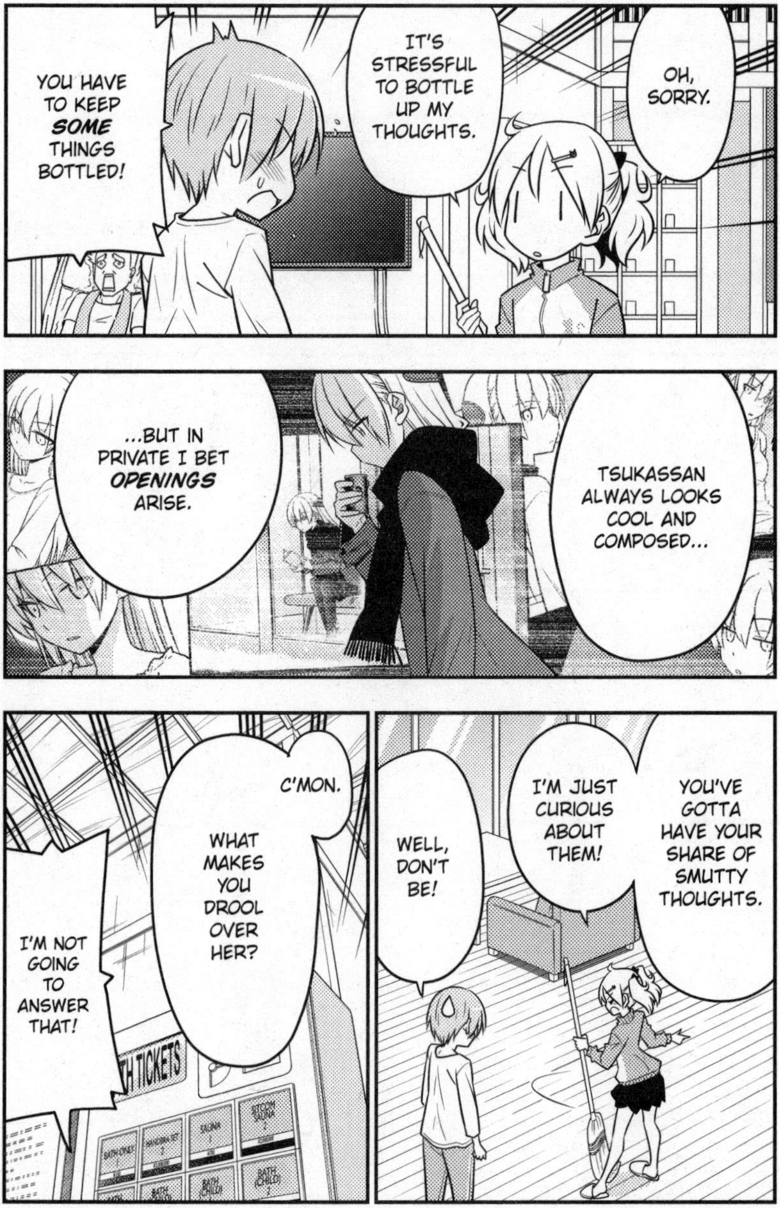
OH, SORRY.
IT'S STRESSFUL TO BOTTLE UP MY THOUGHTS.
YOU HAVE TO KEEP **SOME** THINGS BOTTLED!
TSUKASSAN ALWAYS LOOKS COOL AND COMPOSED...
...BUT IN PRIVATE I BET **OPENINGS** ARISE.
YOU'VE GOTTA HAVE YOUR SHARE OF SMUTTY THOUGHTS.
I'M JUST CURIOUS ABOUT THEM!
WELL, DON'T BE!
C'MON.
WHAT MAKES YOU DROOL OVER HER?
I'M NOT GOING TO ANSWER THAT!

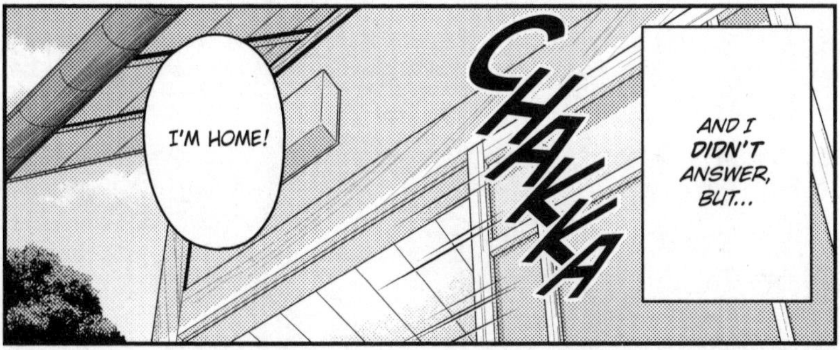
AND I DIDN'T ANSWER, BUT...
CHAKKA
I'M HOME!

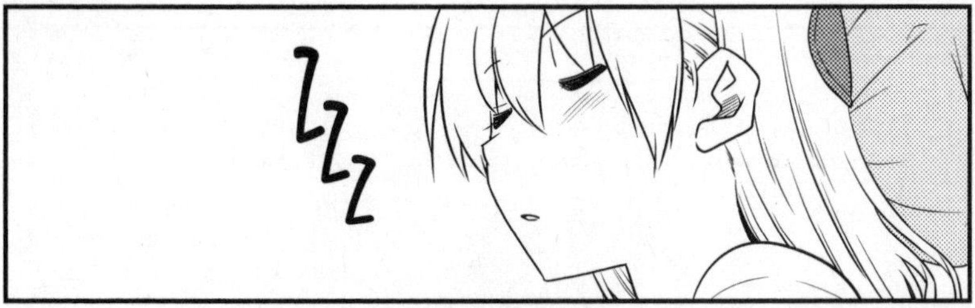
ZZZ

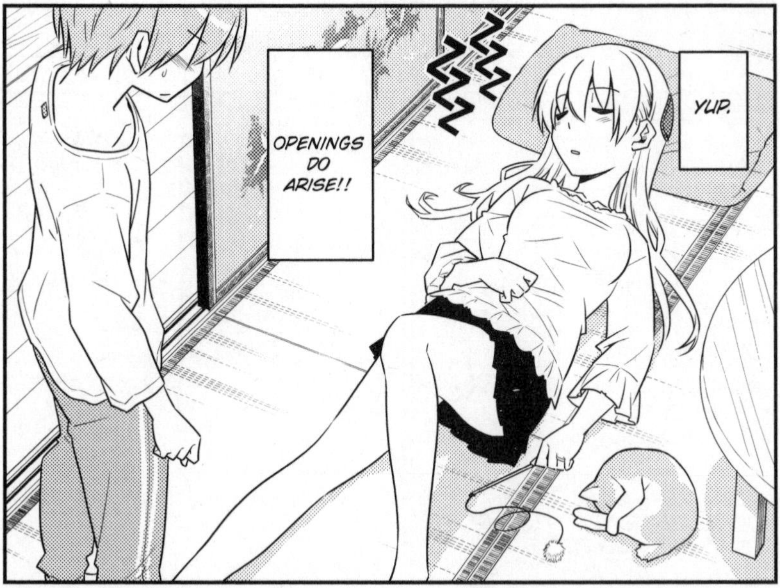
YUP.
ZZZZ
OPENINGS DO ARISE!!

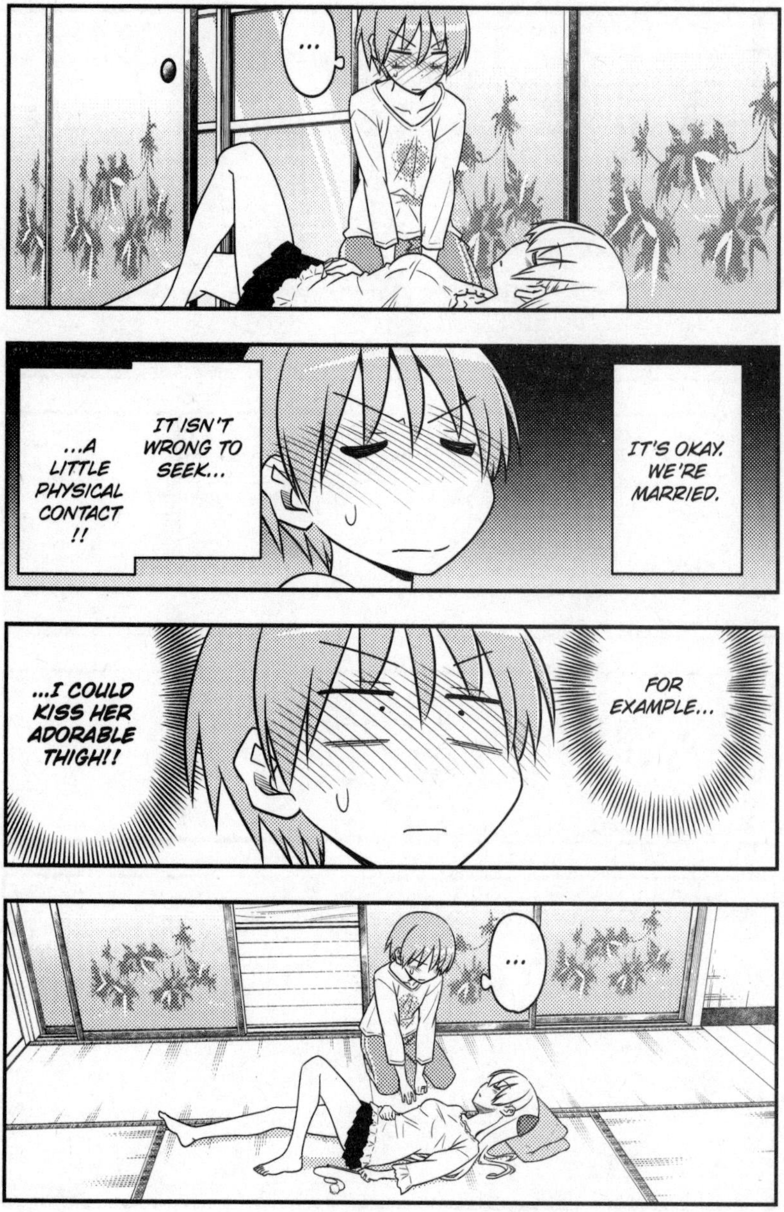
...
IT'S OKAY. WE'RE MARRIED.
IT ISN'T WRONG TO SEEK...
...A LITTLE PHYSICAL CONTACT !!
FOR EXAMPLE...
...I COULD KISS HER ADORABLE THIGH!!
...

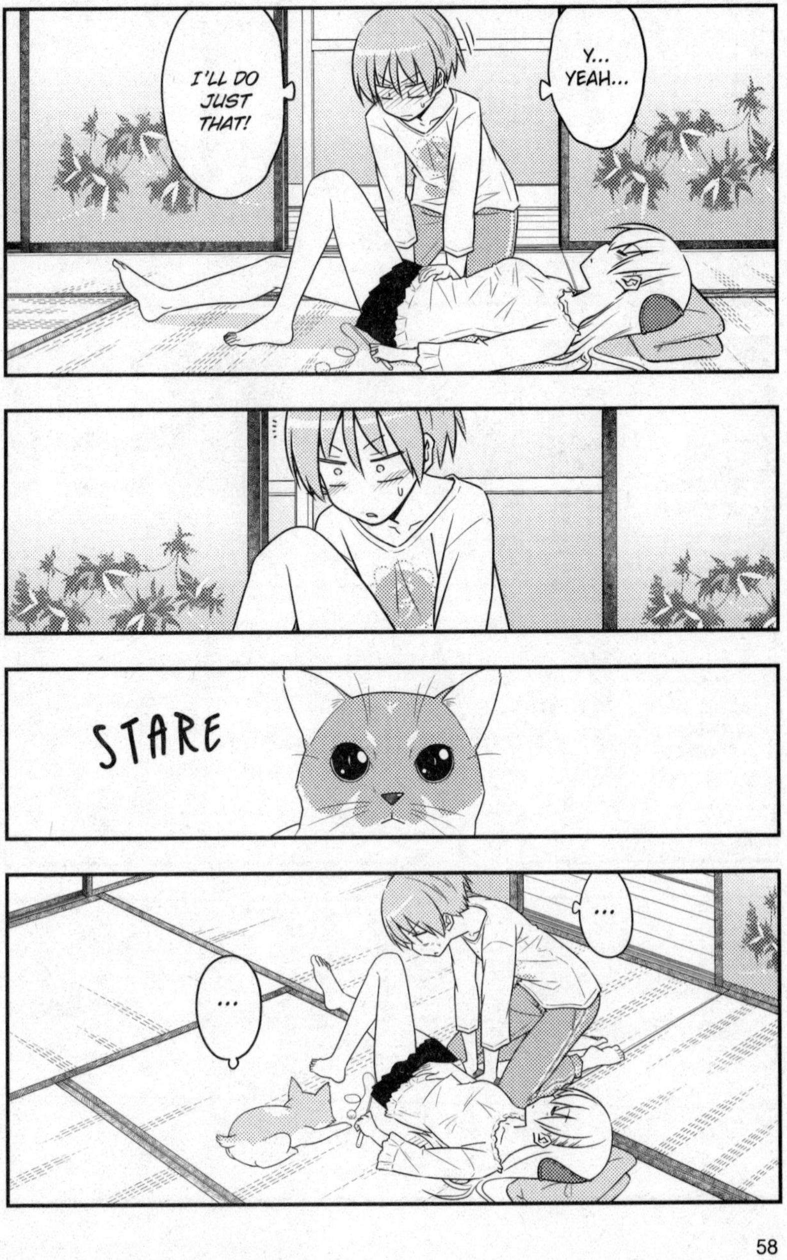
Y... YEAH...
I'LL DO JUST THAT!
STARE
...
...

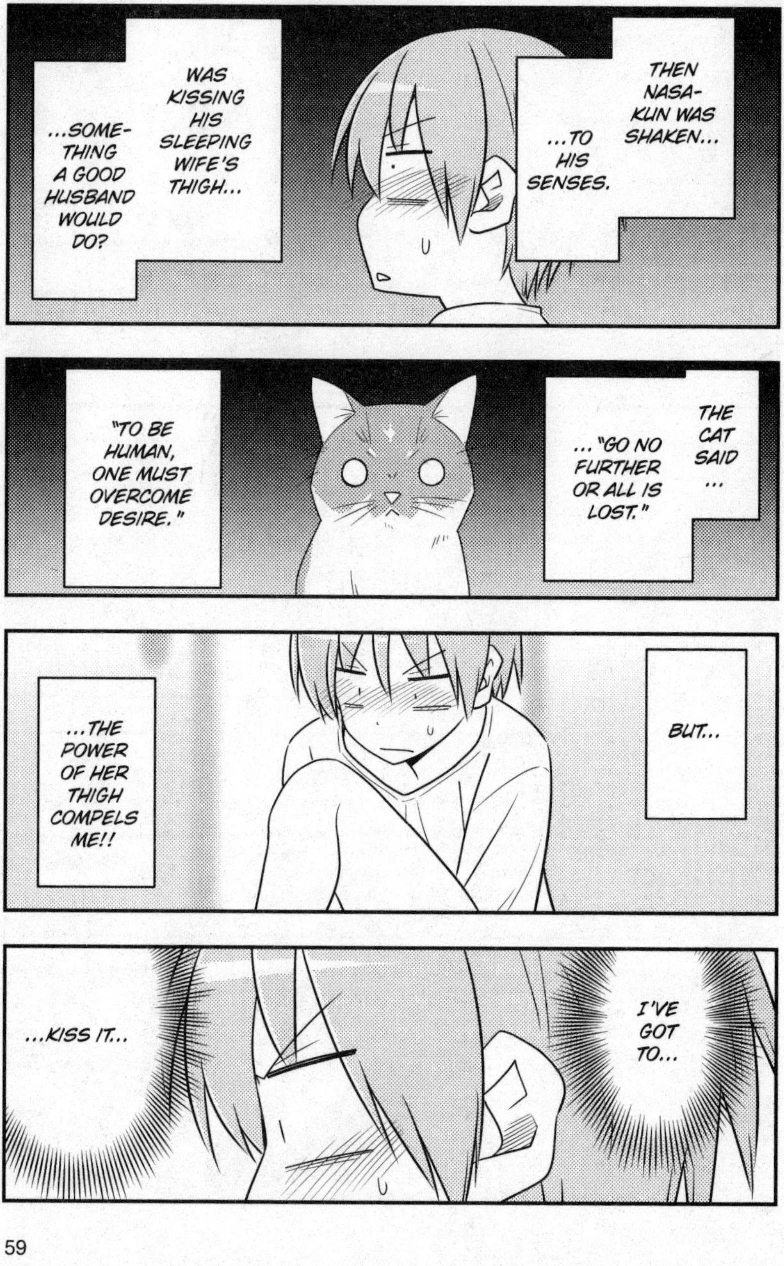
THEN NASA-KUN WAS SHAKEN...
...TO HIS SENSES.
WAS KISSING HIS SLEEPING WIFE'S THIGH...
...SOME-THING A GOOD HUSBAND WOULD DO?
THE CAT SAID ...
..."GO NO FURTHER OR ALL IS LOST."
"TO BE HUMAN, ONE MUST OVERCOME DESIRE."
BUT...
...THE POWER OF HER THIGH COMPELS ME!!
I'VE GOT TO...
...KISS IT...

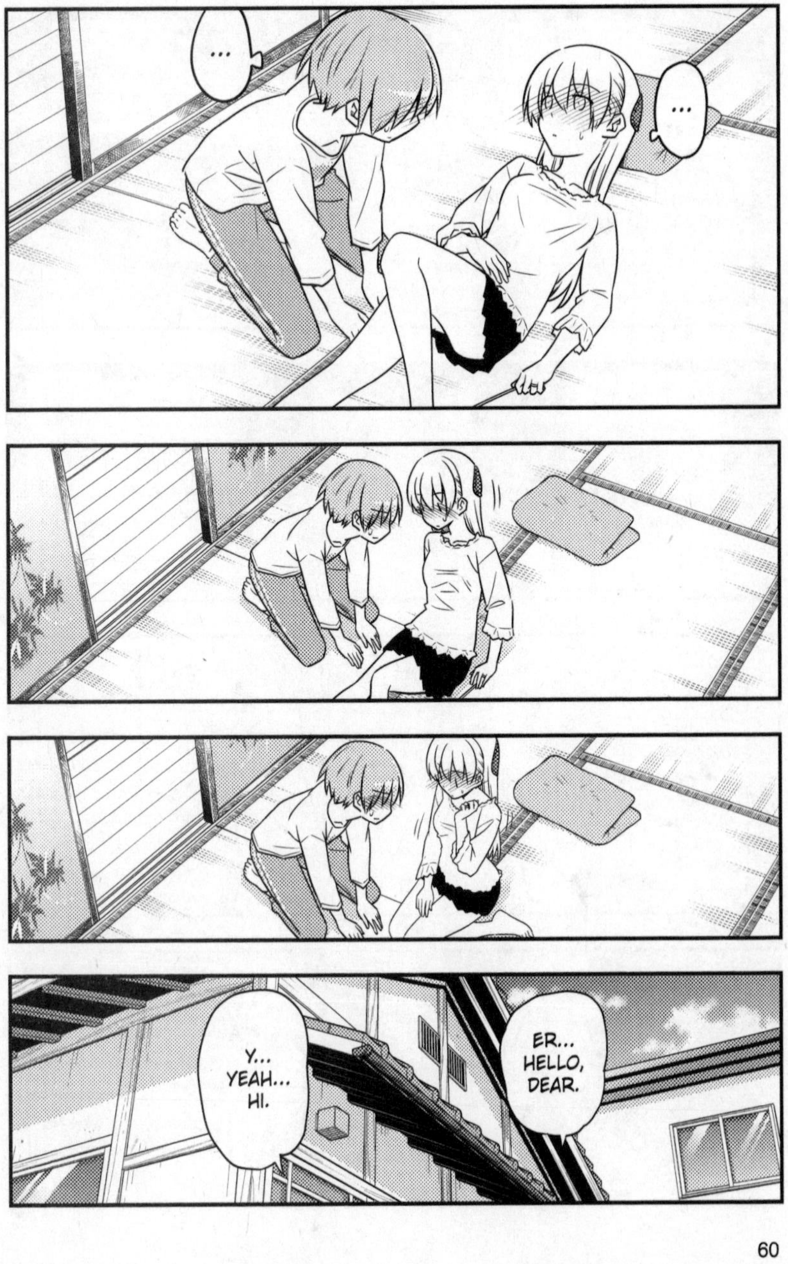
...
...
ER... HELLO, DEAR.
Y... YEAH... HI.

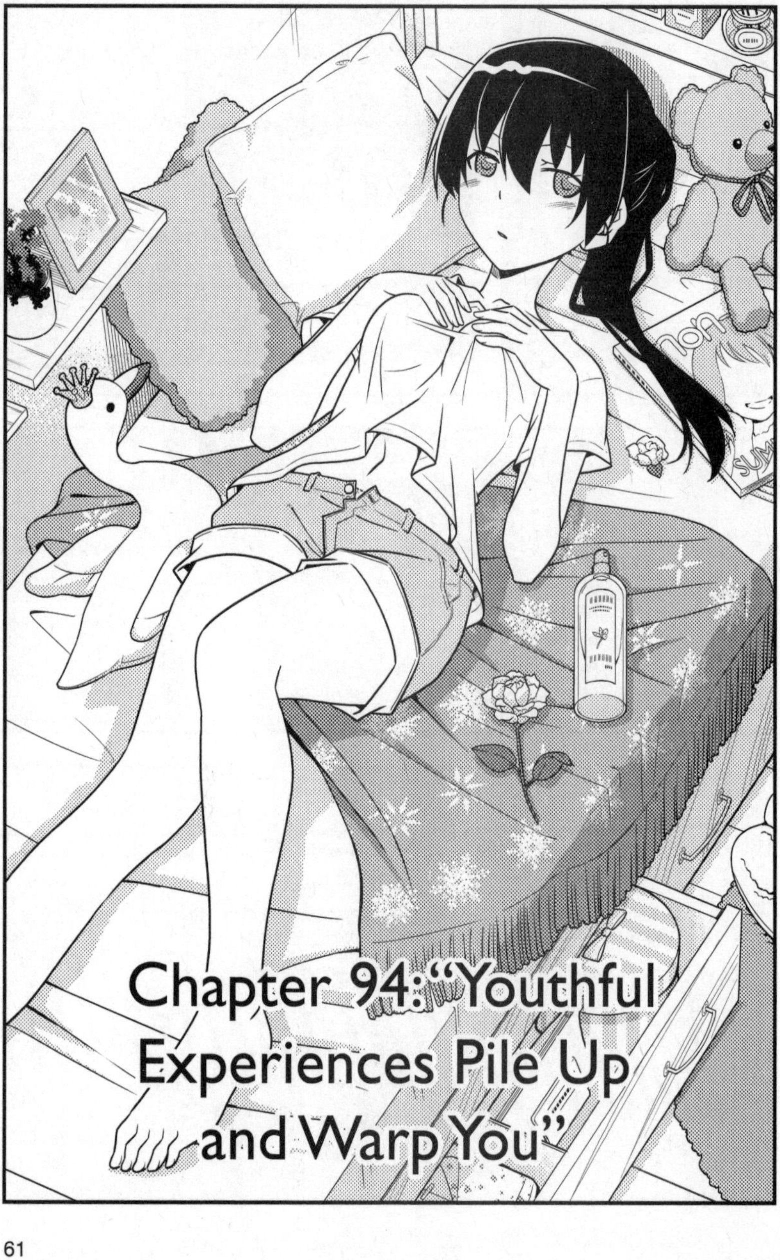
Chapter 94: "Youthful Experiences Pile Up and Warp You"

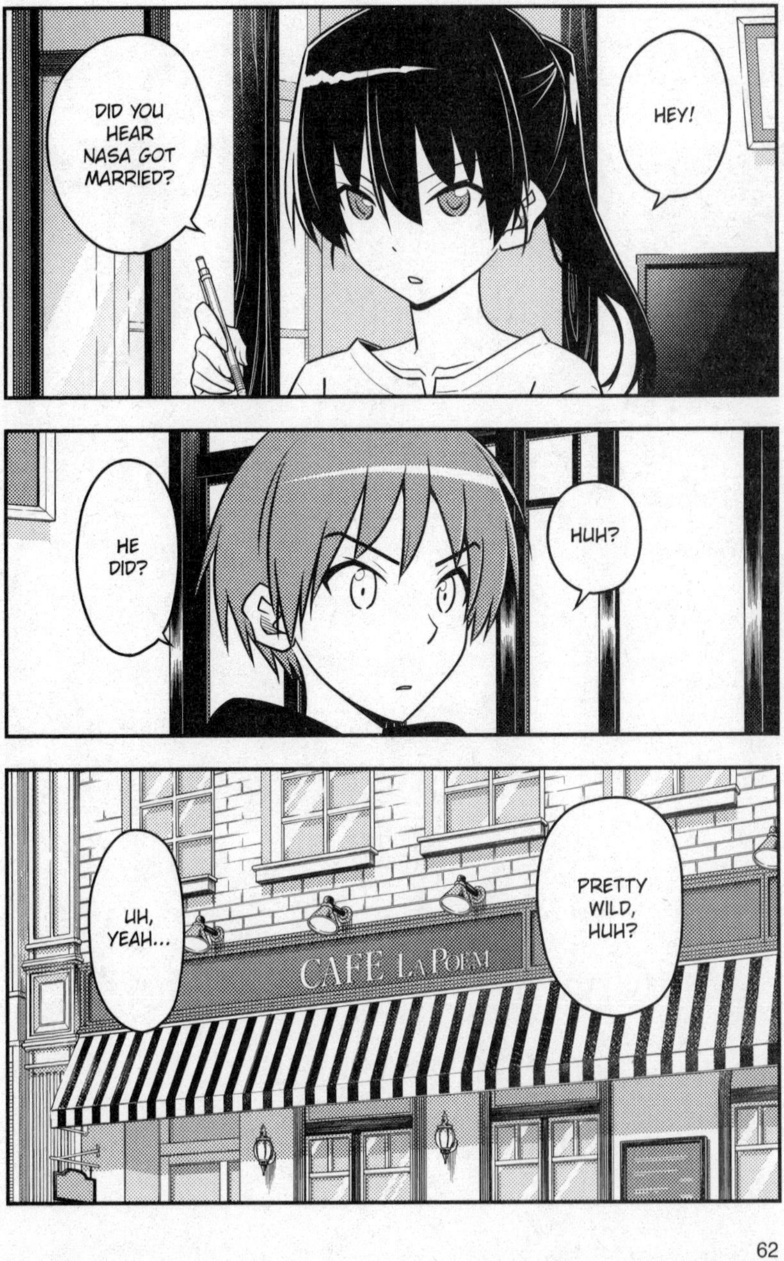
HEY!
DID YOU HEAR NASA GOT MARRIED?
HUH?
HE DID?
PRETTY WILD, HUH?
CAFE LA POEM
UH, YEAH...

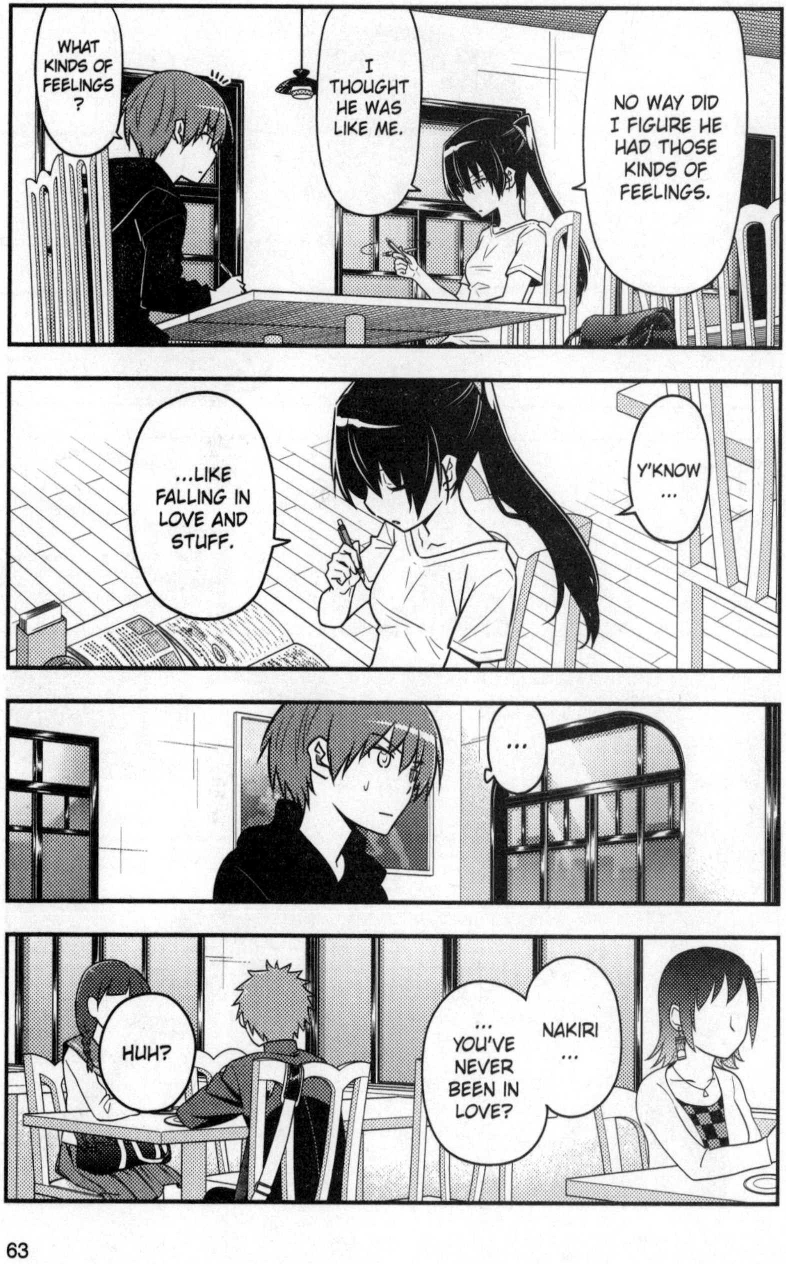
NO WAY DID I FIGURE HE HAD THOSE KINDS OF FEELINGS.
I THOUGHT HE WAS LIKE ME.
WHAT KINDS OF FEELINGS?
Y'KNOW...
...LIKE FALLING IN LOVE AND STUFF.
...
NAKIRI...
...YOU'VE NEVER BEEN IN LOVE?
HUH?

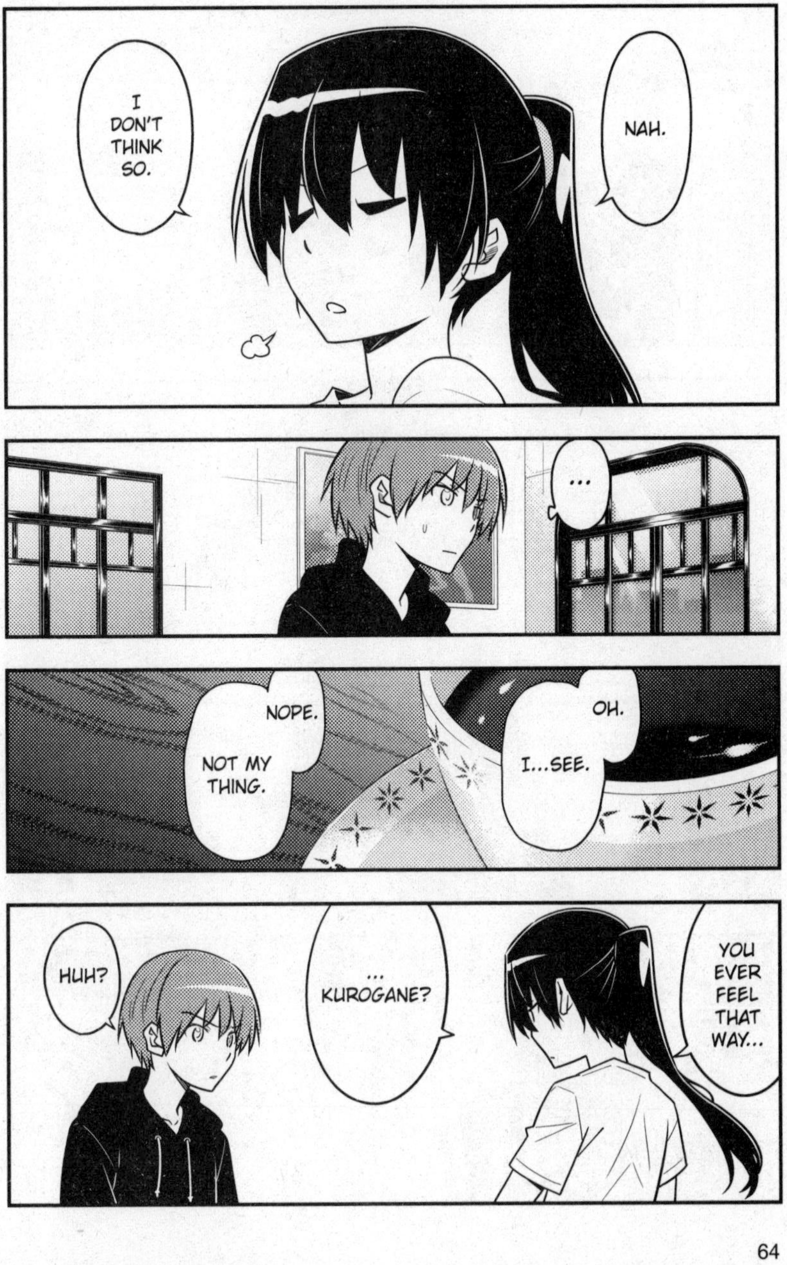
NAH.
I DON'T THINK SO.
...
OH.
I...SEE.
NOPE.
NOT MY THING.
YOU EVER FEEL THAT WAY...
... KUROGANE?
HUH?

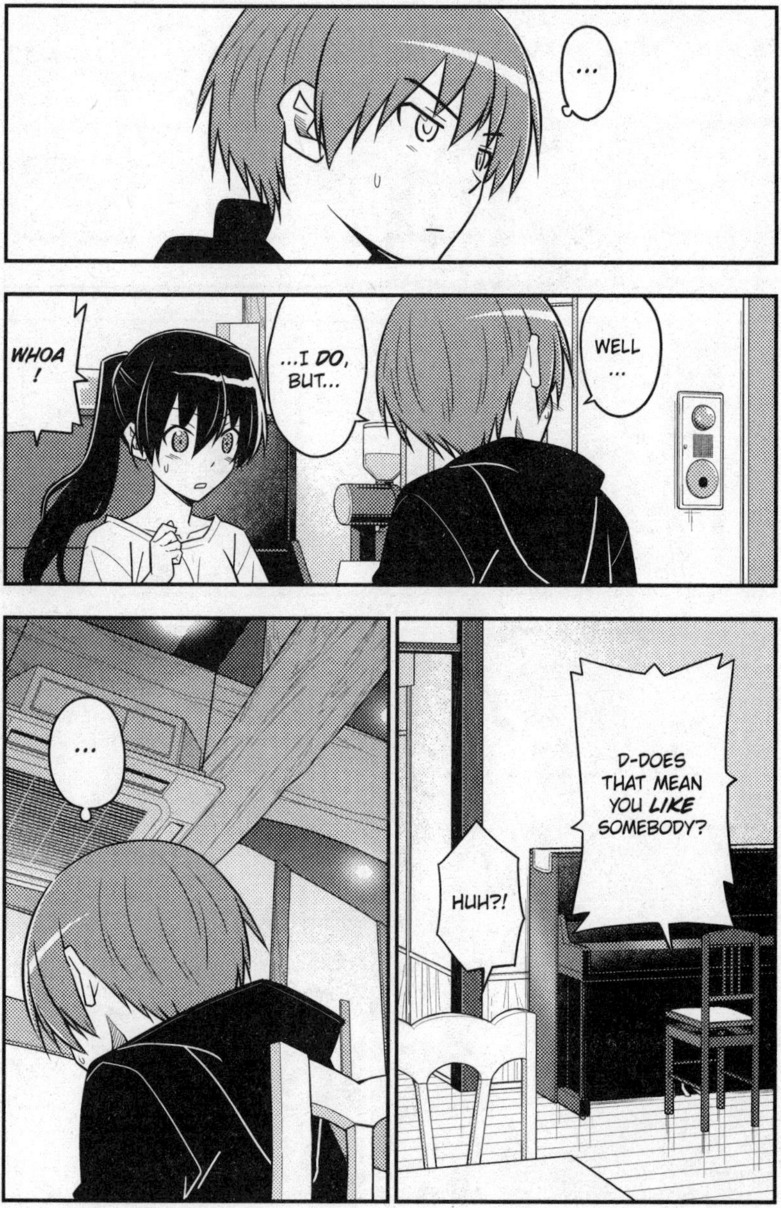
...
WELL ...
...I *DO*, BUT...
WHOA!
D-DOES THAT MEAN YOU *LIKE* SOMEBODY?
HUH?!
...

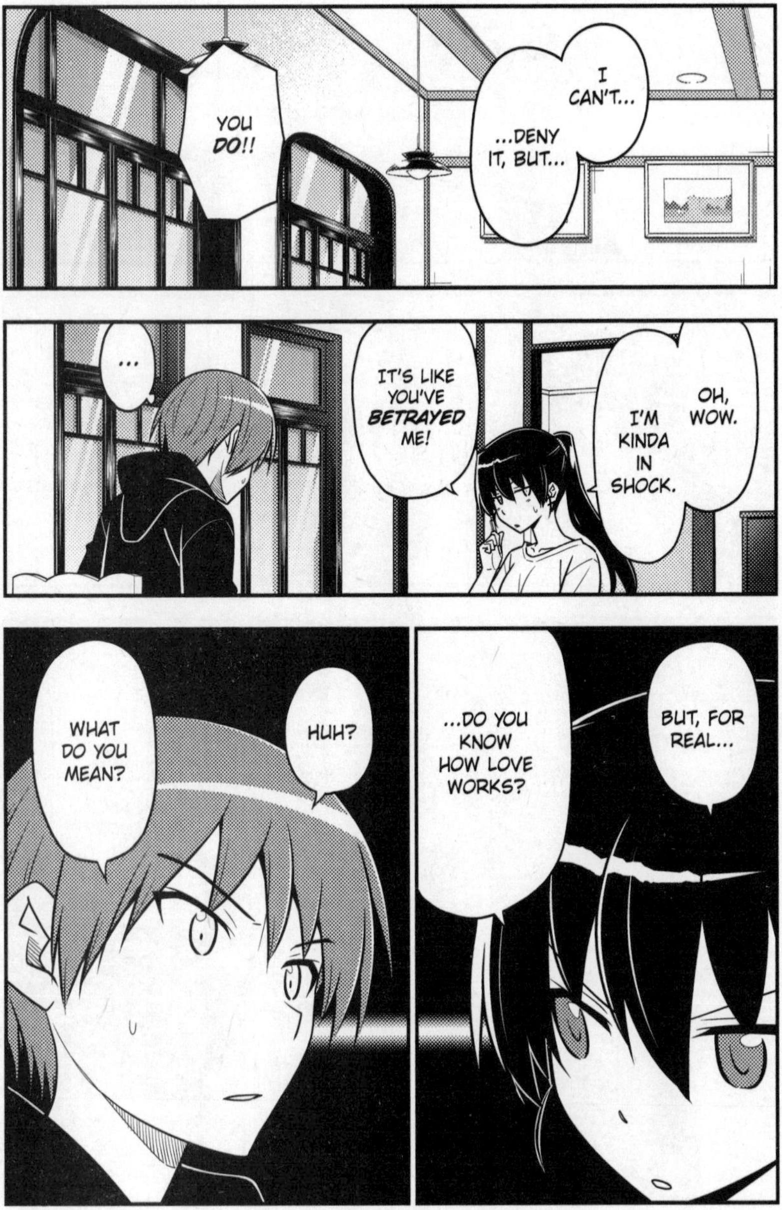
I CAN'T...
...DENY IT, BUT...
YOU DO!!
OH, WOW.
I'M KINDA IN SHOCK.
IT'S LIKE YOU'VE BETRAYED ME!
...
BUT, FOR REAL...
...DO YOU KNOW HOW LOVE WORKS?
HUH?
WHAT DO YOU MEAN?

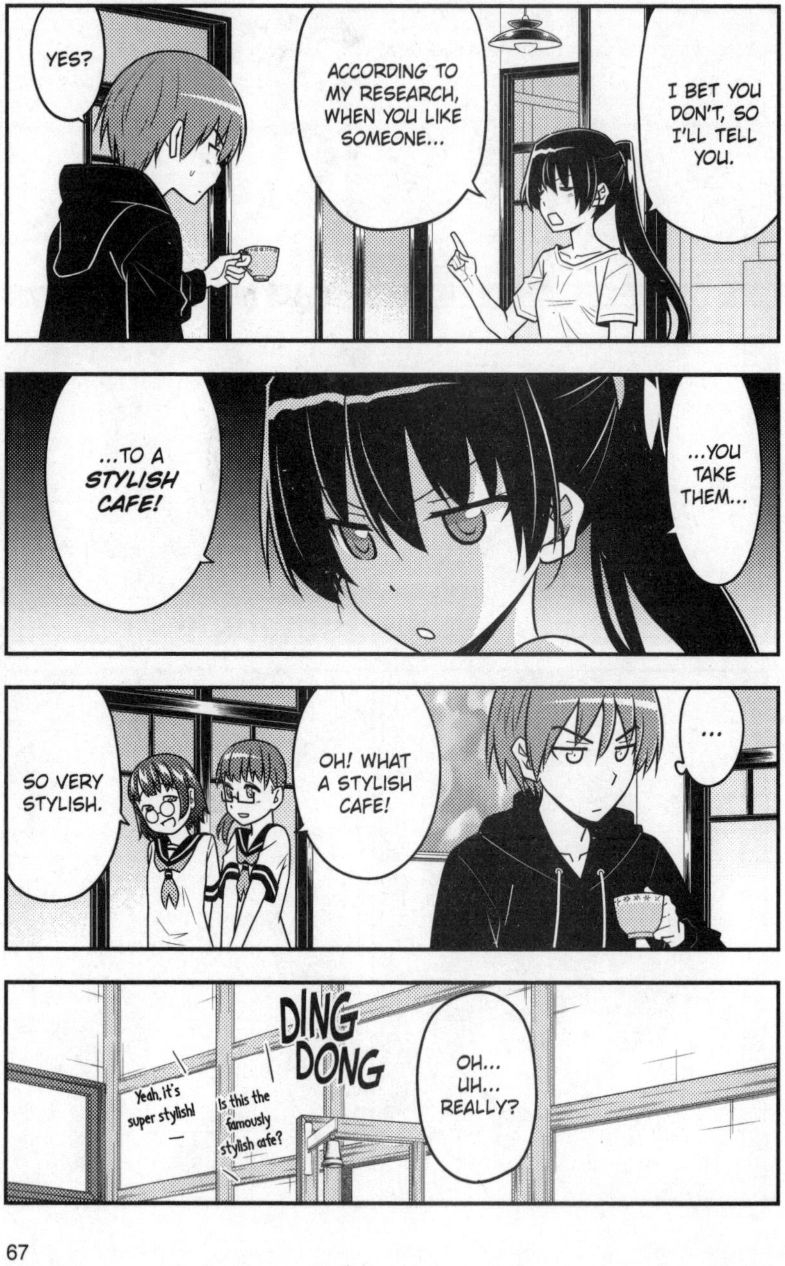
I BET YOU DON'T, SO I'LL TELL YOU.
ACCORDING TO MY RESEARCH, WHEN YOU LIKE SOMEONE...
YES?
...YOU TAKE THEM...
...TO A STYLISH CAFE!
...
OH! WHAT A STYLISH CAFE!
SO VERY STYLISH.
OH... UH... REALLY?
DING DONG
Is this the famously stylish cafe?
Yeah, it's super stylish!

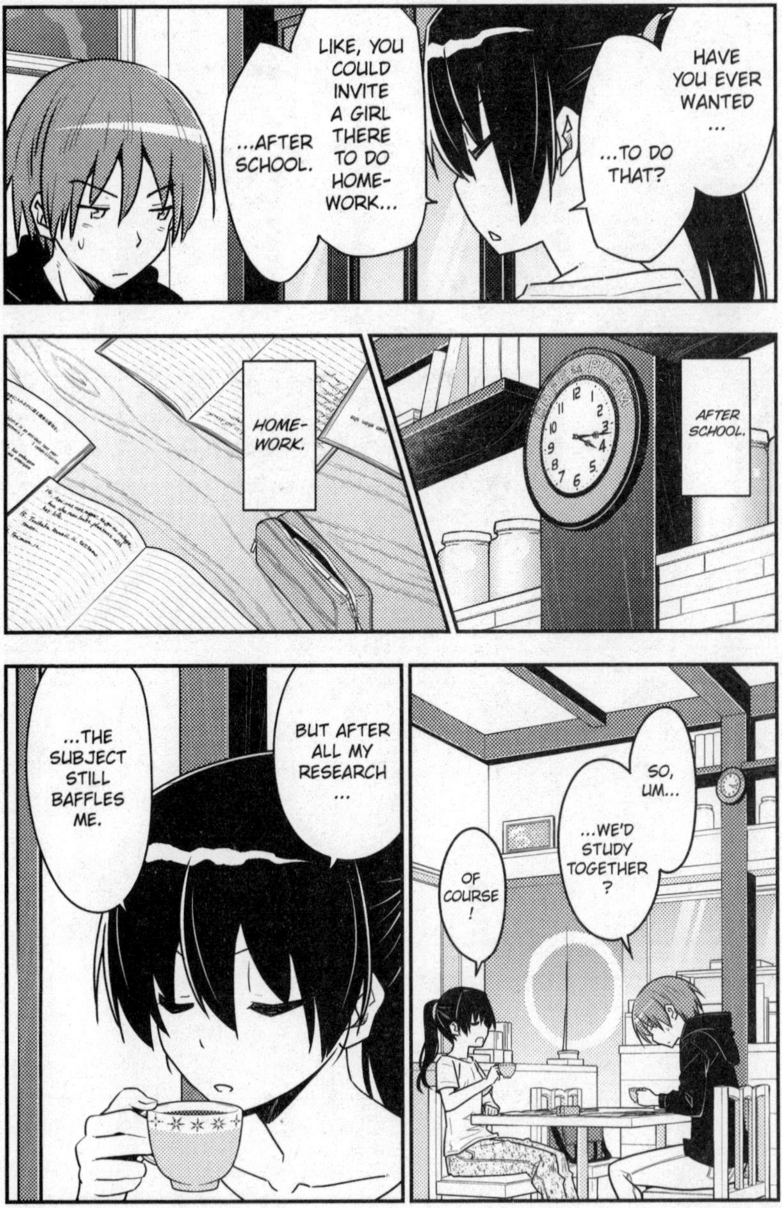
HAVE YOU EVER WANTED ...
...TO DO THAT?
LIKE, YOU COULD INVITE A GIRL THERE TO DO HOME-WORK...
...AFTER SCHOOL.
AFTER SCHOOL.
HOME-WORK.
SO, UM...
...WE'D STUDY TOGETHER ?
OF COURSE !
BUT AFTER ALL MY RESEARCH ...
...THE SUBJECT STILL BAFFLES ME.

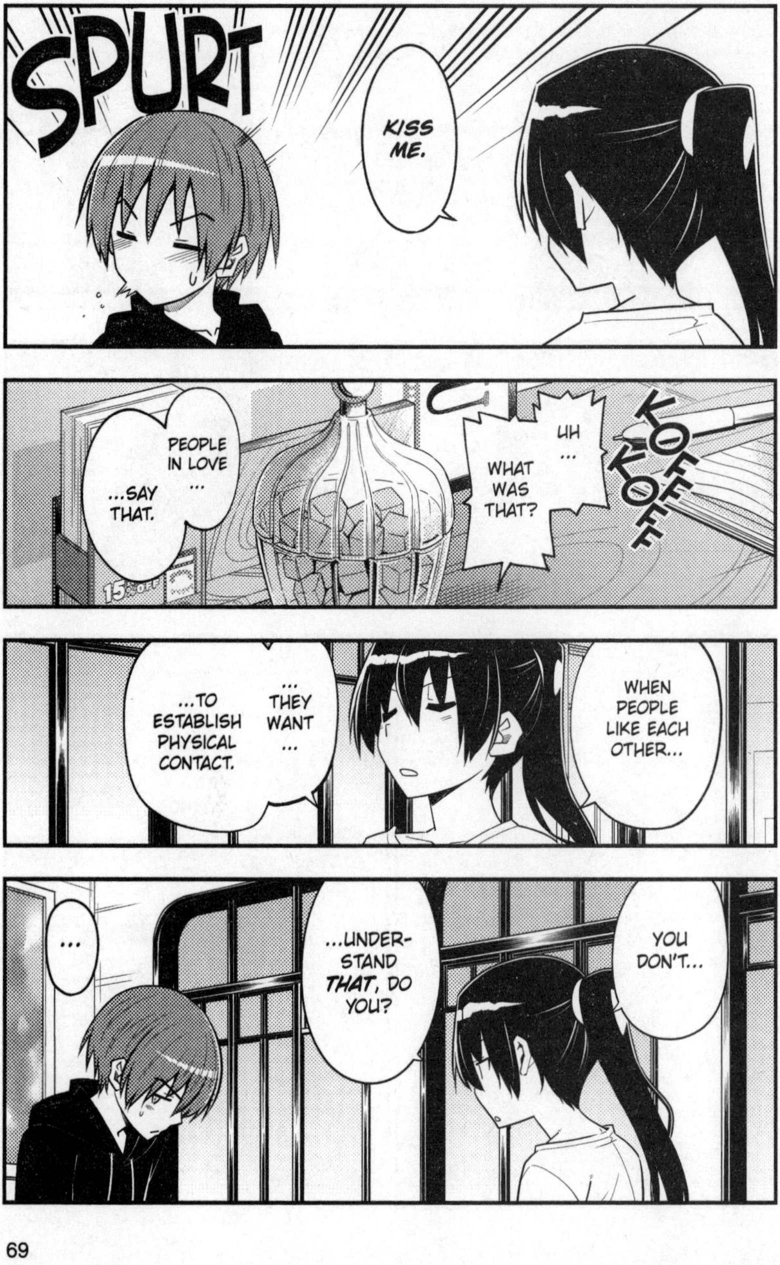
KISS ME.
SPURT
KOFF KOFF
UH ... WHAT WAS THAT?
PEOPLE IN LOVE ... ...SAY THAT.
15% OFF
WHEN PEOPLE LIKE EACH OTHER...
... THEY WANT ...
...TO ESTABLISH PHYSICAL CONTACT.
YOU DON'T...
...UNDER-STAND THAT, DO YOU?
...

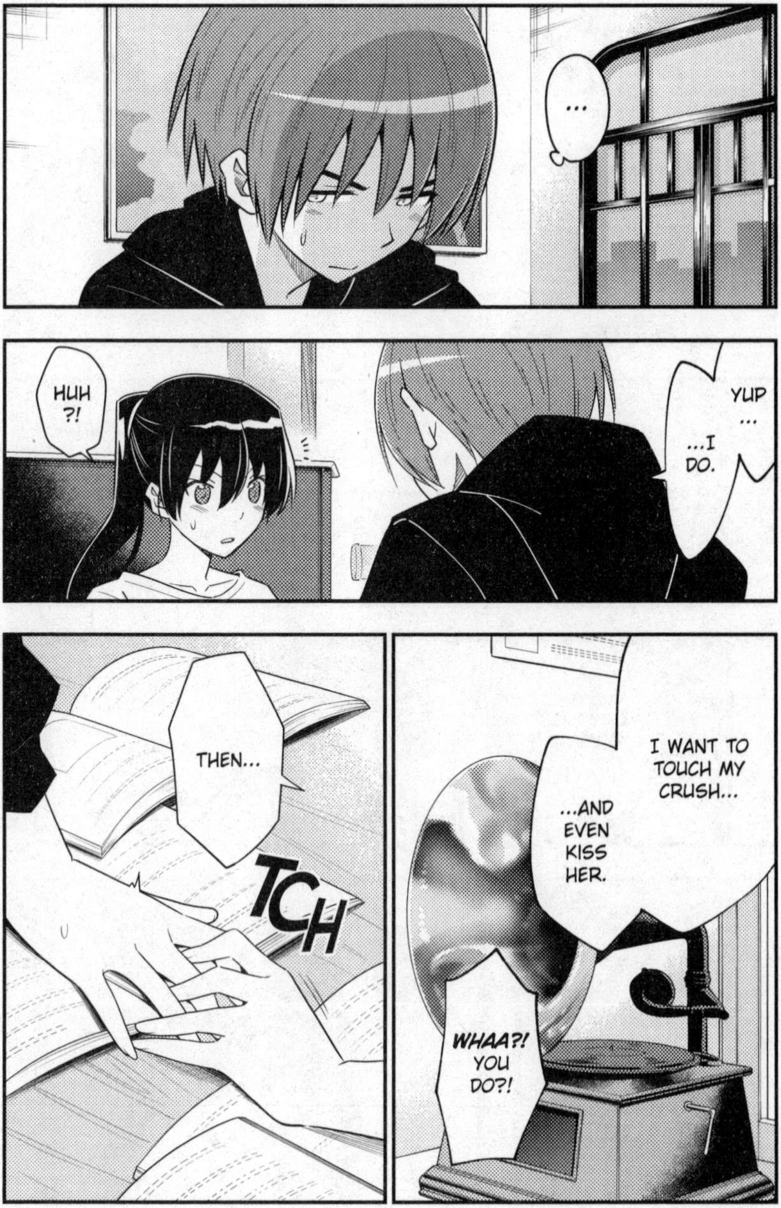
...
YUP ...
...I DO.
HUH ?!
I WANT TO TOUCH MY CRUSH...
...AND EVEN KISS HER.
WHAA?! YOU DO?!
THEN...
TCH

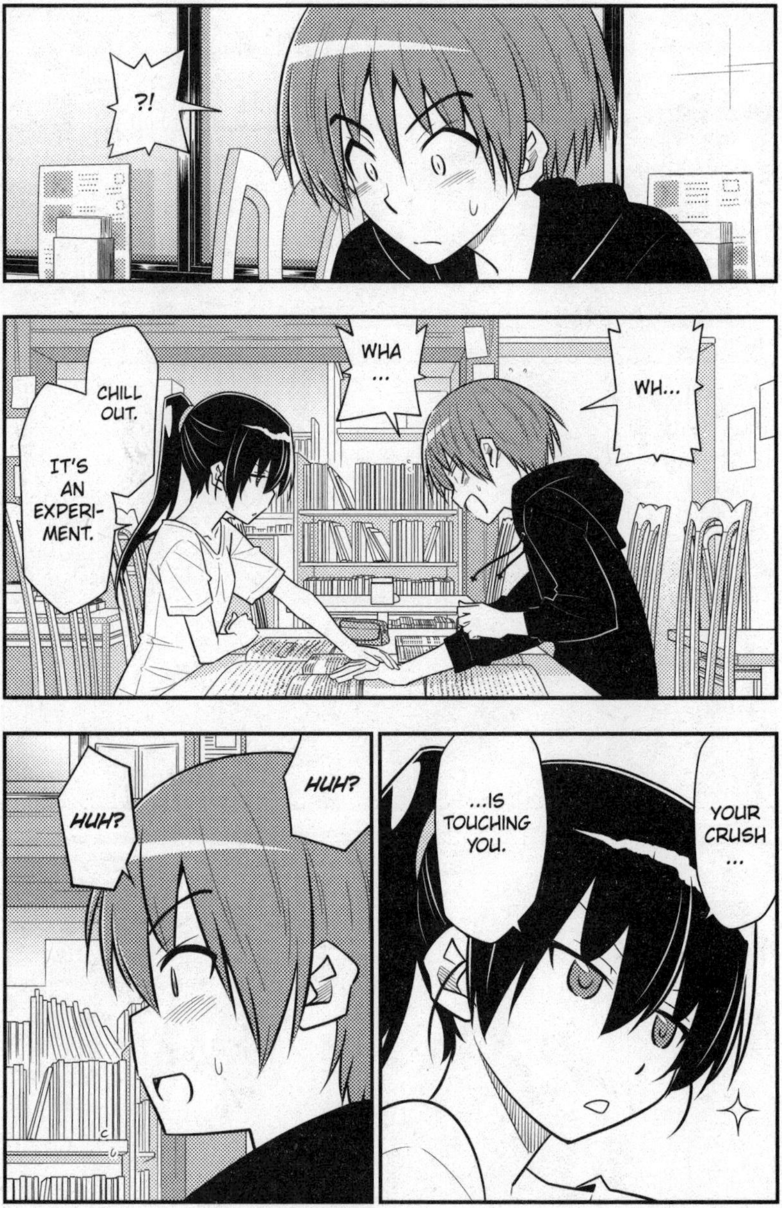
?!
WH...
WHA ...
CHILL OUT.
IT'S AN EXPERI-MENT.
YOUR CRUSH ...
...IS TOUCHING YOU.
HUH?
HUH?

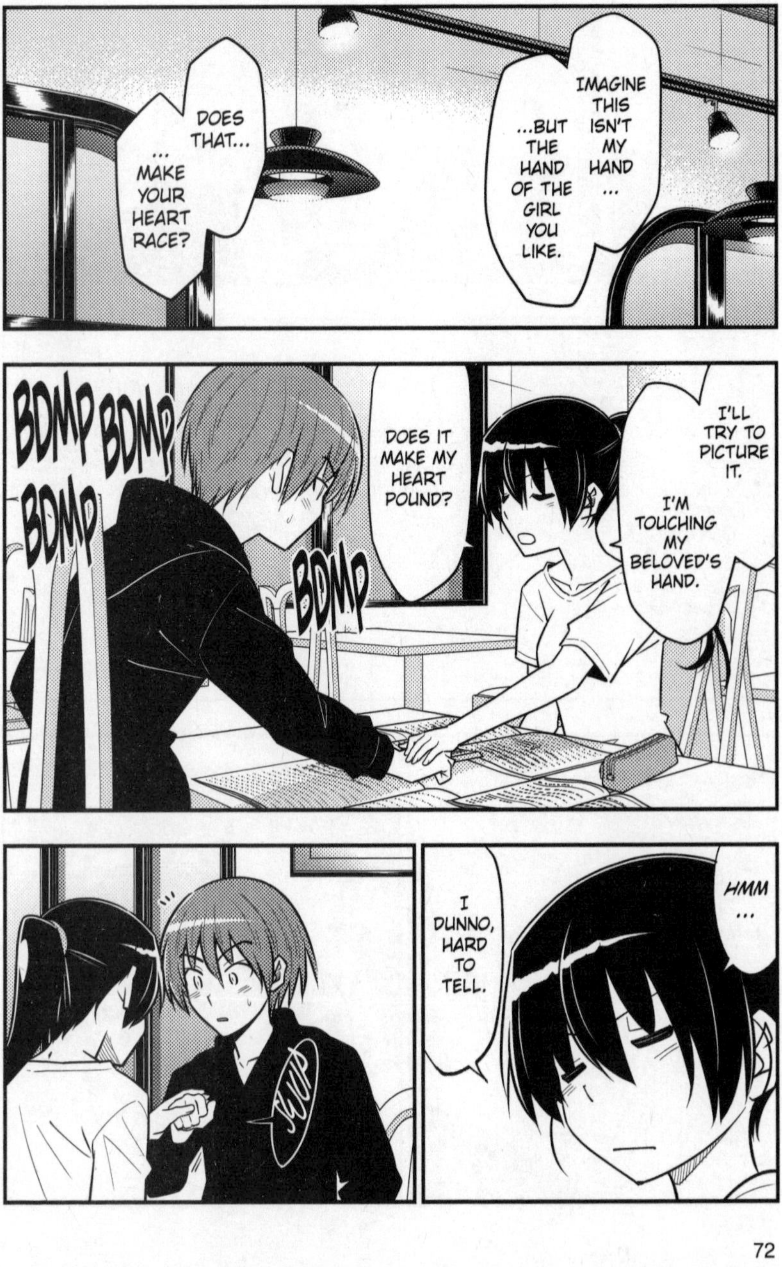
IMAGINE THIS ISN'T MY HAND ...
...BUT THE HAND OF THE GIRL YOU LIKE.
DOES THAT...
...MAKE YOUR HEART RACE?
I'LL TRY TO PICTURE IT.
I'M TOUCHING MY BELOVED'S HAND.
DOES IT MAKE MY HEART POUND?
BDMP BDMP
BDMP
BDMP
HMM ...
I DUNNO, HARD TO TELL.

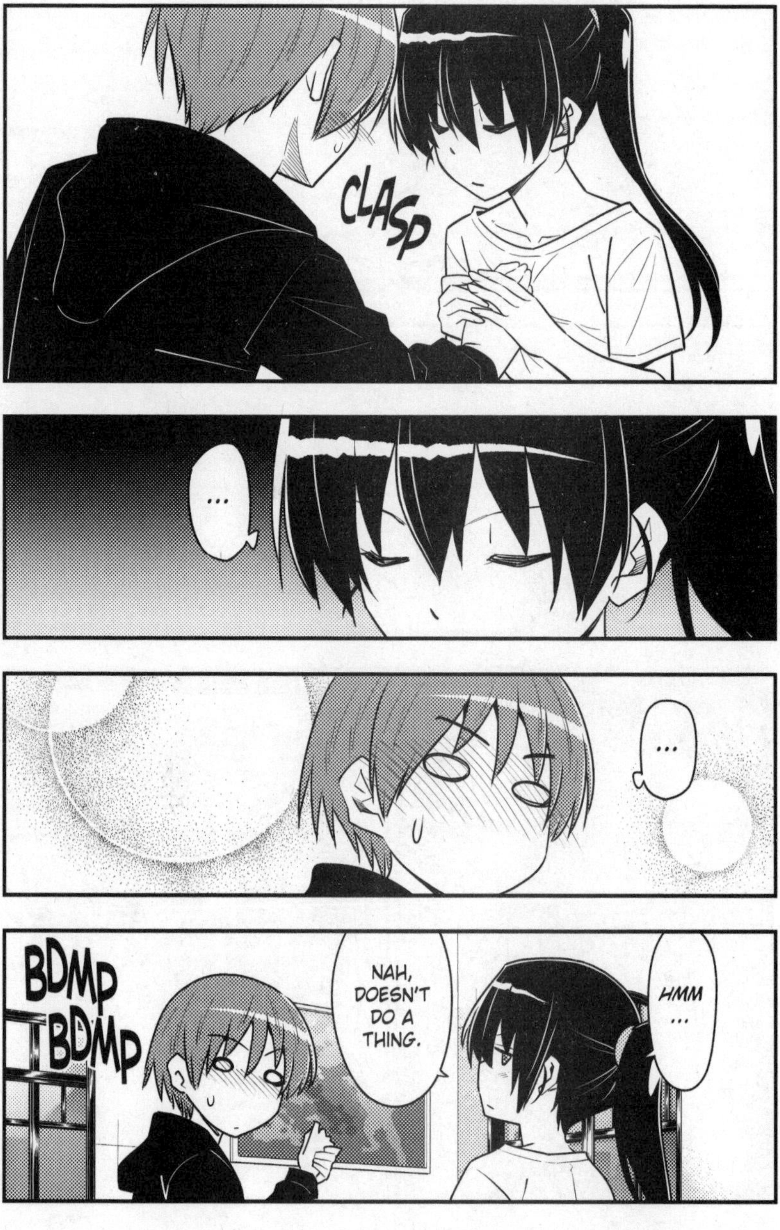
CLASP
...
...
HMM ...
NAH, DOESN'T DO A THING.
BDMP BDMP

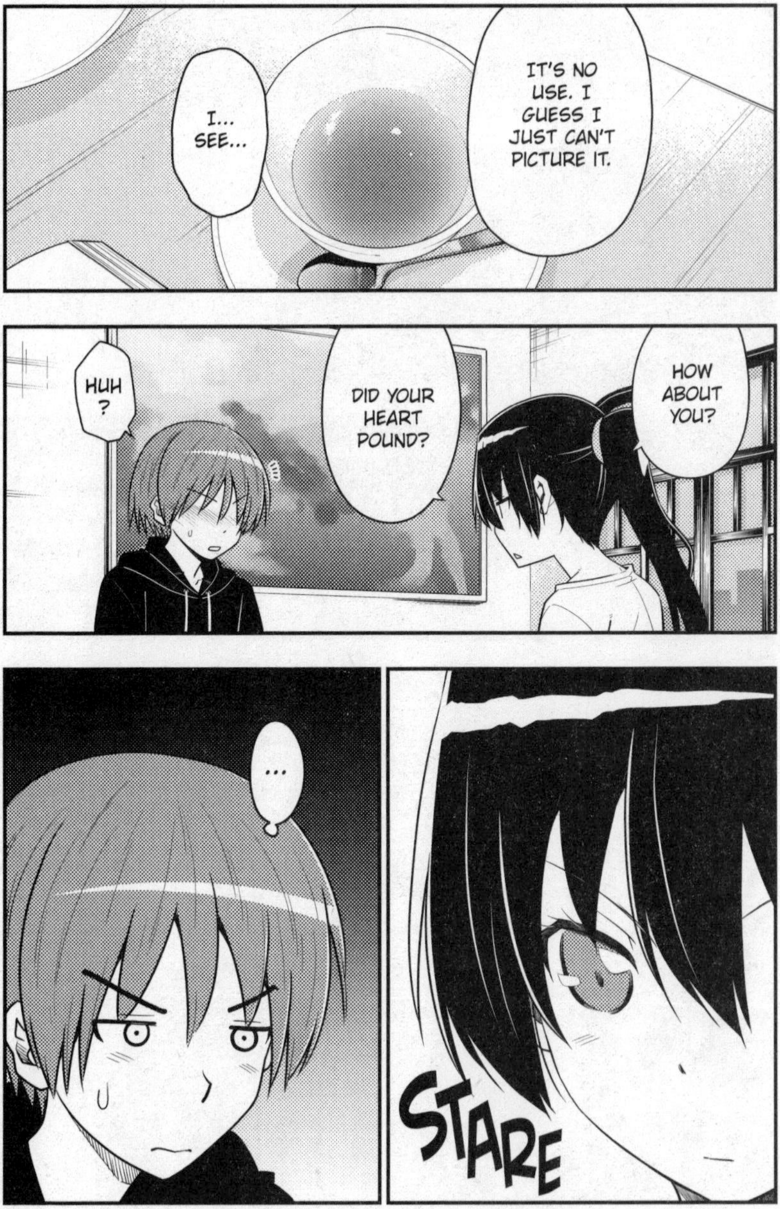
IT'S NO USE. I GUESS I JUST CAN'T PICTURE IT.
I... SEE...
HOW ABOUT YOU?
DID YOUR HEART POUND?
HUH ?
STARE
...

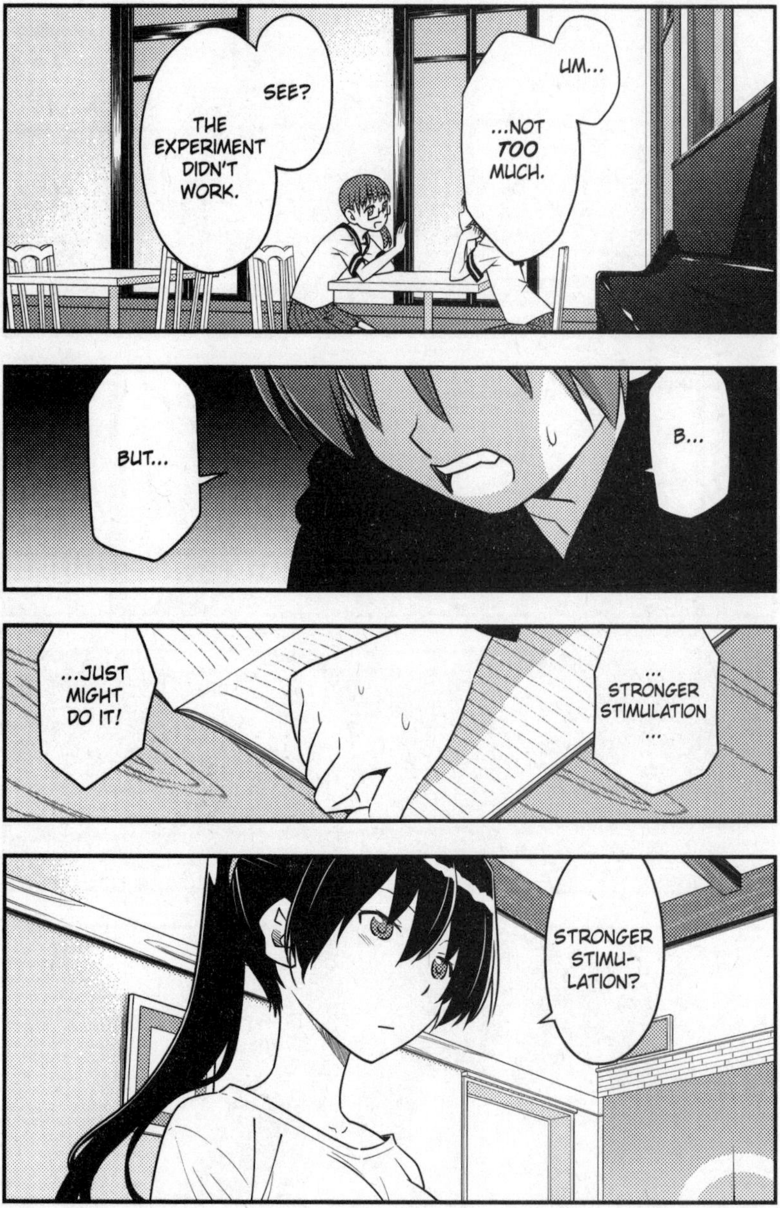
UM...
...NOT *TOO* MUCH.
SEE?
THE EXPERIMENT DIDN'T WORK.
B...
BUT...
... STRONGER STIMULATION ...
...JUST MIGHT DO IT!
STRONGER STIMU- LATION?

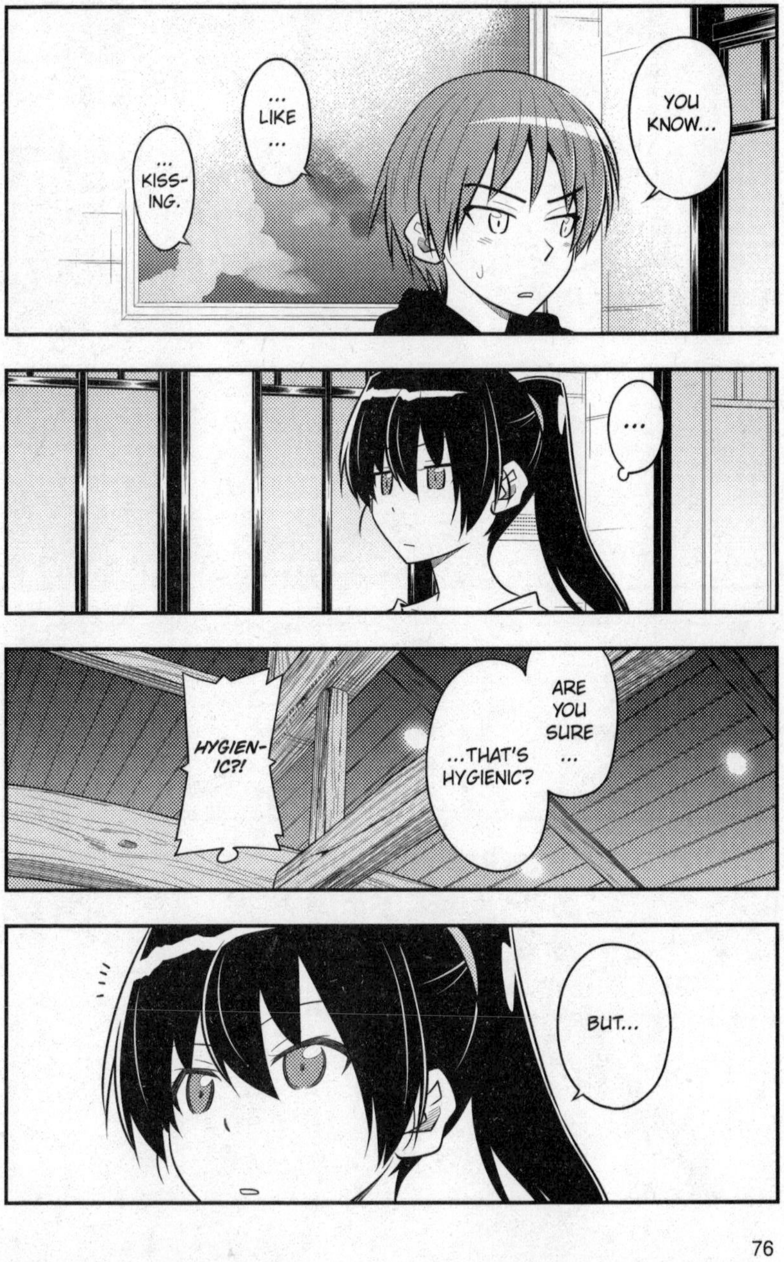
YOU KNOW...
... LIKE ...
... KISS-ING.
...
ARE YOU SURE ...
...THAT'S HYGIENIC?
HYGIEN-IC?!
BUT...

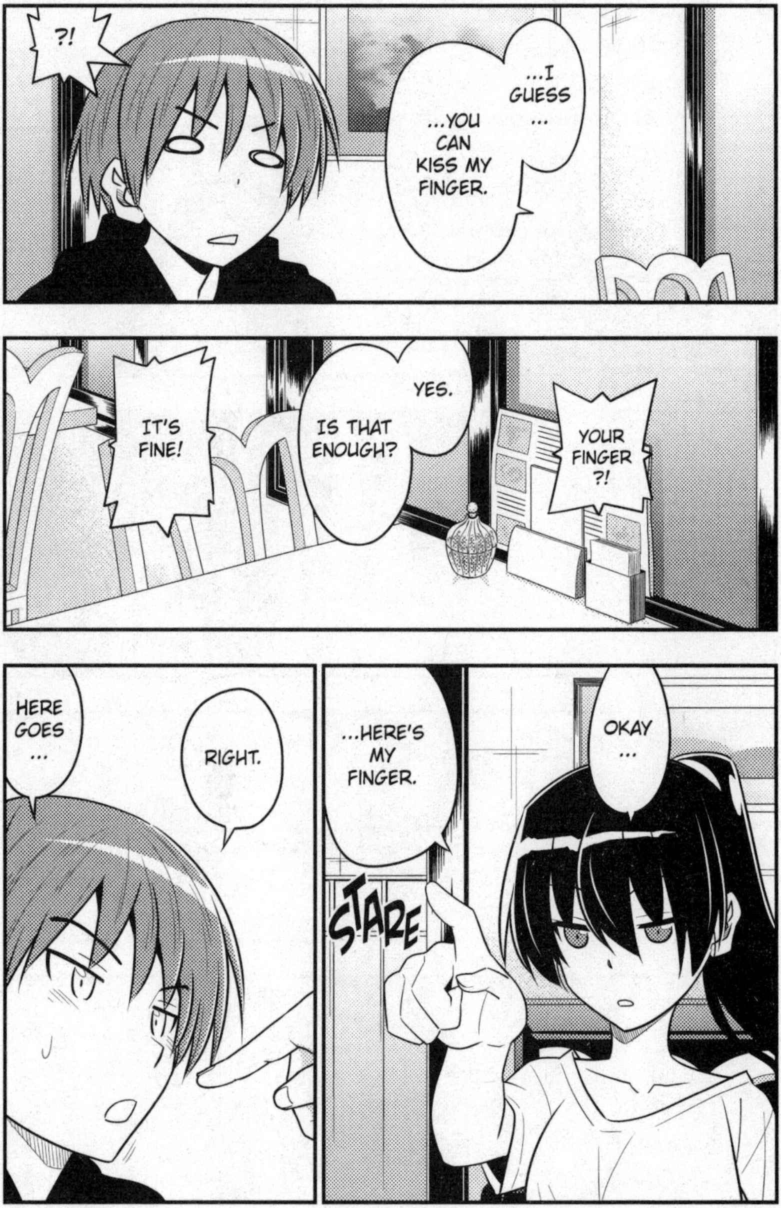
...I GUESS ...
...YOU CAN KISS MY FINGER.
?!
YOUR FINGER ?!
YES.
IS THAT ENOUGH?
IT'S FINE!
OKAY ...
...HERE'S MY FINGER.
STARE
RIGHT.
HERE GOES ...

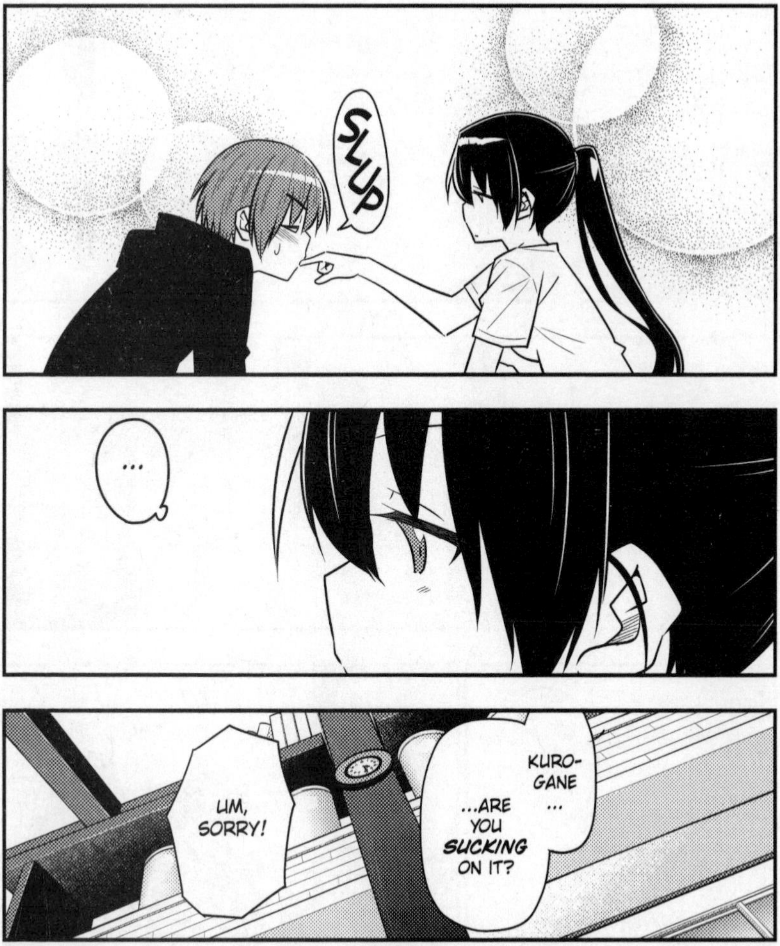
SLUP
...
KURO-GANE ...
...ARE YOU SUCKING ON IT?
UM, SORRY!
WHAT ARE YOUR FRIENDS DOING OVER THERE?
DEAR?
I... HAVE NO IDEA.
THE YUZAKIS DIDN'T MAKE IT INTO THIS CHAPTER.

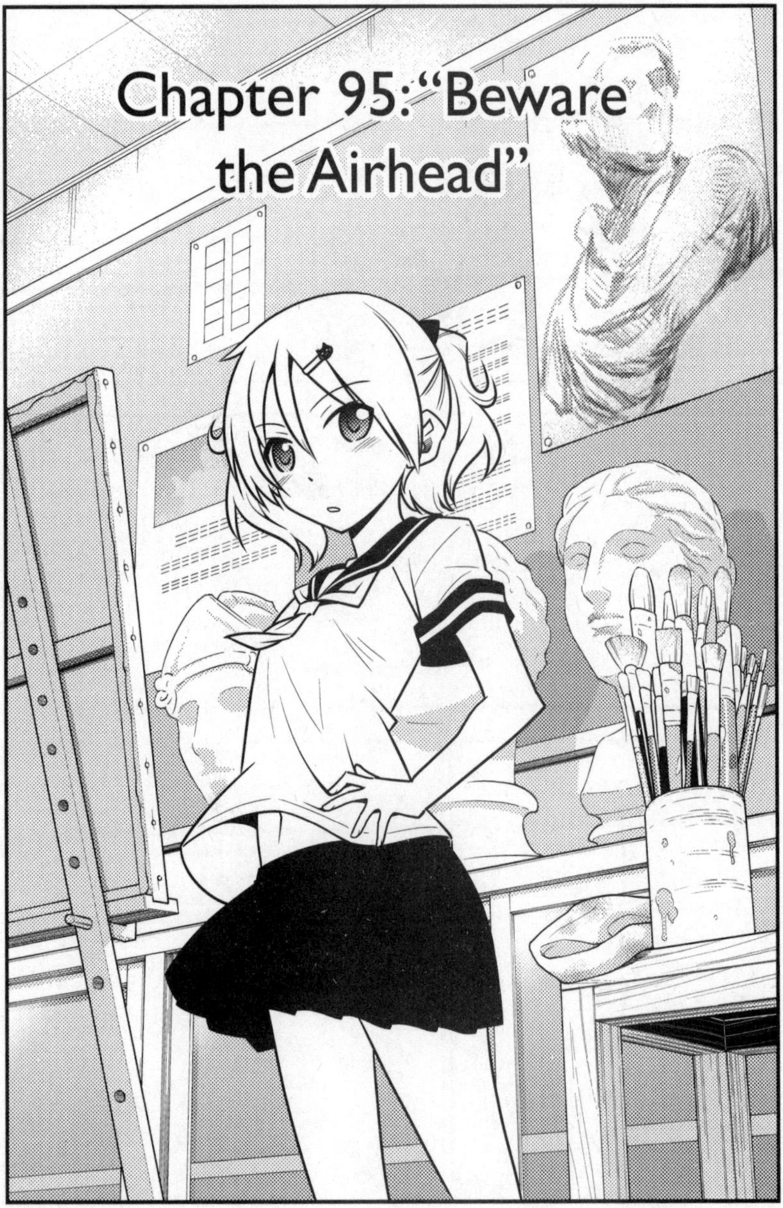
Chapter 95: "Beware the Airhead"

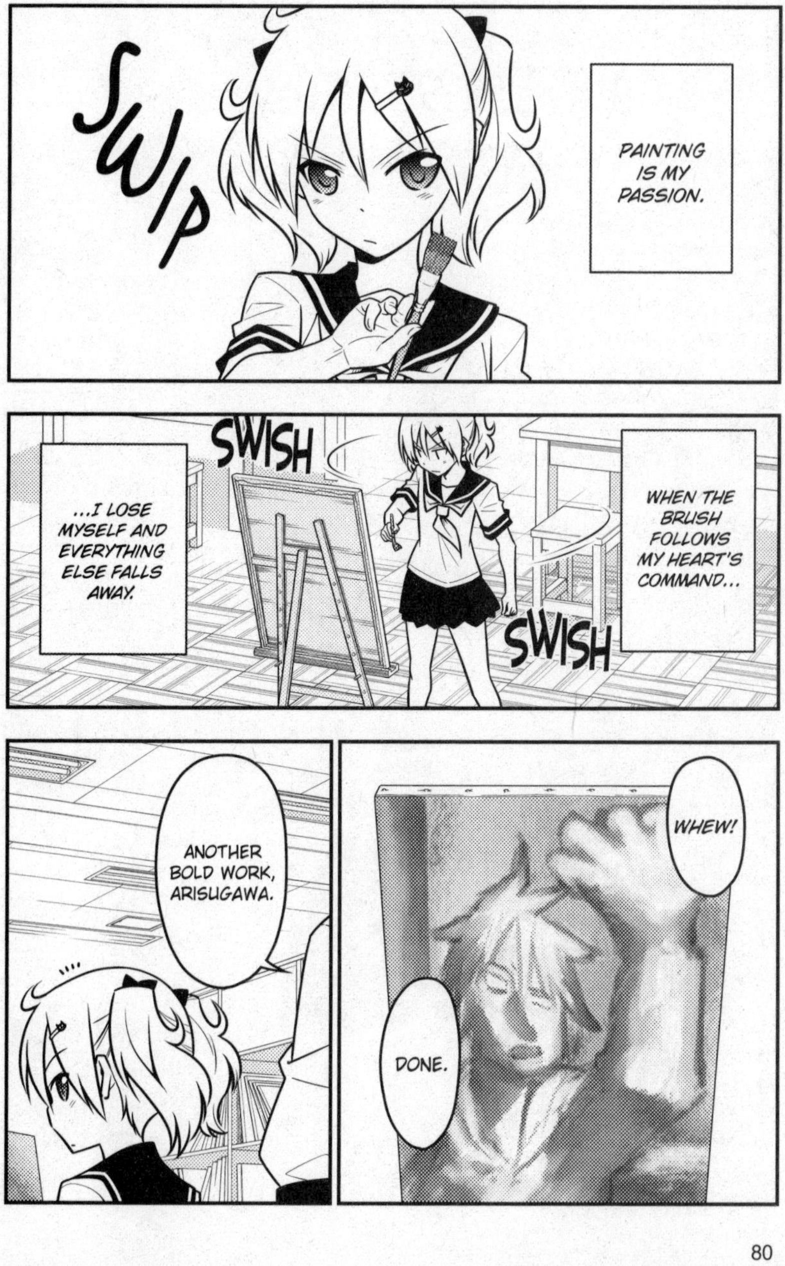
PAINTING IS MY PASSION.
SWIP
WHEN THE BRUSH FOLLOWS MY HEART'S COMMAND...
SWISH
SWISH
...I LOSE MYSELF AND EVERYTHING ELSE FALLS AWAY.
WHEW!
DONE.
ANOTHER BOLD WORK, ARISUGAWA.

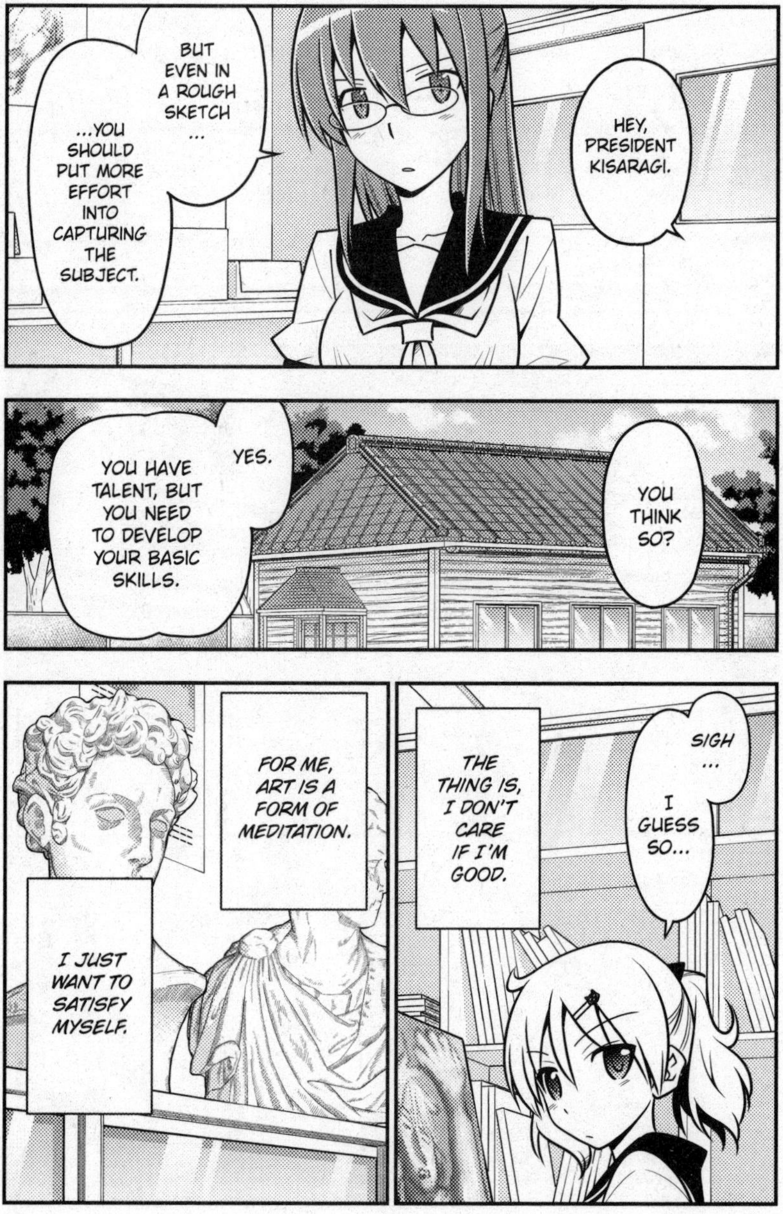
HEY, PRESIDENT KISARAGI.
BUT EVEN IN A ROUGH SKETCH ...
...YOU SHOULD PUT MORE EFFORT INTO CAPTURING THE SUBJECT.
YOU THINK SO?
YES.
YOU HAVE TALENT, BUT YOU NEED TO DEVELOP YOUR BASIC SKILLS.
SIGH ...
I GUESS SO...
THE THING IS, I DON'T CARE IF I'M GOOD.
FOR ME, ART IS A FORM OF MEDITATION.
I JUST WANT TO SATISFY MYSELF.

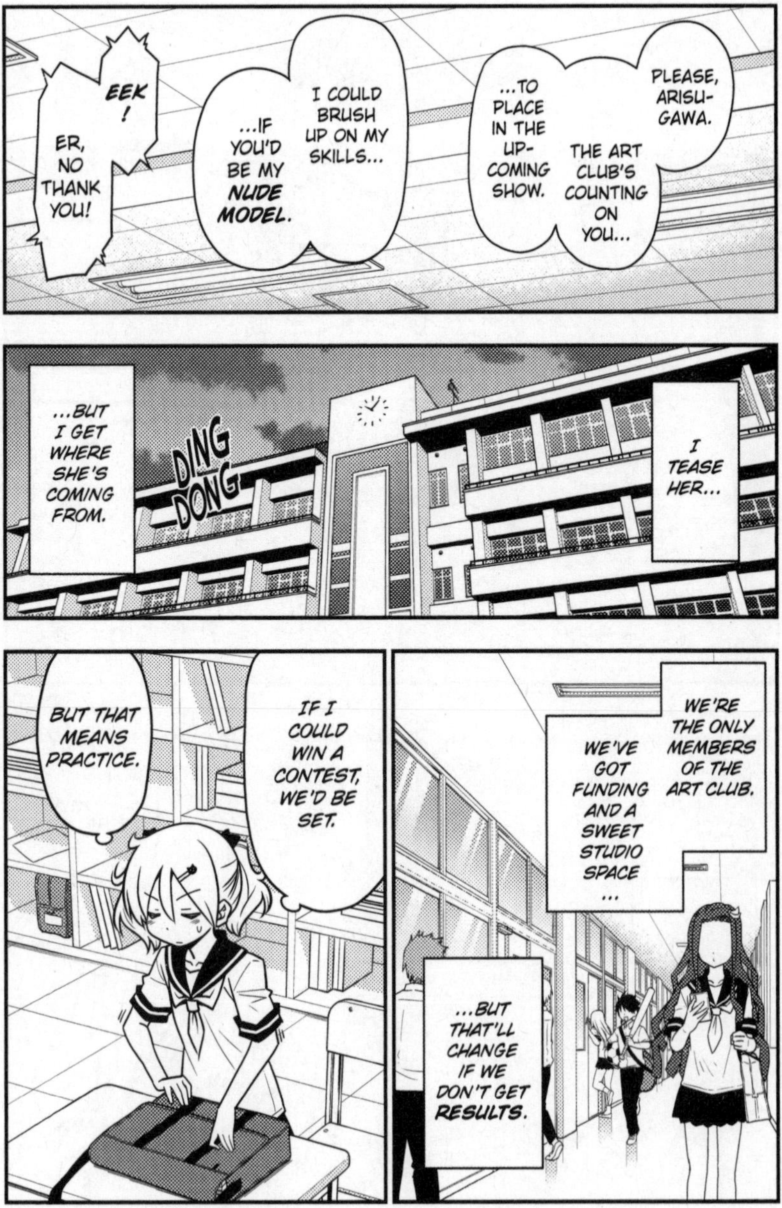
PLEASE, ARISU-GAWA.
THE ART CLUB'S COUNTING ON YOU...
...TO PLACE IN THE UP-COMING SHOW.
I COULD BRUSH UP ON MY SKILLS...
...IF YOU'D BE MY NUDE MODEL.
EEK!
ER, NO THANK YOU!
I TEASE HER...
DING DONG
...BUT I GET WHERE SHE'S COMING FROM.
WE'RE THE ONLY MEMBERS OF THE ART CLUB.
WE'VE GOT FUNDING AND A SWEET STUDIO SPACE ...
...BUT THAT'LL CHANGE IF WE DON'T GET RESULTS.
IF I COULD WIN A CONTEST, WE'D BE SET.
BUT THAT MEANS PRACTICE.

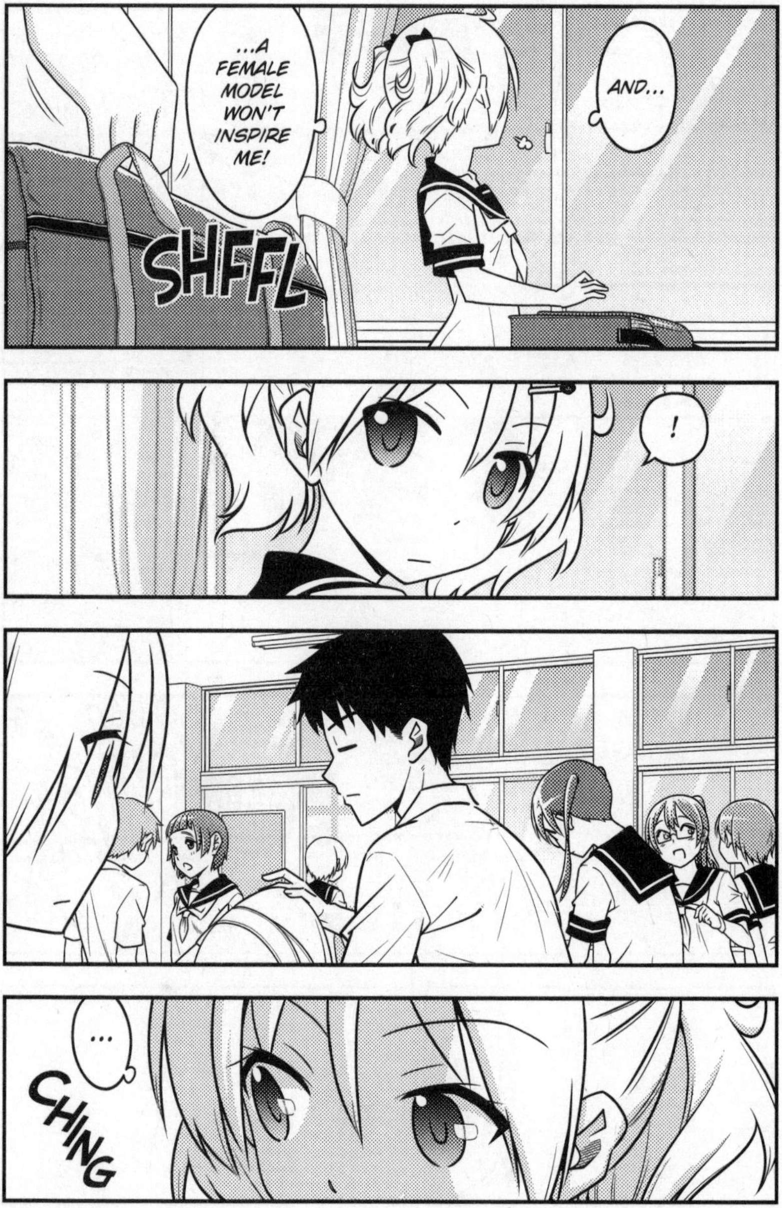
AND...
...A FEMALE MODEL WON'T INSPIRE ME!
SHFFL
!
...
CHING

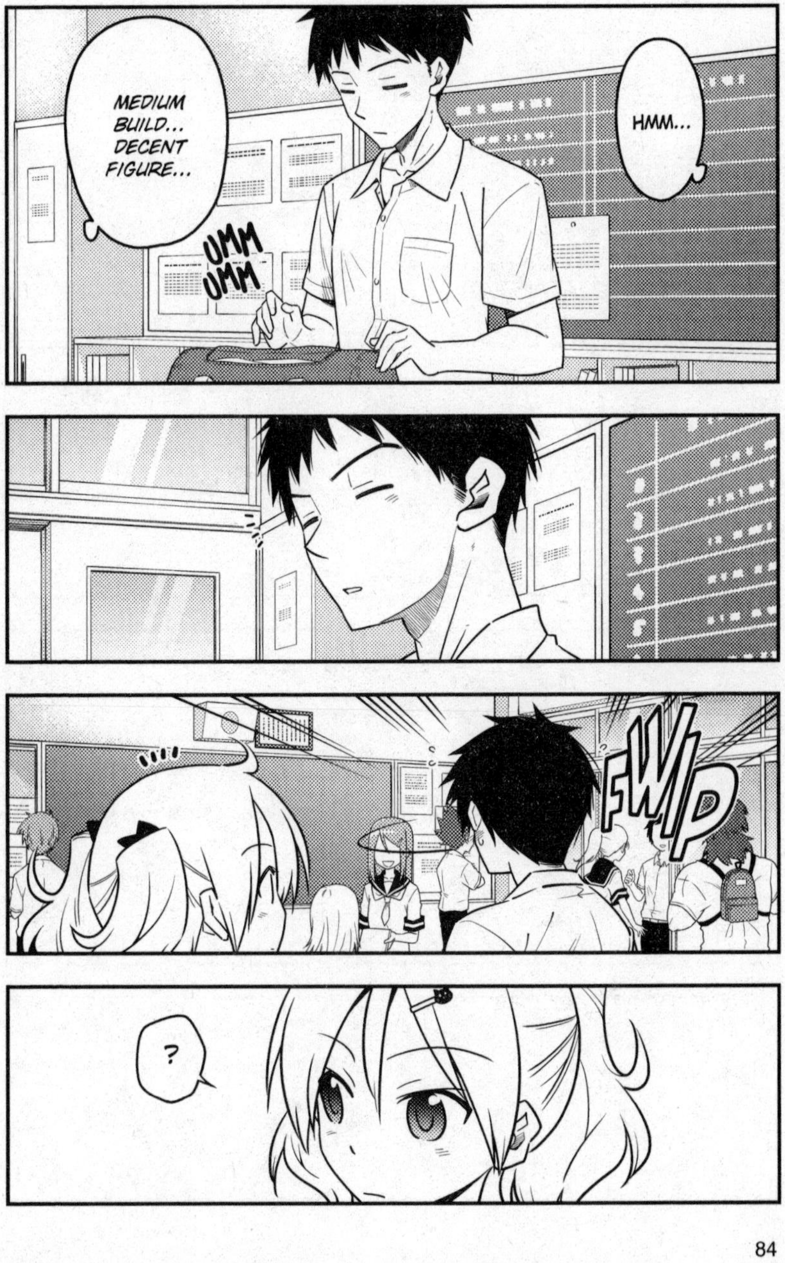
HMM...
MEDIUM BUILD... DECENT FIGURE...
UMM UMM
FWIP
?

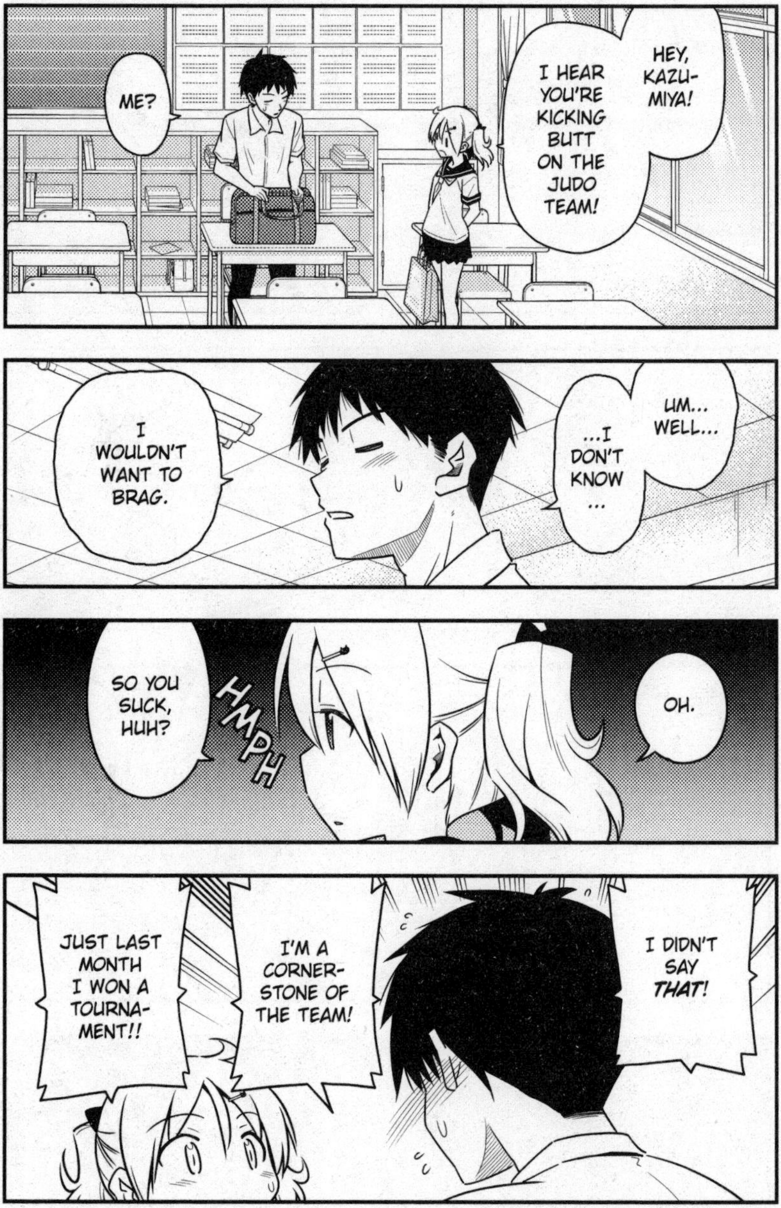
HEY, KAZU-MIYA!
I HEAR YOU'RE KICKING BUTT ON THE JUDO TEAM!
ME?
UM... WELL...
...I DON'T KNOW ...
I WOULDN'T WANT TO BRAG.
OH.
HMPH
SO YOU SUCK, HUH?
I DIDN'T SAY *THAT*!
I'M A CORNER-STONE OF THE TEAM!
JUST LAST MONTH I WON A TOURNA-MENT!!

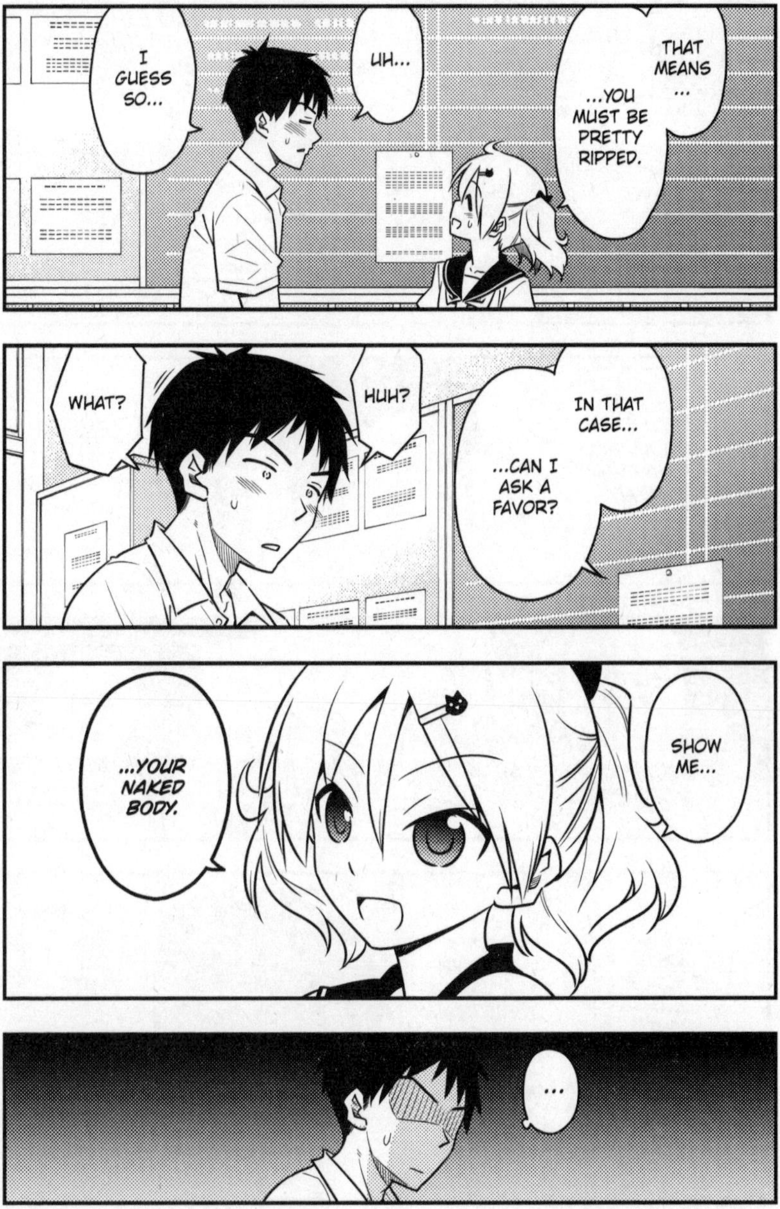
THAT MEANS ...
...YOU MUST BE PRETTY RIPPED.
UH...
I GUESS SO...
IN THAT CASE...
...CAN I ASK A FAVOR?
HUH?
WHAT?
SHOW ME...
...YOUR NAKED BODY.
...

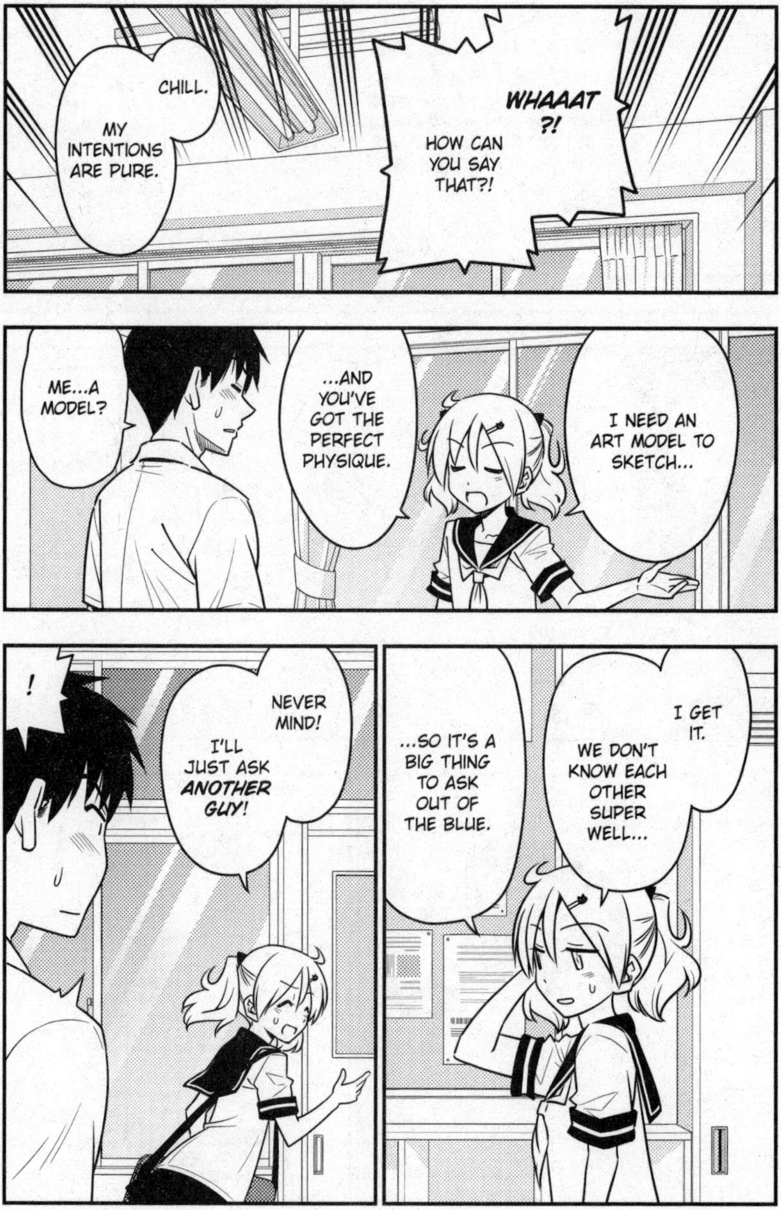
WHAAAT ?!
HOW CAN YOU SAY THAT?!
CHILL.
MY INTENTIONS ARE PURE.
I NEED AN ART MODEL TO SKETCH...
...AND YOU'VE GOT THE PERFECT PHYSIQUE.
ME...A MODEL?
I GET IT.
WE DON'T KNOW EACH OTHER SUPER WELL...
...SO IT'S A BIG THING TO ASK OUT OF THE BLUE.
NEVER MIND!
I'LL JUST ASK ANOTHER GUY!
!

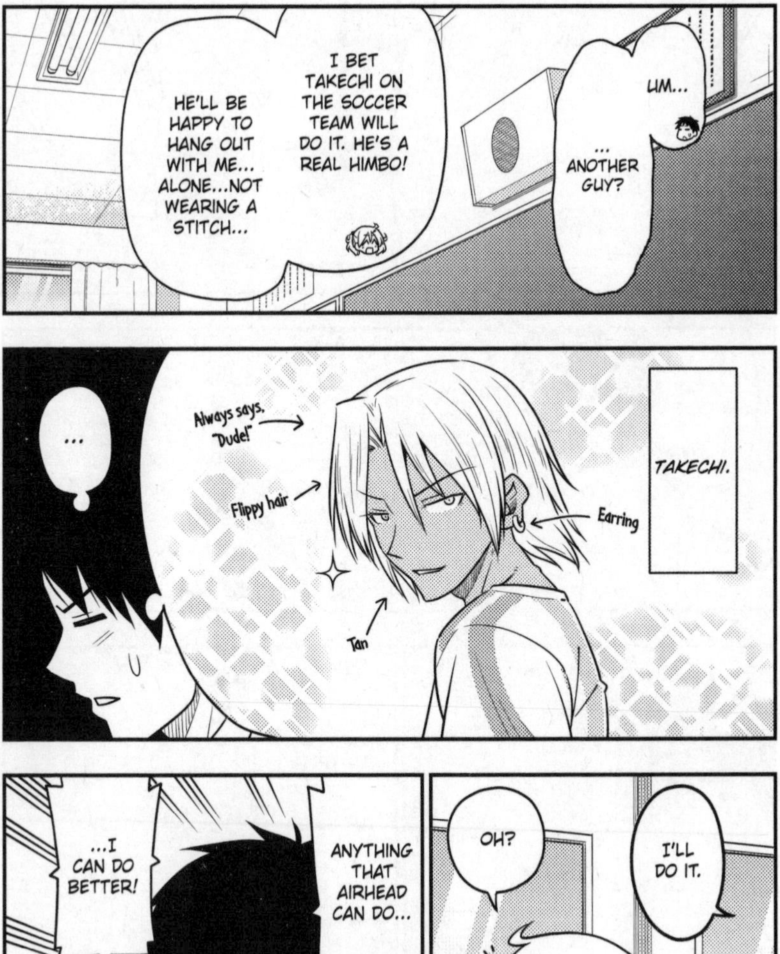
UM...
...ANOTHER GUY?
I BET TAKECHI ON THE SOCCER TEAM WILL DO IT. HE'S A REAL HIMBO!
HE'LL BE HAPPY TO HANG OUT WITH ME... ALONE...NOT WEARING A STITCH...
TAKECHI.
Earring
Always says, "Dude!"
Flippy hair
Tan
...
I'LL DO IT.
OH?
ANYTHING THAT AIRHEAD CAN DO...
...I CAN DO BETTER!

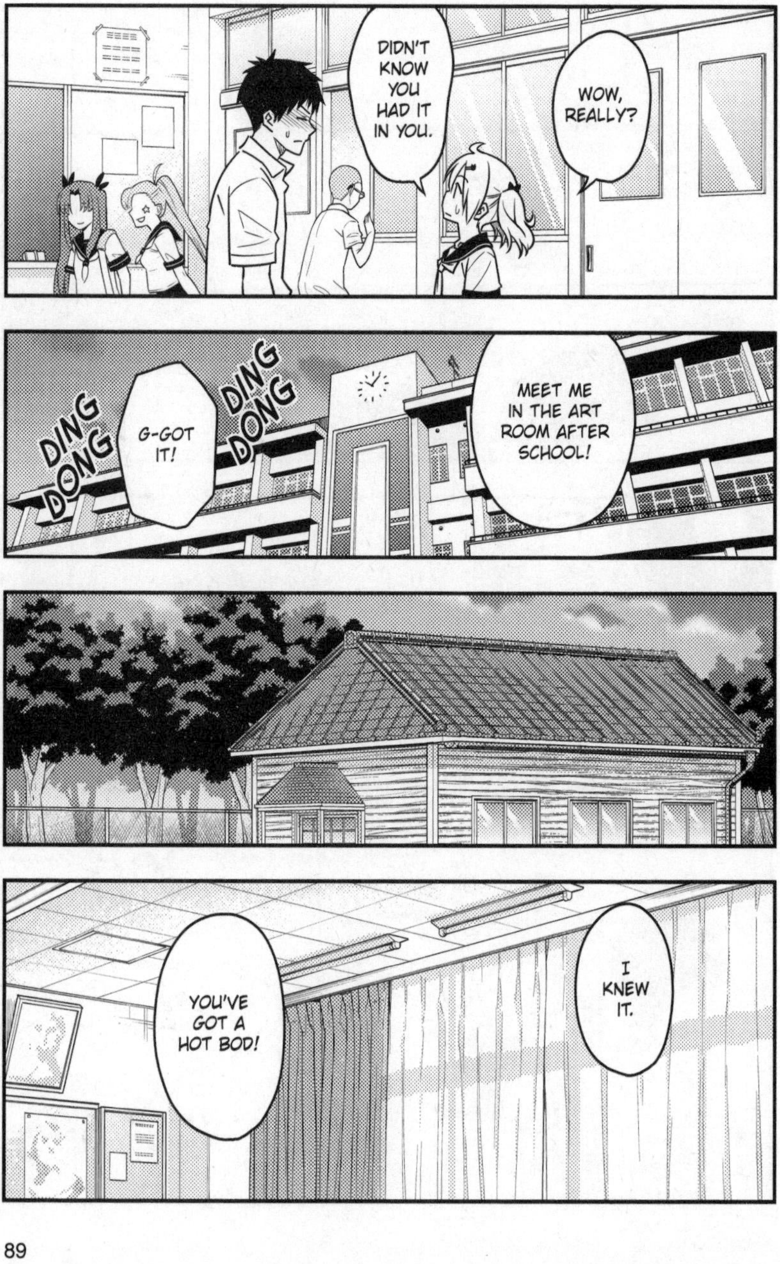
WOW, REALLY?
DIDN'T KNOW YOU HAD IT IN YOU.
MEET ME IN THE ART ROOM AFTER SCHOOL!
DING DONG
G-GOT IT!
DING DONG
I KNEW IT.
YOU'VE GOT A HOT BOD!

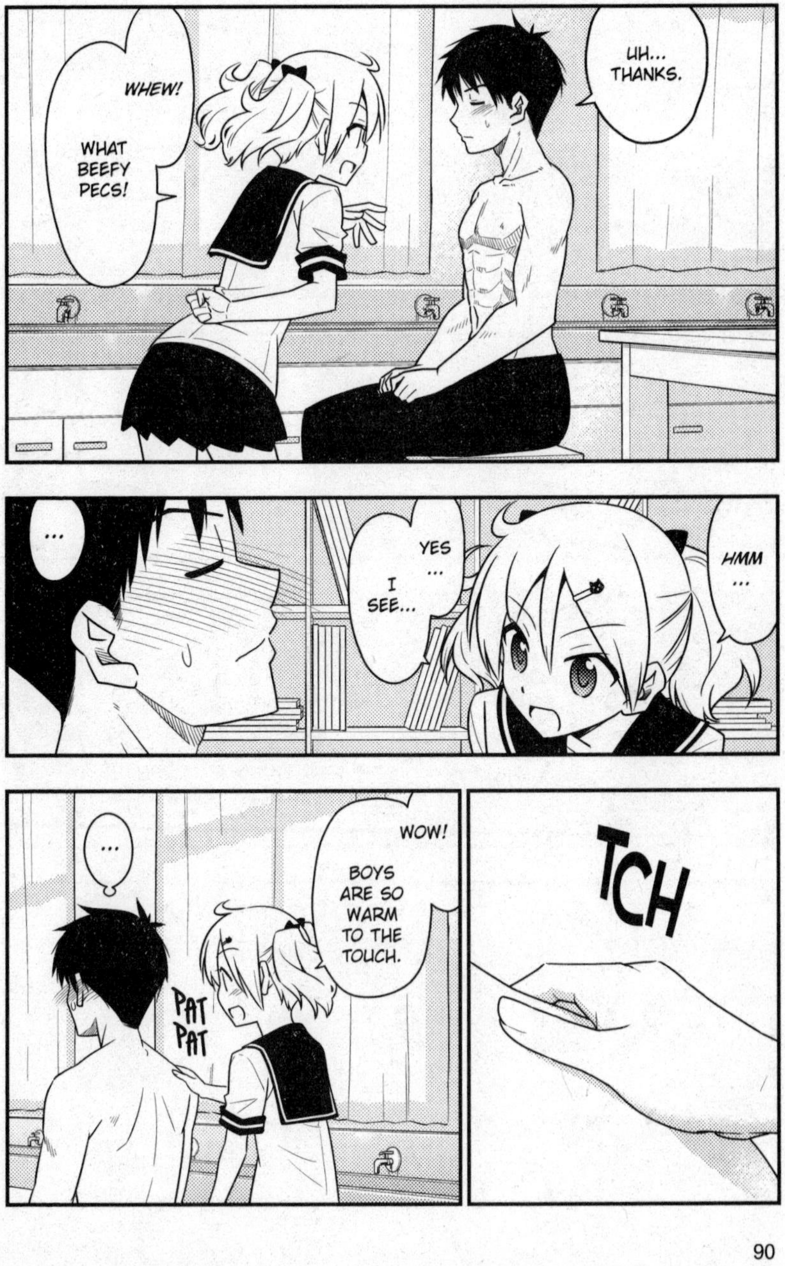
UH... THANKS.
WHEW!
WHAT BEEFY PECS!
HMM ...
YES ...
I SEE...
...
TCH
WOW!
BOYS ARE SO WARM TO THE TOUCH.
PAT PAT
...

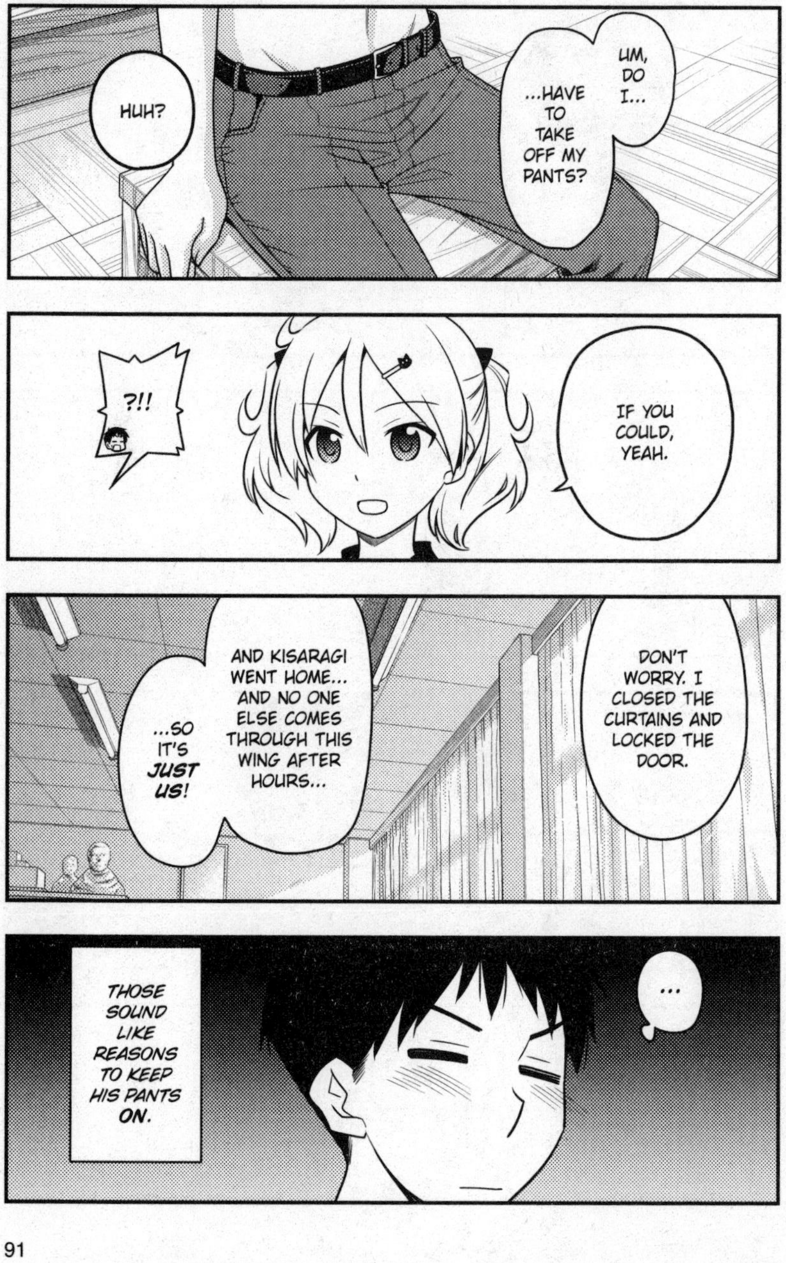
UM, DO I... ...HAVE TO TAKE OFF MY PANTS?
HUH?
IF YOU COULD, YEAH.
?!!
DON'T WORRY. I CLOSED THE CURTAINS AND LOCKED THE DOOR.
AND KISARAGI WENT HOME... AND NO ONE ELSE COMES THROUGH THIS WING AFTER HOURS...
...SO IT'S ***JUST US***!
...
THOSE SOUND LIKE REASONS TO KEEP HIS PANTS ***ON***.

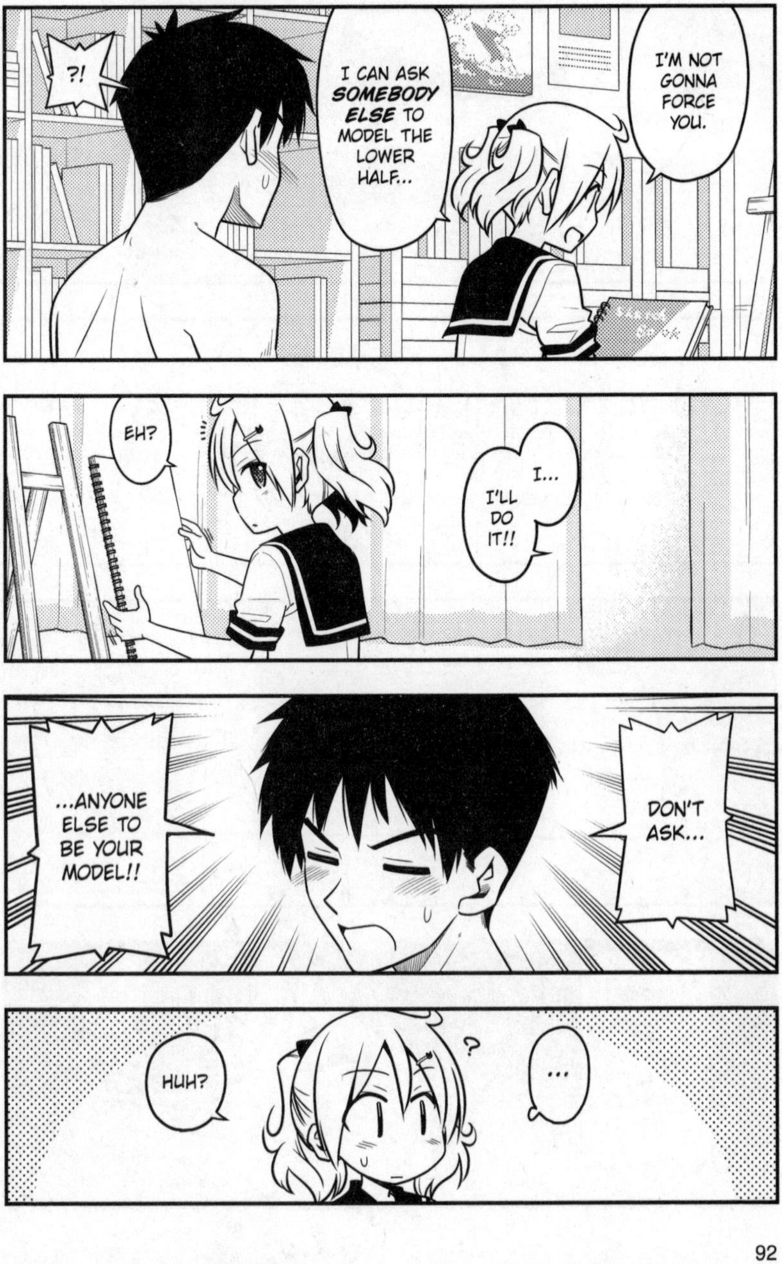
I'M NOT GONNA FORCE YOU.
I CAN ASK SOMEBODY ELSE TO MODEL THE LOWER HALF...
?!
I... I'LL DO IT!!
EH?
DON'T ASK...
...ANYONE ELSE TO BE YOUR MODEL!!
...
HUH?

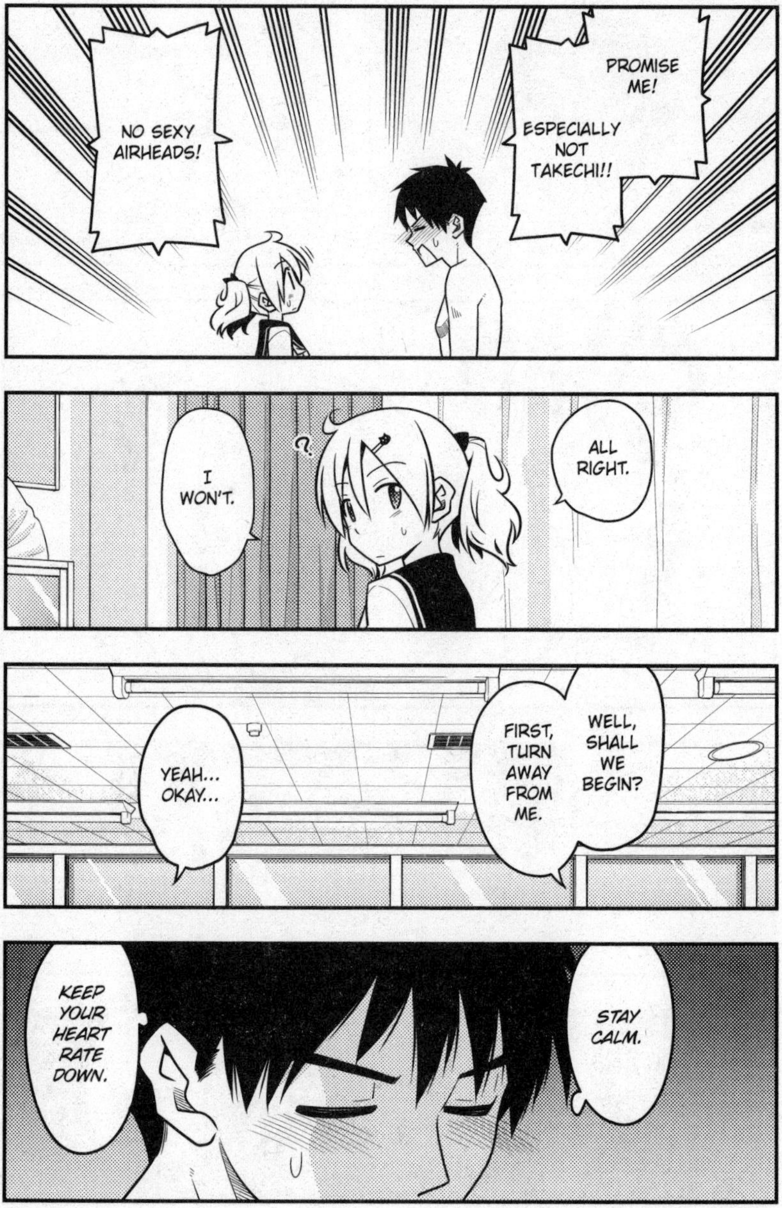
PROMISE ME!
ESPECIALLY NOT TAKECHI!!
NO SEXY AIRHEADS!
ALL RIGHT.
I WON'T.
WELL, SHALL WE BEGIN?
FIRST, TURN AWAY FROM ME.
YEAH... OKAY...
STAY CALM.
KEEP YOUR HEART RATE DOWN.

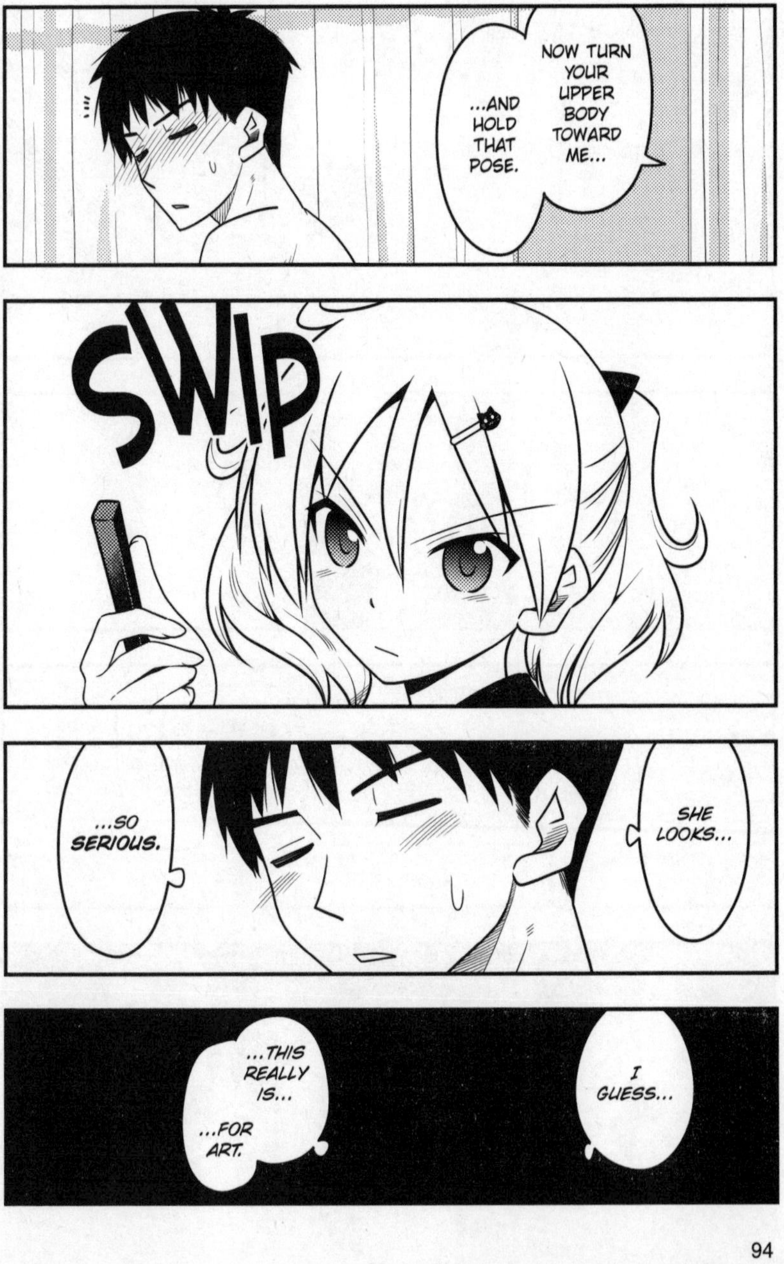
NOW TURN YOUR UPPER BODY TOWARD ME...
...AND HOLD THAT POSE.
SWIP
SHE LOOKS...
...SO SERIOUS.
I GUESS...
...THIS REALLY IS...
...FOR ART.

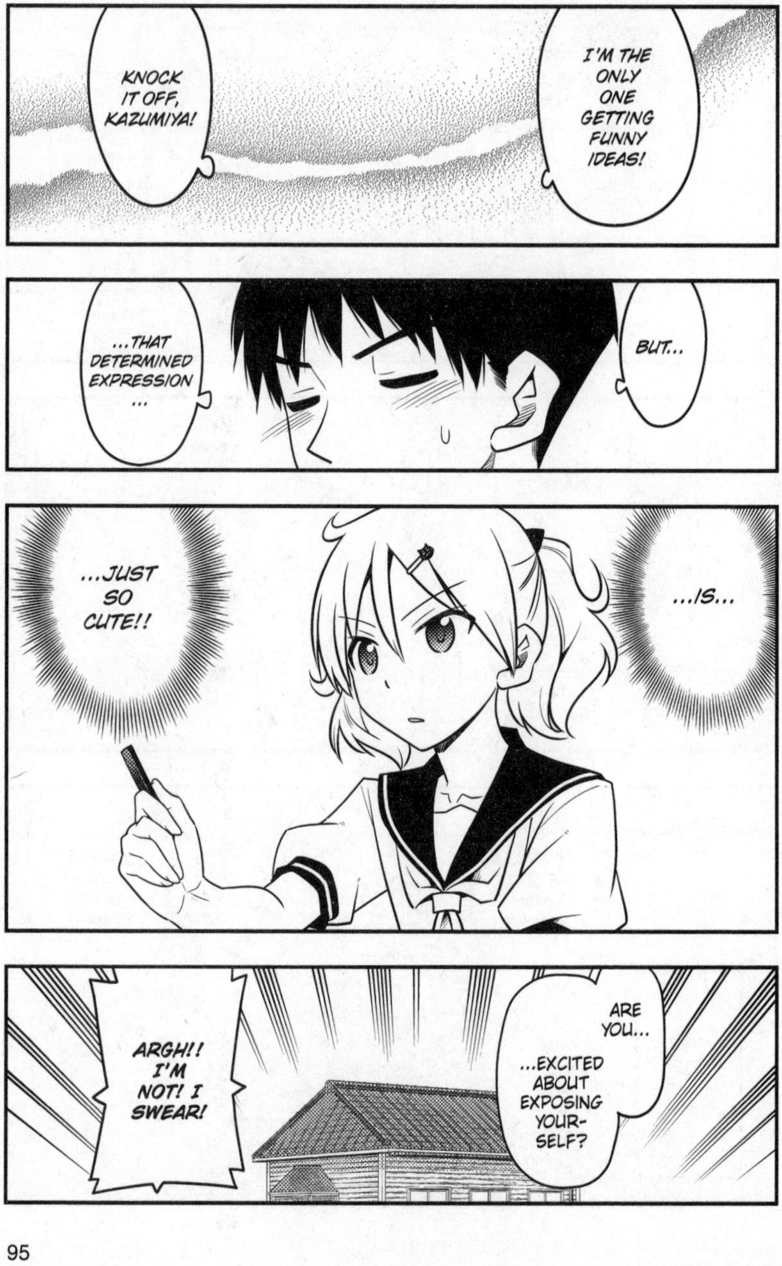
I'M THE ONLY ONE GETTING FUNNY IDEAS!
KNOCK IT OFF, KAZUMIYA!
BUT...
...THAT DETERMINED EXPRESSION ...
...IS...
...JUST SO CUTE!!
ARE YOU...
...EXCITED ABOUT EXPOSING YOUR-SELF?
ARGH!! I'M NOT! I SWEAR!

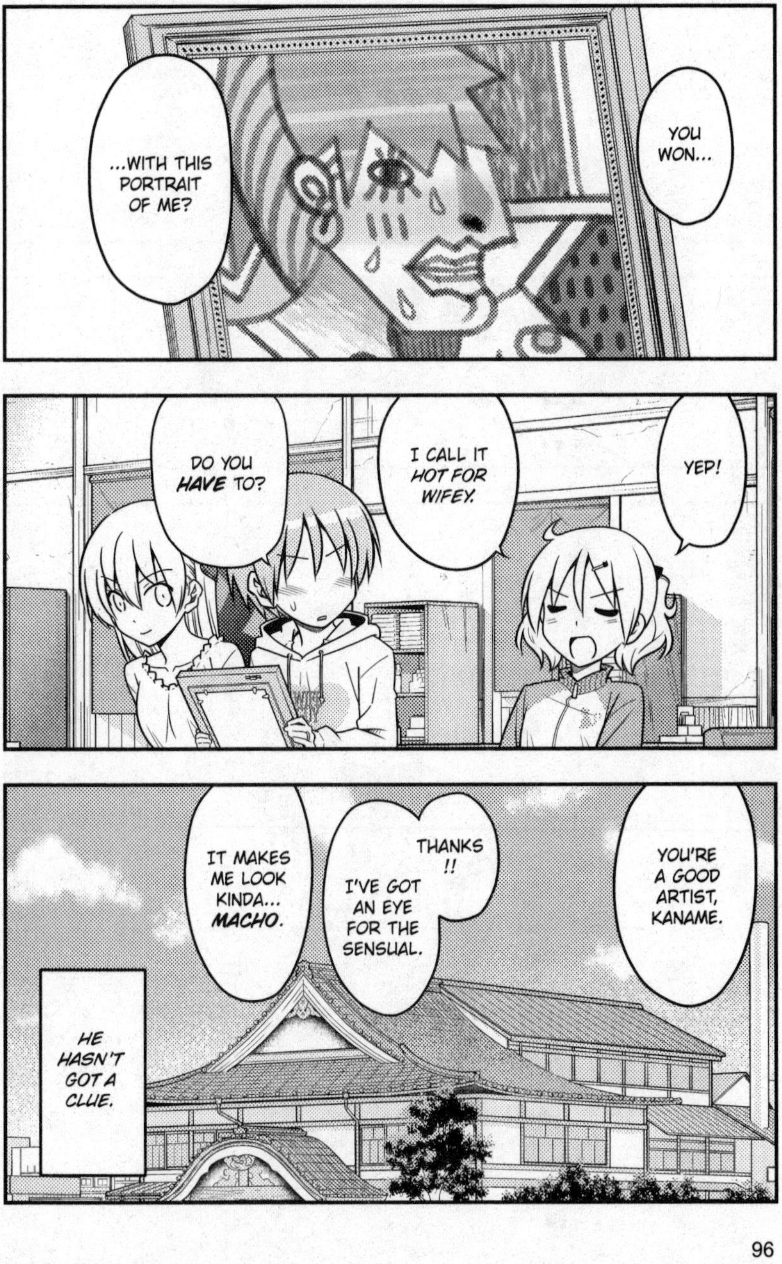
YOU WON...
...WITH THIS PORTRAIT OF ME?
YEP!
I CALL IT *HOT FOR WIFEY.*
DO YOU ***HAVE*** TO?
YOU'RE A GOOD ARTIST, KANAME.
THANKS !!
I'VE GOT AN EYE FOR THE SENSUAL.
IT MAKES ME LOOK KINDA... ***MACHO.***
HE HASN'T GOT A CLUE.

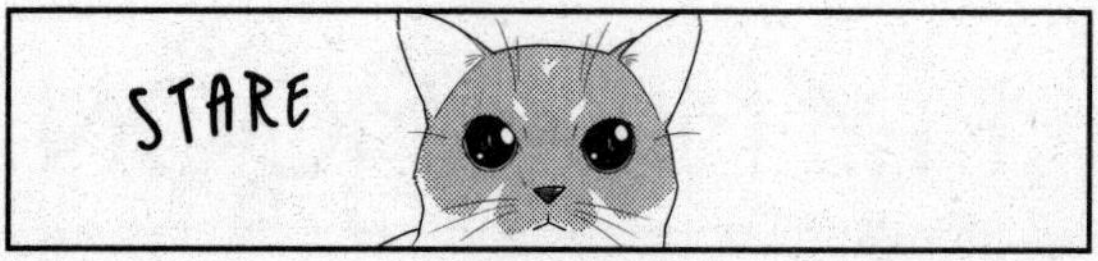
STARE

FLY ME TO THE MOON

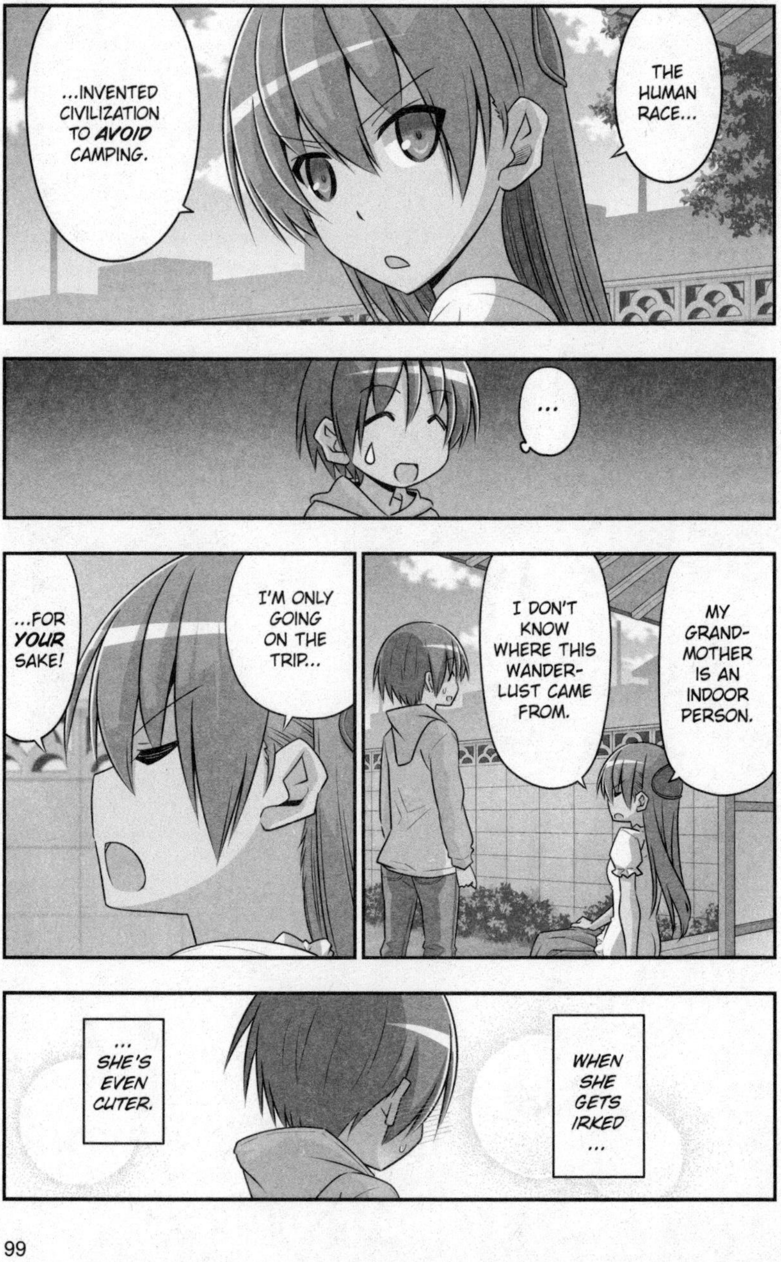
THE HUMAN RACE...
...INVENTED CIVILIZATION TO **AVOID** CAMPING.
...
MY GRAND-MOTHER IS AN INDOOR PERSON.
I DON'T KNOW WHERE THIS WANDER-LUST CAME FROM.
I'M ONLY GOING ON THE TRIP...
...FOR **YOUR** SAKE!
WHEN SHE GETS IRKED...
...SHE'S EVEN CUTER.

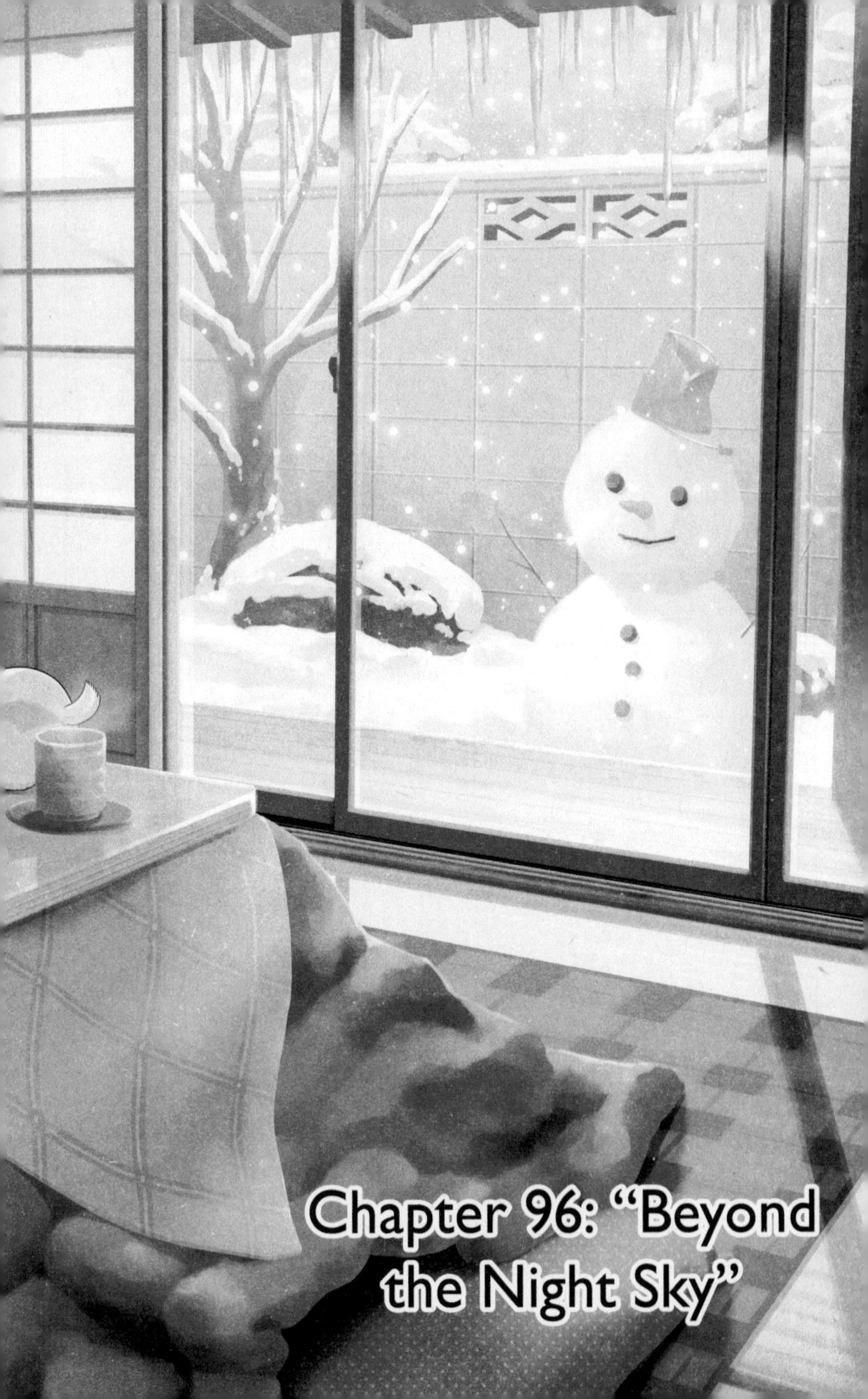
Chapter 96: "Beyond the Night Sky"

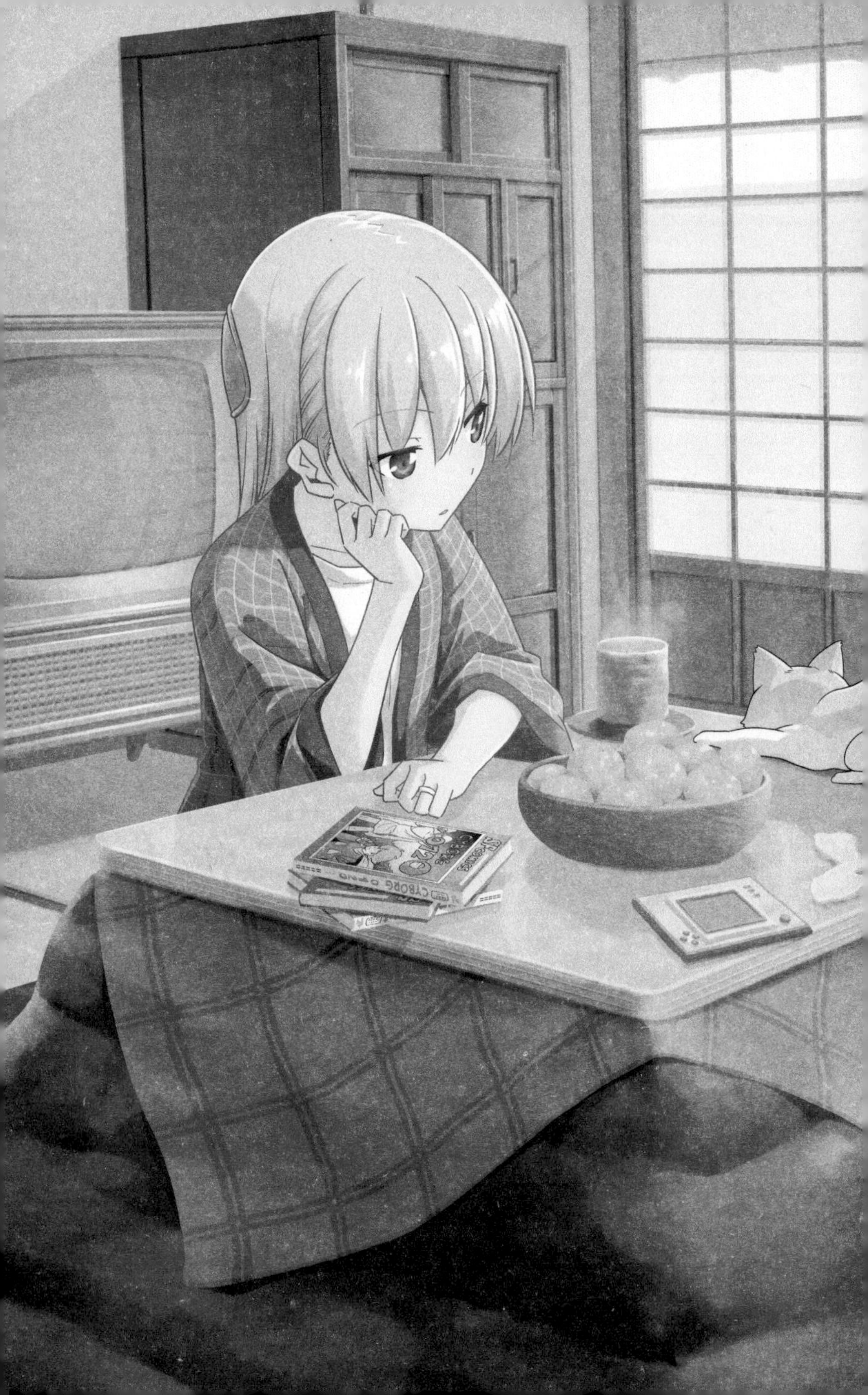
CYBORG

FLY ME _{TO} _{THE} MOON

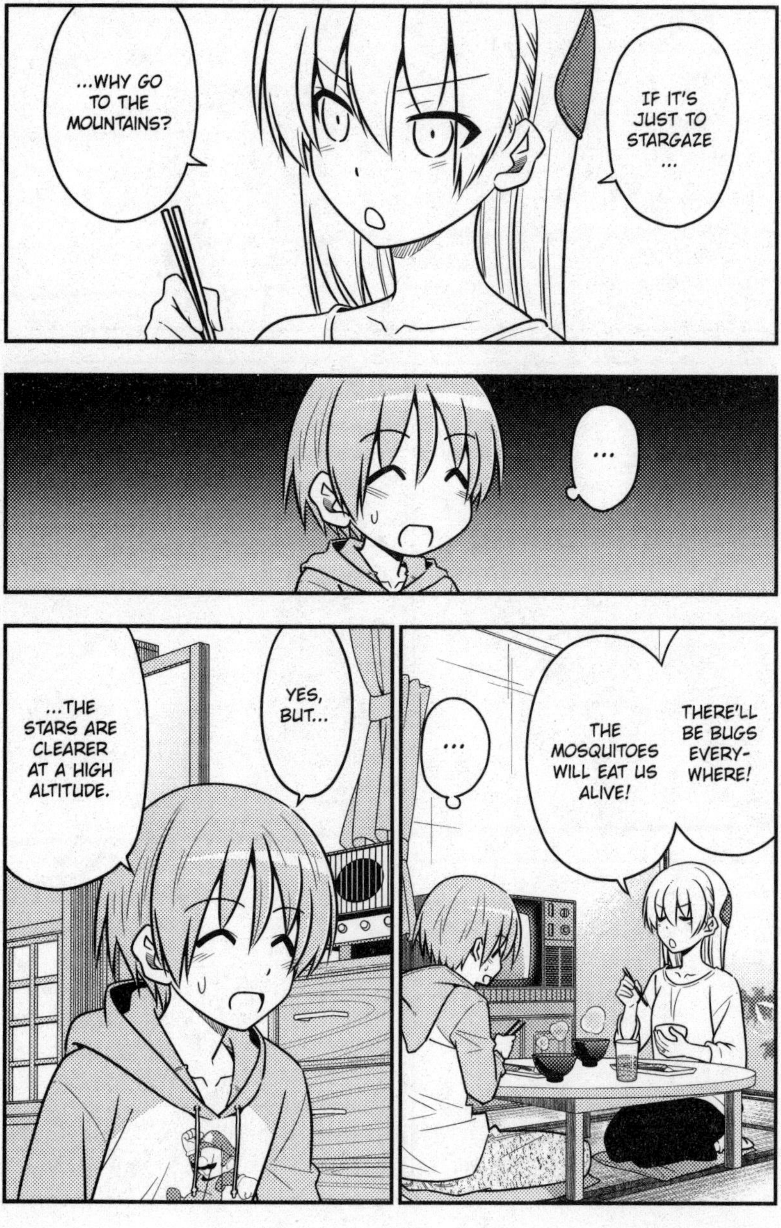
IF IT'S JUST TO STARGAZE ...
...WHY GO TO THE MOUNTAINS?
...
THERE'LL BE BUGS EVERY-WHERE!
THE MOSQUITOES WILL EAT US ALIVE!
...
YES, BUT...
...THE STARS ARE CLEARER AT A HIGH ALTITUDE.

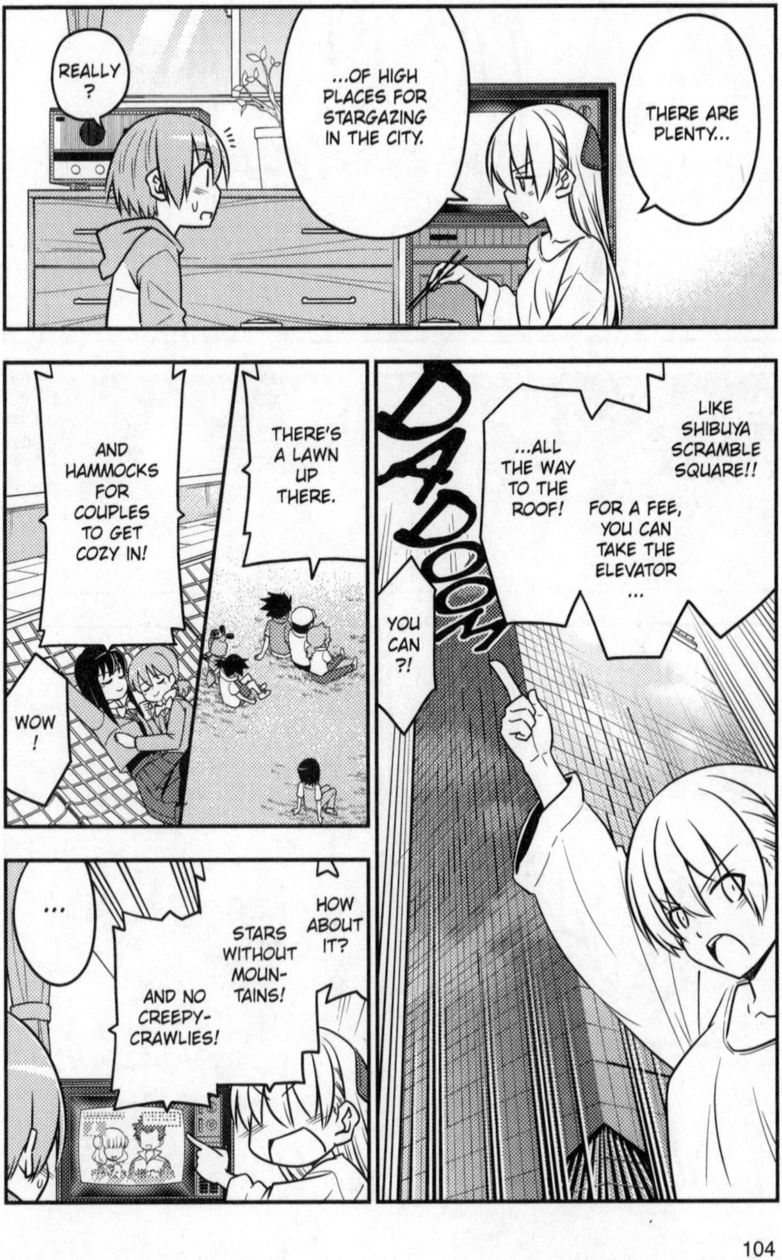
THERE ARE PLENTY...
...OF HIGH PLACES FOR STARGAZING IN THE CITY.
REALLY?
LIKE SHIBUYA SCRAMBLE SQUARE!!
FOR A FEE, YOU CAN TAKE THE ELEVATOR...
...ALL THE WAY TO THE ROOF!
DADOOM
YOU CAN?!
THERE'S A LAWN UP THERE.
AND HAMMOCKS FOR COUPLES TO GET COZY IN!
WOW!
HOW ABOUT IT?
STARS WITHOUT MOUN-TAINS!
AND NO CREEPY-CRAWLIES!
...

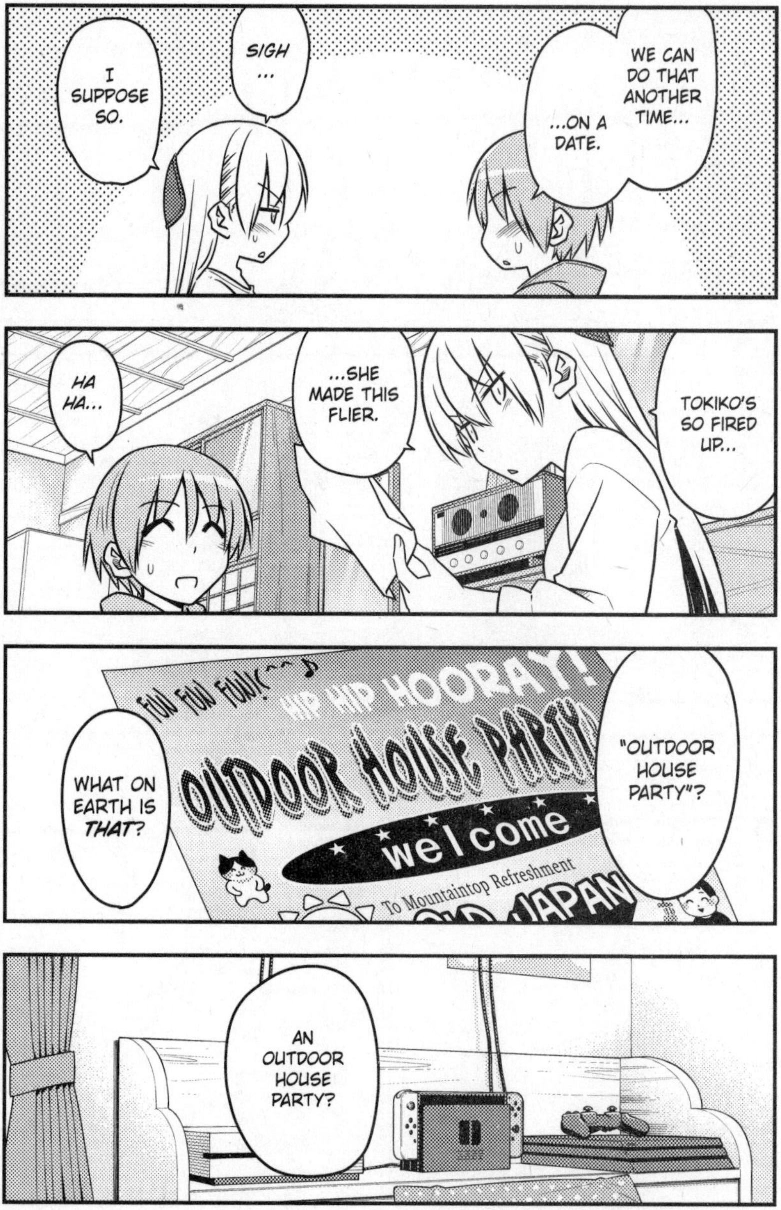
WE CAN DO THAT ANOTHER TIME...
...ON A DATE.
SIGH ...
I SUPPOSE SO.
TOKIKO'S SO FIRED UP...
...SHE MADE THIS FLIER.
HA HA...
"OUTDOOR HOUSE PARTY"?
HIP HIP HOORAY!
FUN FUN FUN(^^♪
OUTDOOR HOUSE PARTY
welcome
To Mountaintop Refreshment
WHAT ON EARTH IS THAT?
AN OUTDOOR HOUSE PARTY?

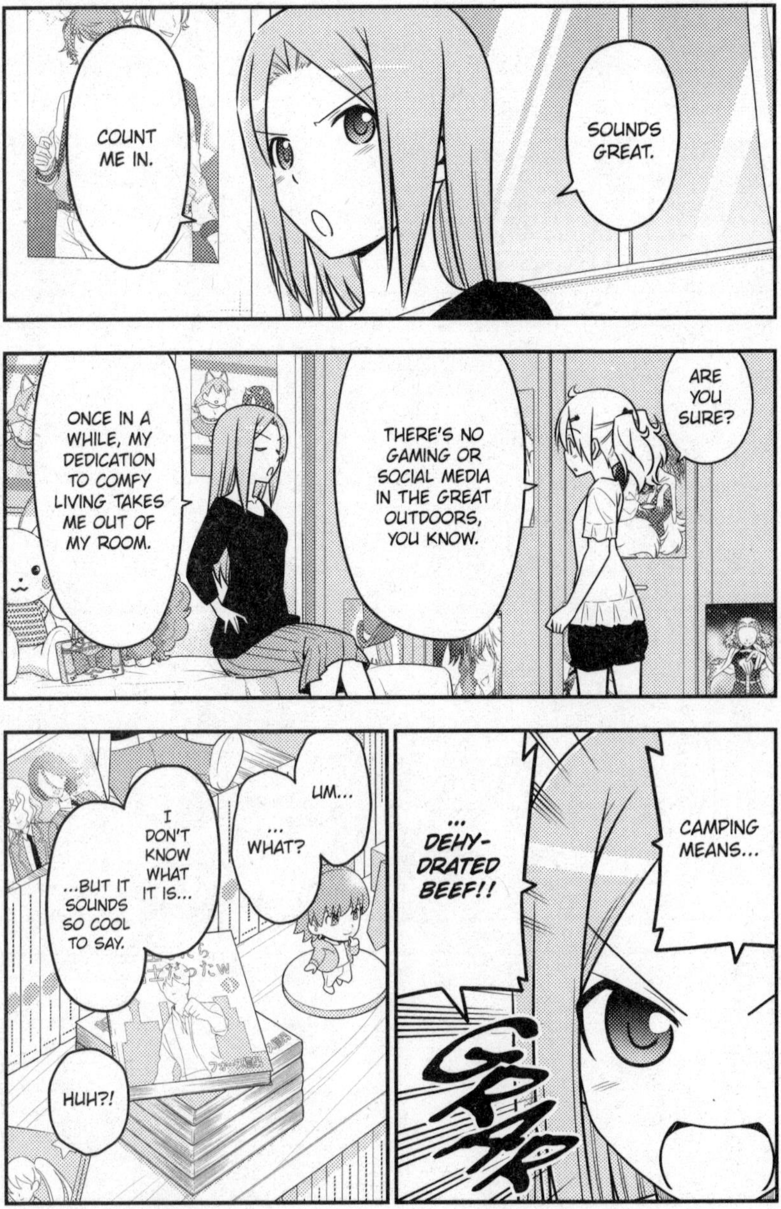
SOUNDS GREAT.
COUNT ME IN.
ARE YOU SURE?
THERE'S NO GAMING OR SOCIAL MEDIA IN THE GREAT OUTDOORS, YOU KNOW.
ONCE IN A WHILE, MY DEDICATION TO COMFY LIVING TAKES ME OUT OF MY ROOM.
CAMPING MEANS...
...DEHY-DRATED BEEF!!
UM...
...WHAT?
I DON'T KNOW WHAT IT IS...
...BUT IT SOUNDS SO COOL TO SAY.
HUH?!

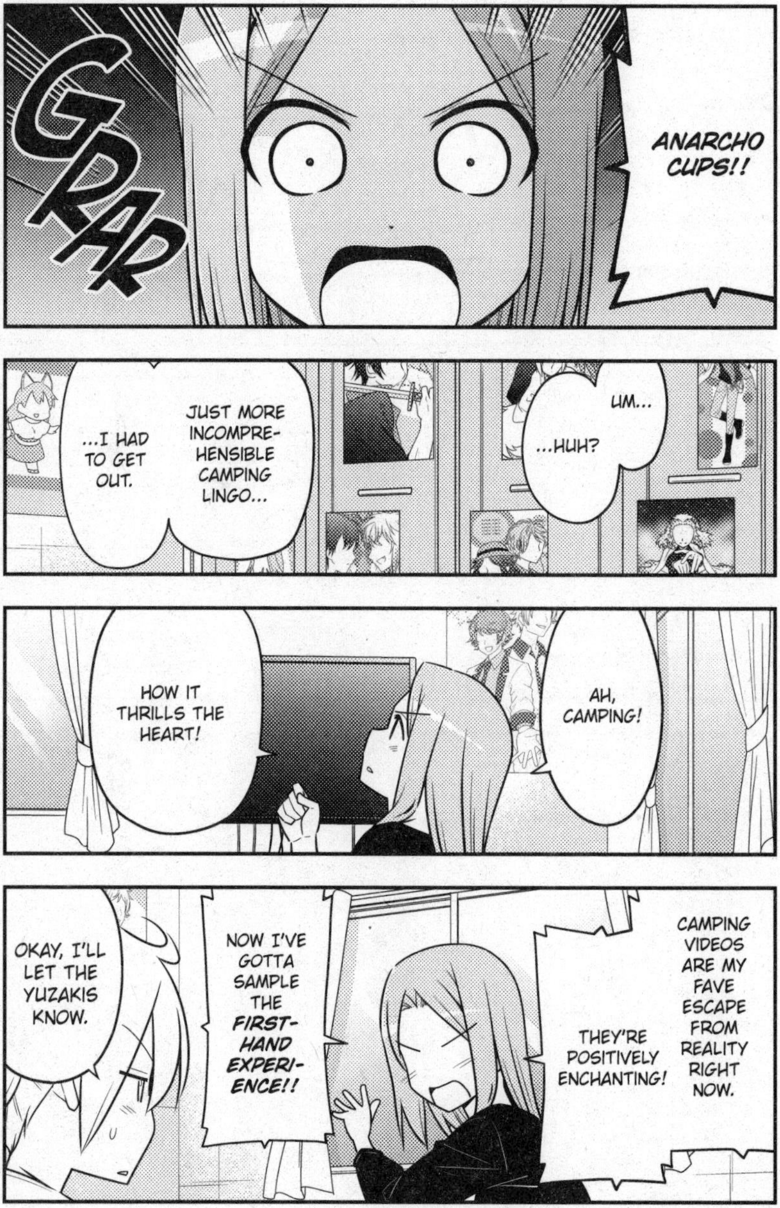
ANARCHO CUPS!!
GRAR
UM...
...HUH?
JUST MORE INCOMPRE-HENSIBLE CAMPING LINGO...
...I HAD TO GET OUT.
AH, CAMPING!
HOW IT THRILLS THE HEART!
CAMPING VIDEOS ARE MY FAVE ESCAPE FROM REALITY RIGHT NOW.
THEY'RE POSITIVELY ENCHANTING!
NOW I'VE GOTTA SAMPLE THE FIRST-HAND EXPERI-ENCE!!
OKAY, I'LL LET THE YUZAKIS KNOW.

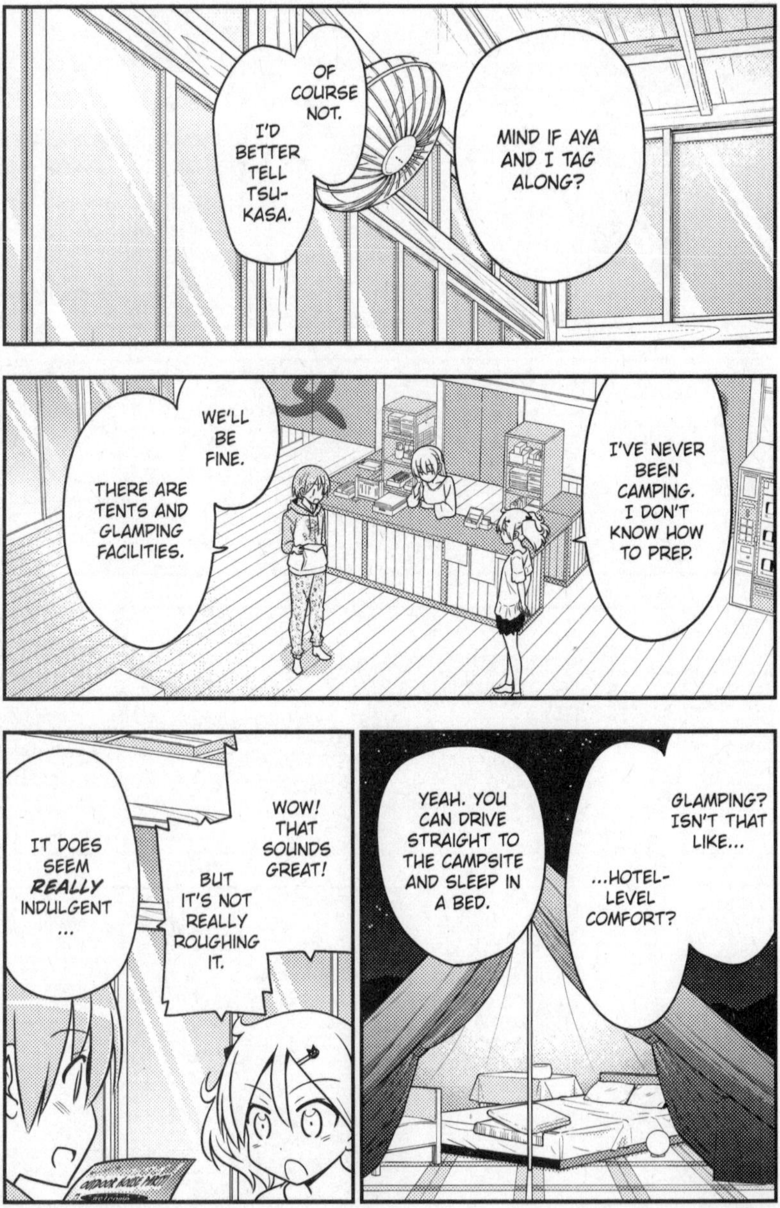
MIND IF AYA AND I TAG ALONG?
OF COURSE NOT.
I'D BETTER TELL TSU-KASA.
I'VE NEVER BEEN CAMPING. I DON'T KNOW HOW TO PREP.
WE'LL BE FINE.
THERE ARE TENTS AND GLAMPING FACILITIES.
GLAMPING? ISN'T THAT LIKE...
...HOTEL-LEVEL COMFORT?
YEAH. YOU CAN DRIVE STRAIGHT TO THE CAMPSITE AND SLEEP IN A BED.
WOW! THAT SOUNDS GREAT!
BUT IT'S NOT REALLY ROUGHING IT.
IT DOES SEEM ***REALLY*** INDULGENT ...

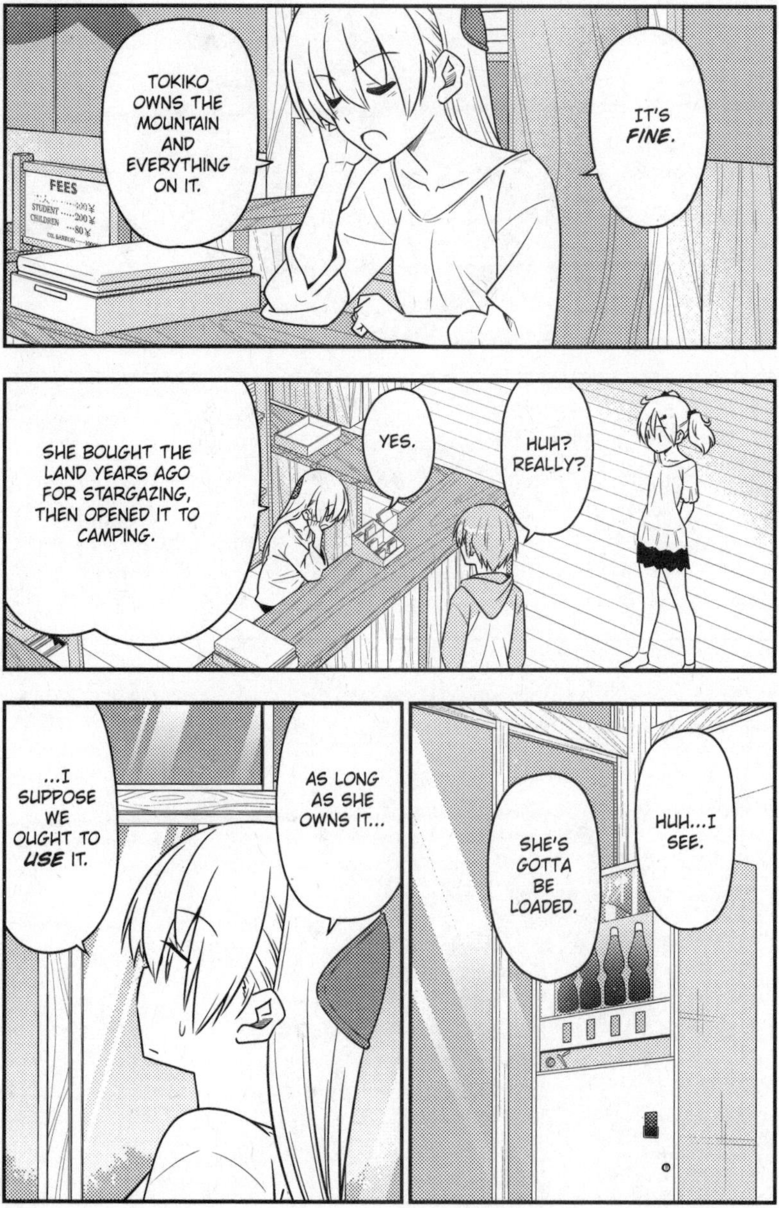
IT'S *FINE*.
TOKIKO OWNS THE MOUNTAIN AND EVERYTHING ON IT.
FEES
HUH? REALLY?
YES.
SHE BOUGHT THE LAND YEARS AGO FOR STARGAZING, THEN OPENED IT TO CAMPING.
HUH...I SEE.
SHE'S GOTTA BE LOADED.
AS LONG AS SHE OWNS IT...
...I SUPPOSE WE OUGHT TO *USE* IT.

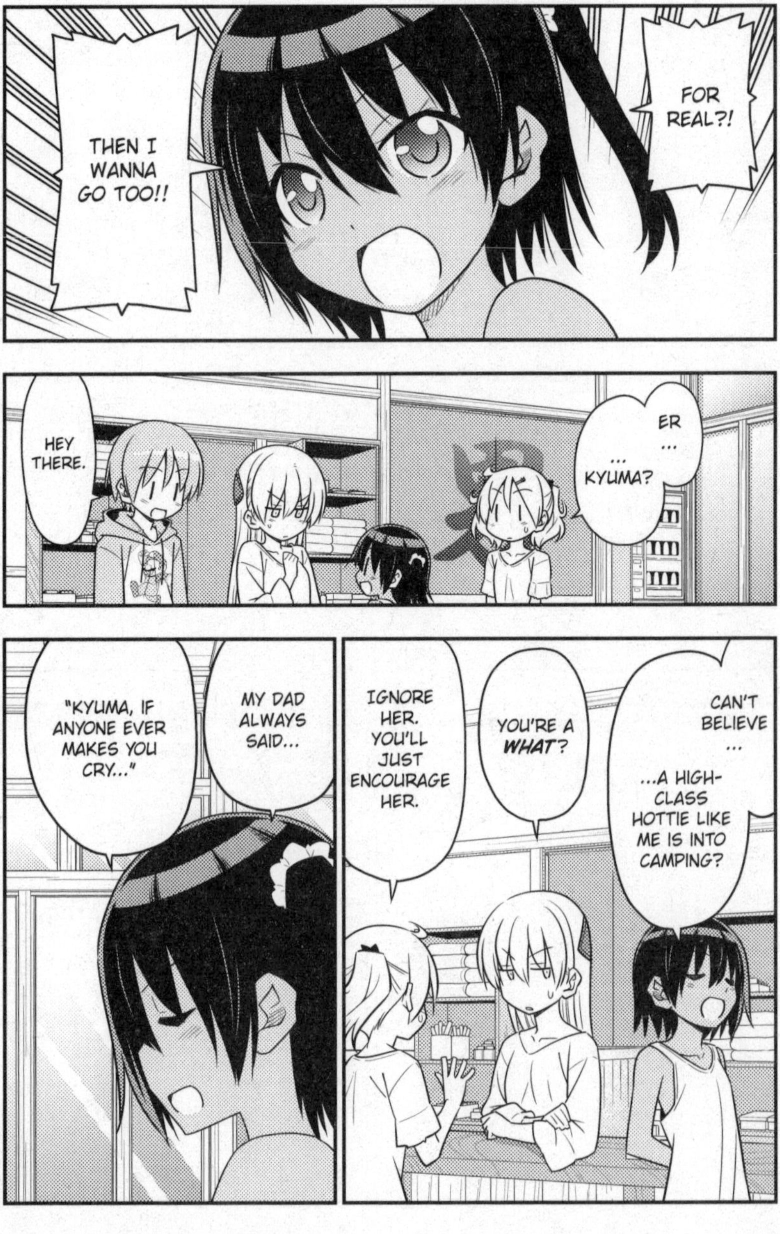
FOR REAL?!
THEN I WANNA GO TOO!!
ER ...
... KYUMA?
HEY THERE.
CAN'T BELIEVE ...
...A HIGH-CLASS HOTTIE LIKE ME IS INTO CAMPING?
YOU'RE A *WHAT*?
IGNORE HER. YOU'LL JUST ENCOURAGE HER.
MY DAD ALWAYS SAID...
"KYUMA, IF ANYONE EVER MAKES YOU CRY..."

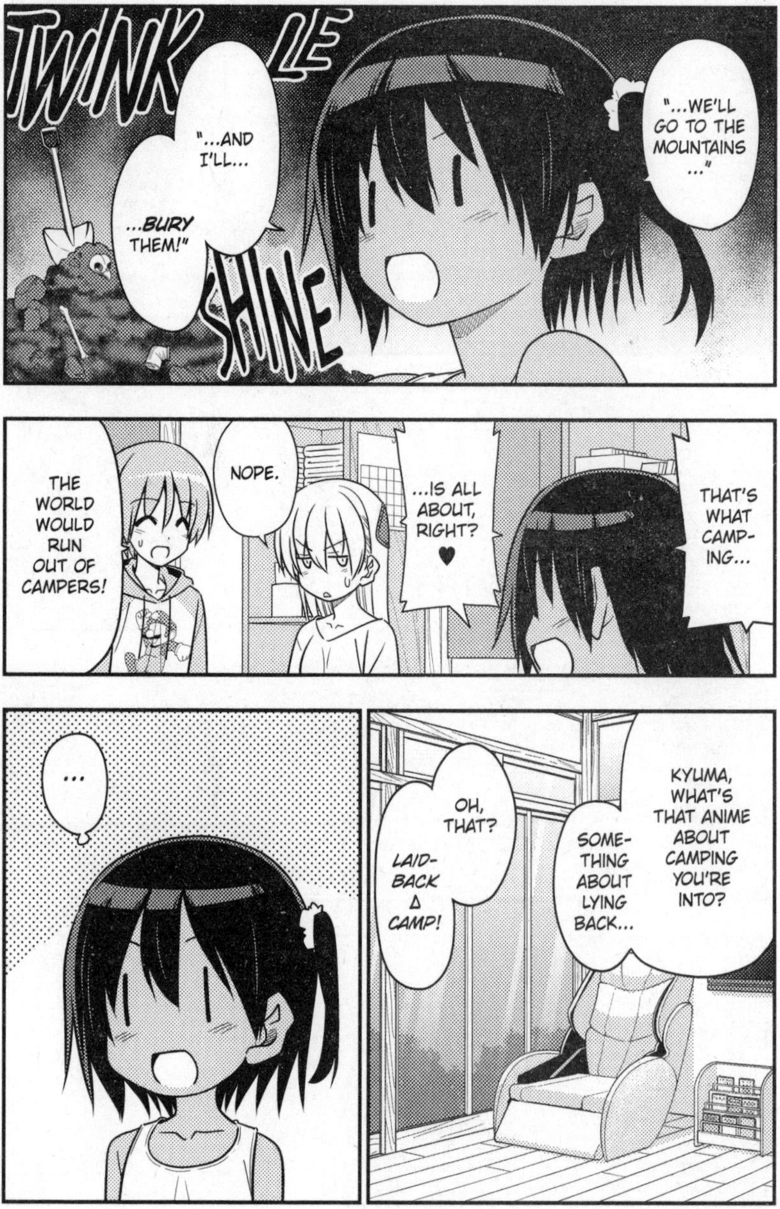
"...WE'LL GO TO THE MOUNTAINS ..."
"...AND I'LL...
...BURY THEM!"
TWINKLE
SHINE
THAT'S WHAT CAMP-ING...
...IS ALL ABOUT, RIGHT? ♥
NOPE.
THE WORLD WOULD RUN OUT OF CAMPERS!
KYUMA, WHAT'S THAT ANIME ABOUT CAMPING YOU'RE INTO?
SOME-THING ABOUT LYING BACK...
OH, THAT?
LAID-BACK Δ CAMP!
...

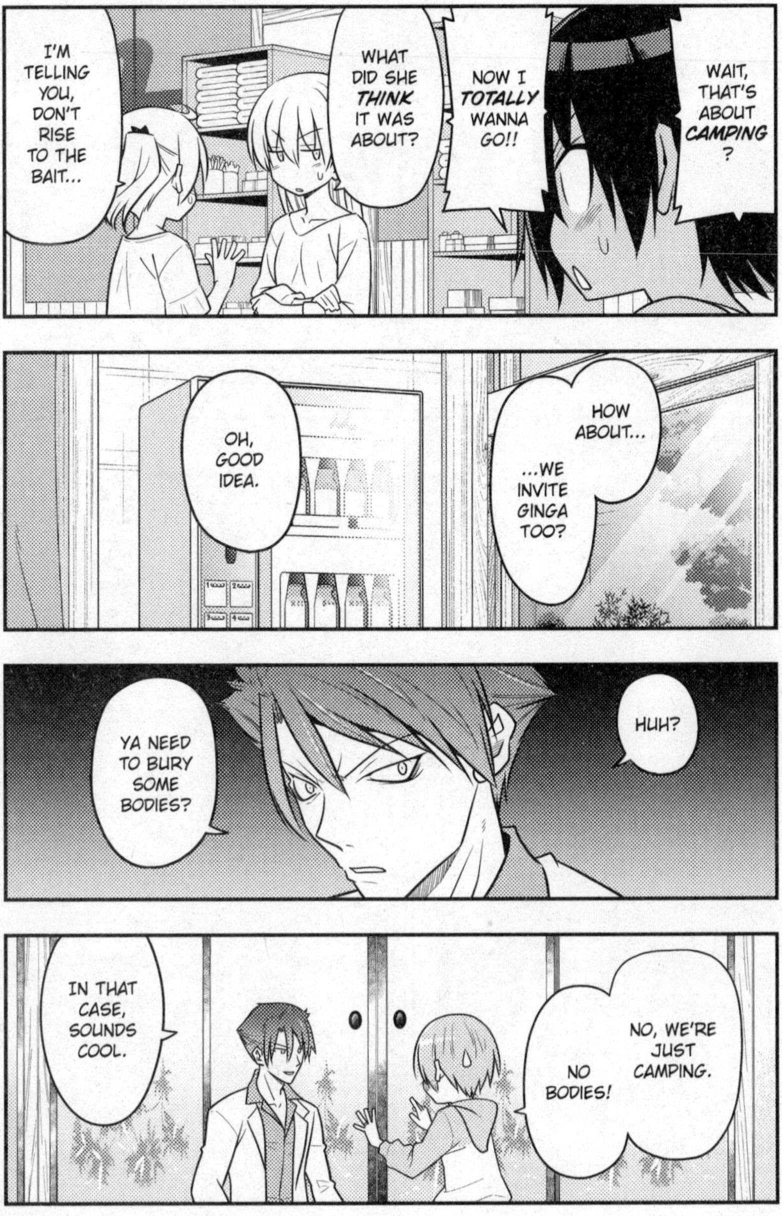
WAIT, THAT'S ABOUT CAMPING?
NOW I TOTALLY WANNA GO!!
WHAT DID SHE THINK IT WAS ABOUT?
I'M TELLING YOU, DON'T RISE TO THE BAIT...
HOW ABOUT...
...WE INVITE GINGA TOO?
OH, GOOD IDEA.
HUH?
YA NEED TO BURY SOME BODIES?
NO, WE'RE JUST CAMPING.
NO BODIES!
IN THAT CASE, SOUNDS COOL.

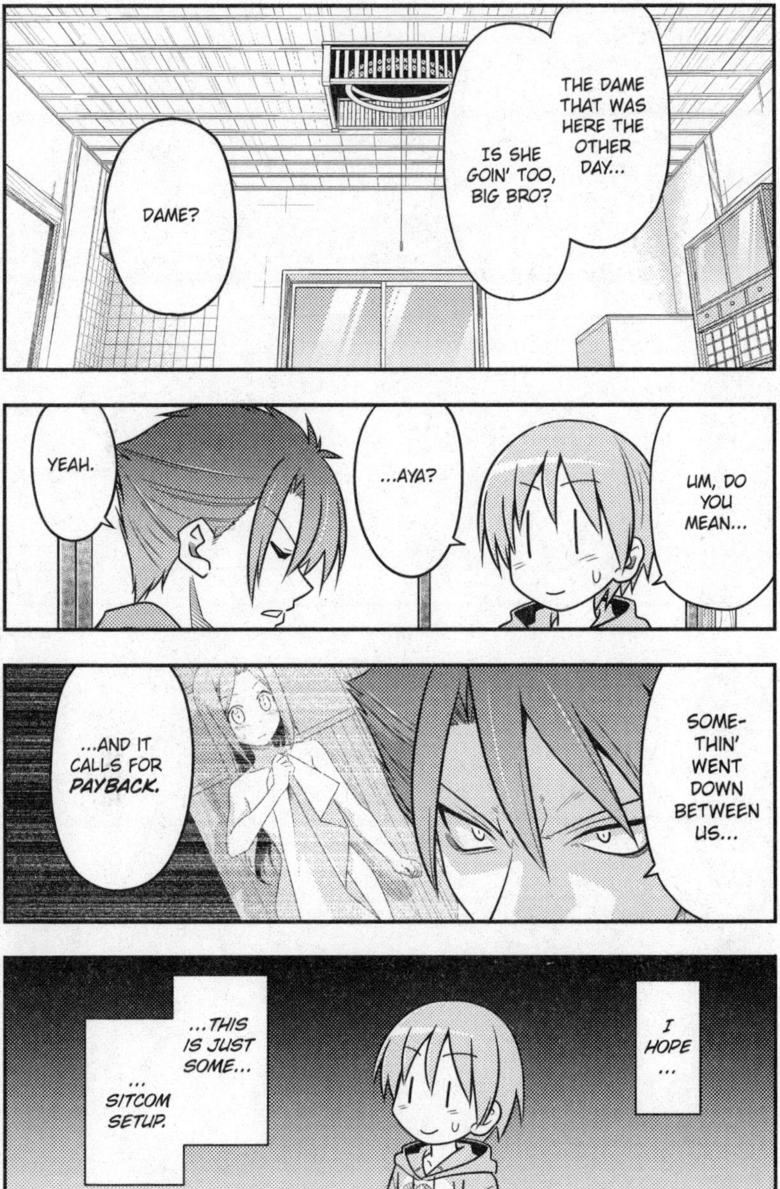
THE DAME THAT WAS HERE THE OTHER DAY...
IS SHE GOIN' TOO, BIG BRO?
DAME?
UM, DO YOU MEAN...
...AYA?
YEAH.
SOME-THIN' WENT DOWN BETWEEN US...
...AND IT CALLS FOR **PAYBACK.**
I HOPE ...
...THIS IS JUST SOME...
... SITCOM SETUP.

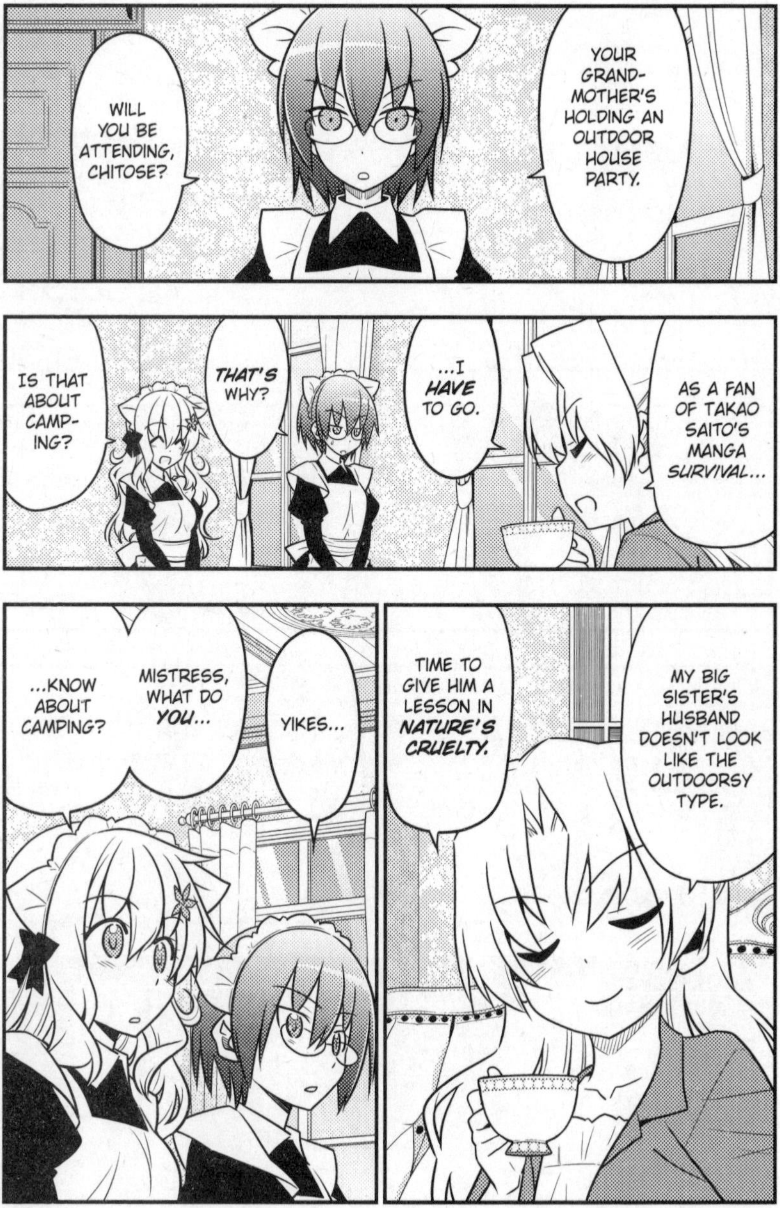
YOUR GRAND-MOTHER'S HOLDING AN OUTDOOR HOUSE PARTY.
WILL YOU BE ATTENDING, CHITOSE?
AS A FAN OF TAKAO SAITO'S MANGA *SURVIVAL*...
...I **HAVE** TO GO.
THAT'S WHY?
IS THAT ABOUT CAMP-ING?
MY BIG SISTER'S HUSBAND DOESN'T LOOK LIKE THE OUTDOORSY TYPE.
TIME TO GIVE HIM A LESSON IN ***NATURE'S CRUELTY.***
YIKES...
MISTRESS, WHAT DO ***YOU***...
...KNOW ABOUT CAMPING?

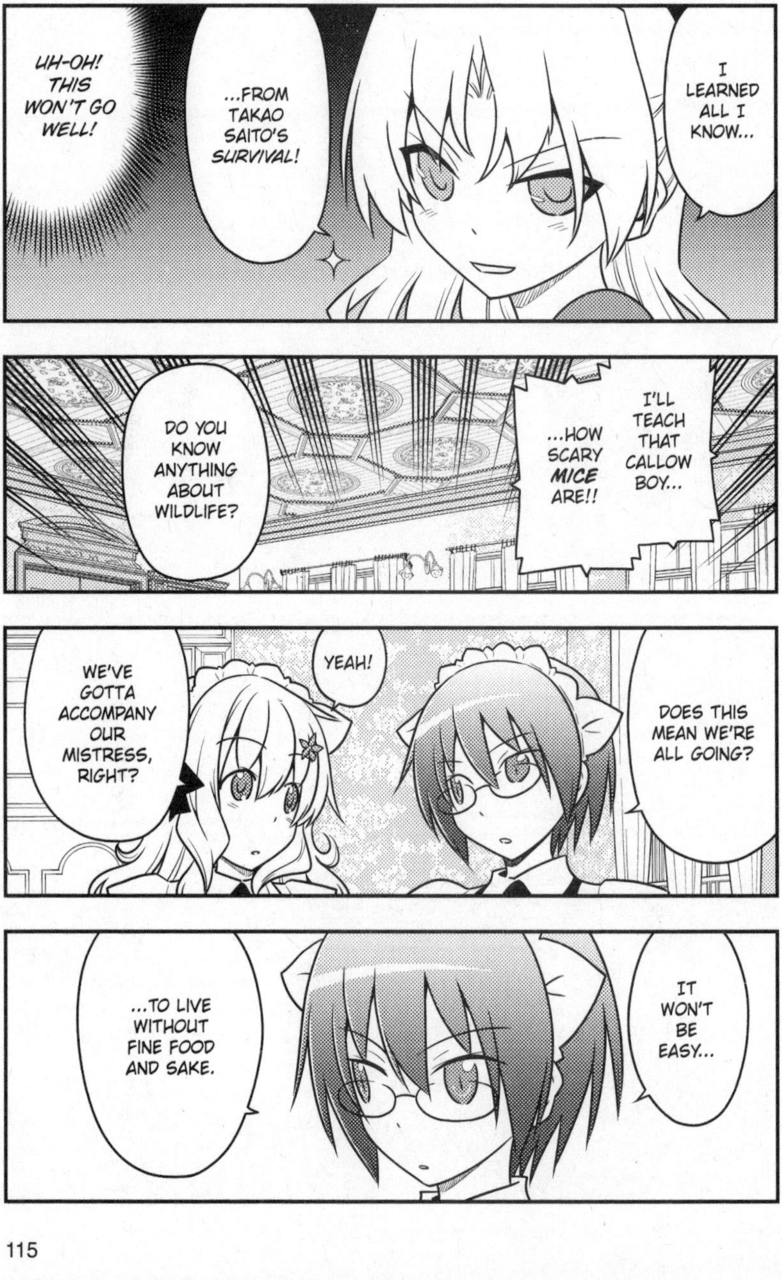
I LEARNED ALL I KNOW...
...FROM TAKAO SAITO'S *SURVIVAL!*
UH-OH! THIS WON'T GO WELL!
I'LL TEACH THAT CALLOW BOY...
...HOW SCARY ***MICE*** ARE!!
DO YOU KNOW ANYTHING ABOUT WILDLIFE?
DOES THIS MEAN WE'RE ALL GOING?
YEAH!
WE'VE GOTTA ACCOMPANY OUR MISTRESS, RIGHT?
IT WON'T BE EASY...
...TO LIVE WITHOUT FINE FOOD AND SAKE.

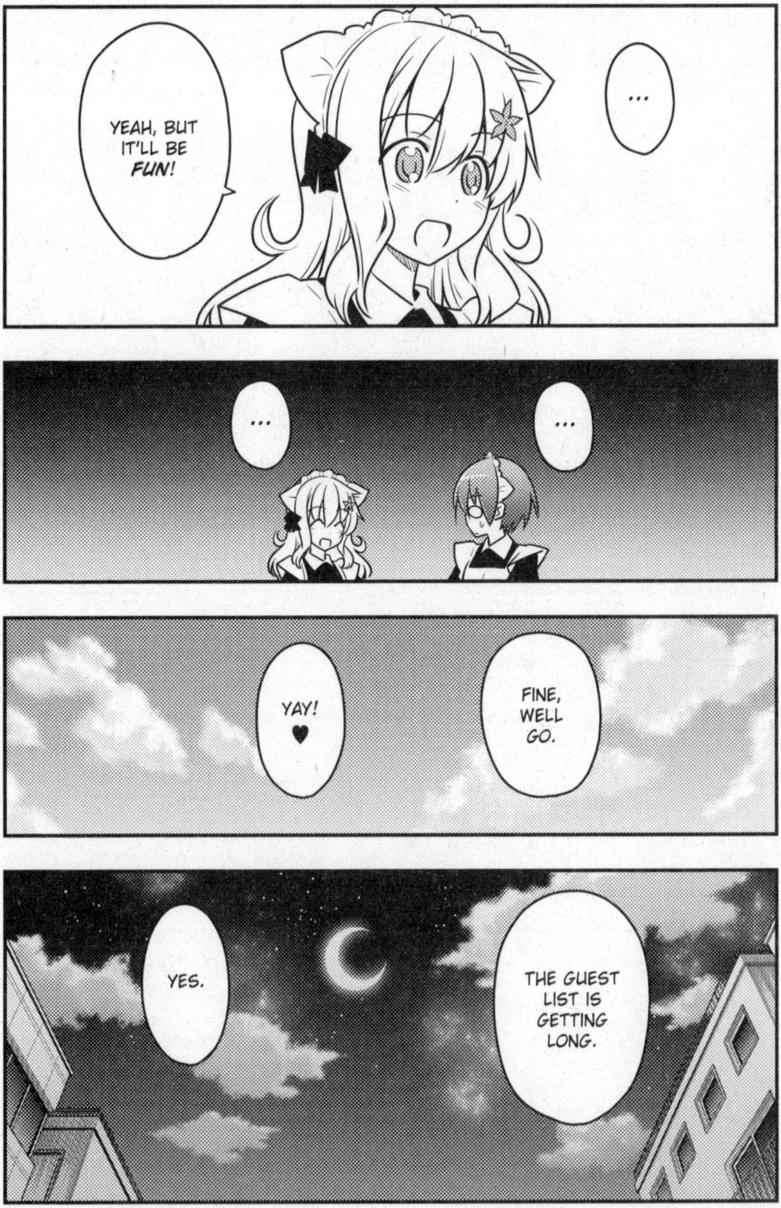
...
YEAH, BUT IT'LL BE *FUN*!
...
...
FINE, WELL GO.
YAY! ♥
THE GUEST LIST IS GETTING LONG.
YES.

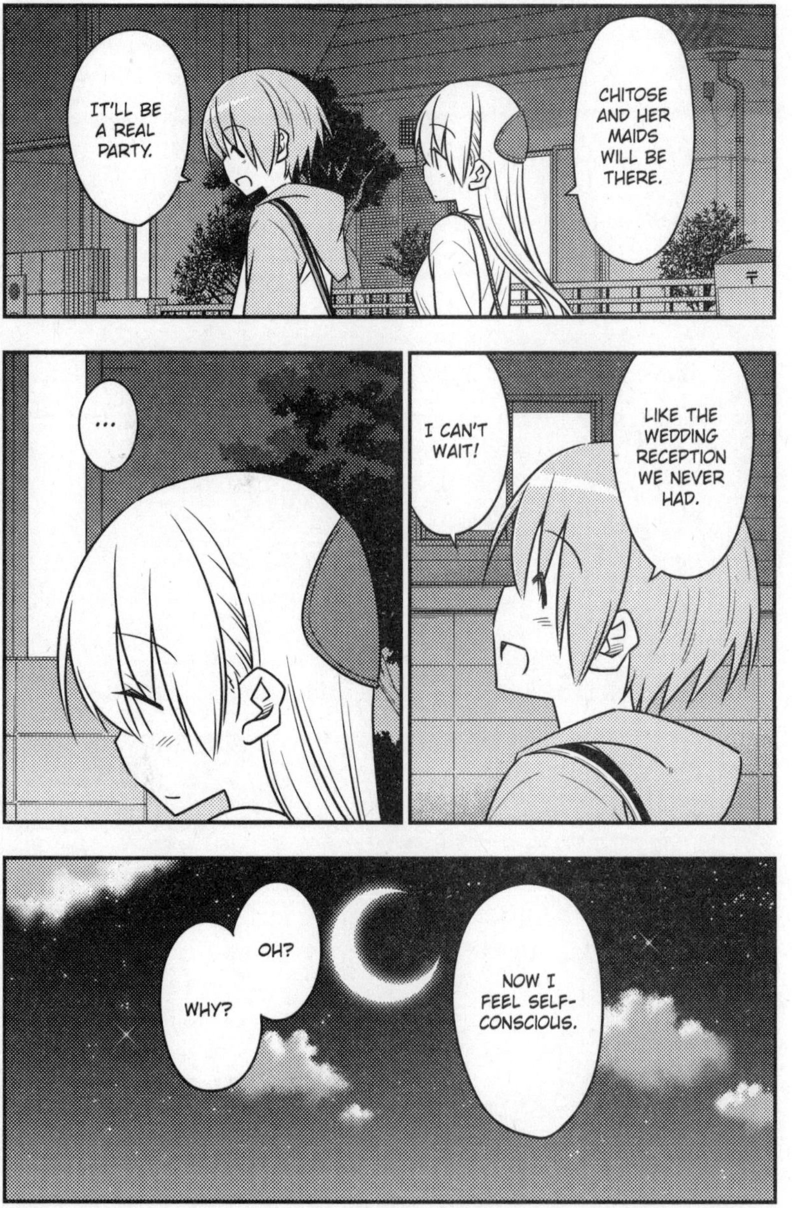
CHITOSE AND HER MAIDS WILL BE THERE.
IT'LL BE A REAL PARTY.
LIKE THE WEDDING RECEPTION WE NEVER HAD.
I CAN'T WAIT!
...
NOW I FEEL SELF-CONSCIOUS.
OH?
WHY?

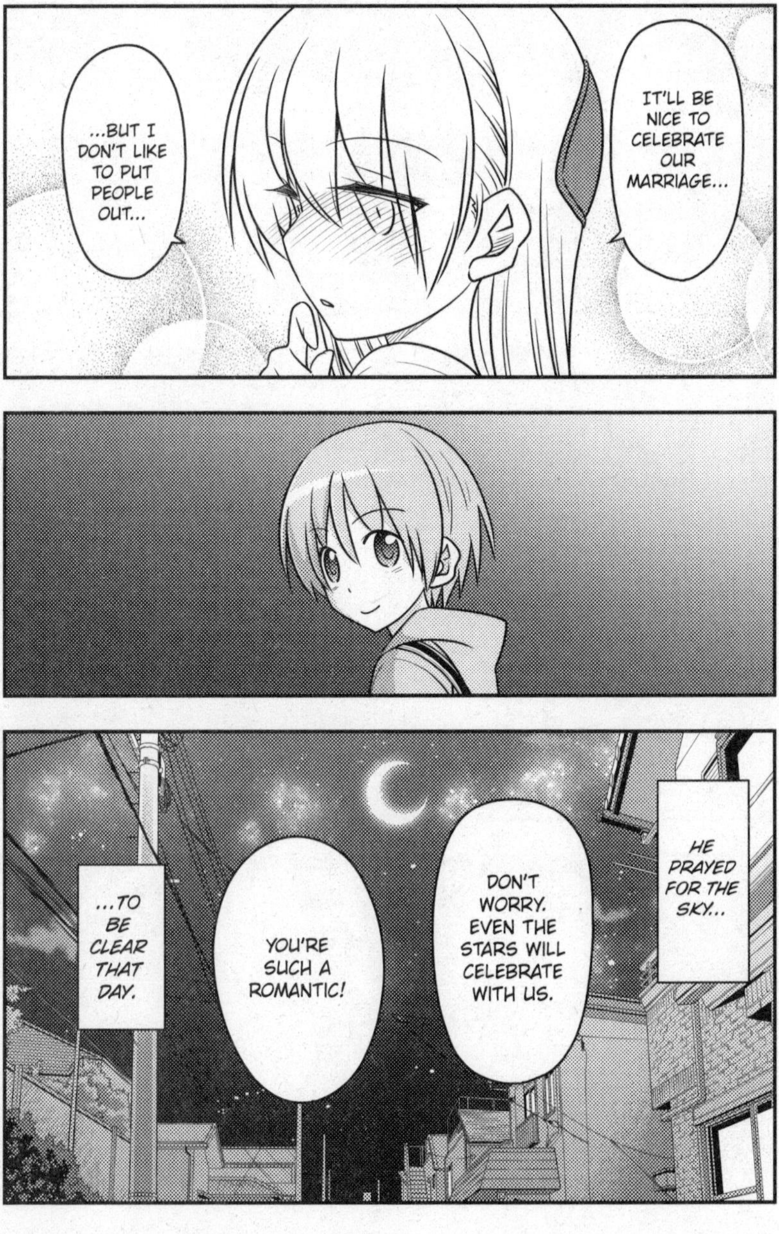
IT'LL BE NICE TO CELEBRATE OUR MARRIAGE...
...BUT I DON'T LIKE TO PUT PEOPLE OUT...
HE PRAYED FOR THE SKY...
DON'T WORRY. EVEN THE STARS WILL CELEBRATE WITH US.
YOU'RE SUCH A ROMANTIC!
...TO BE CLEAR THAT DAY.

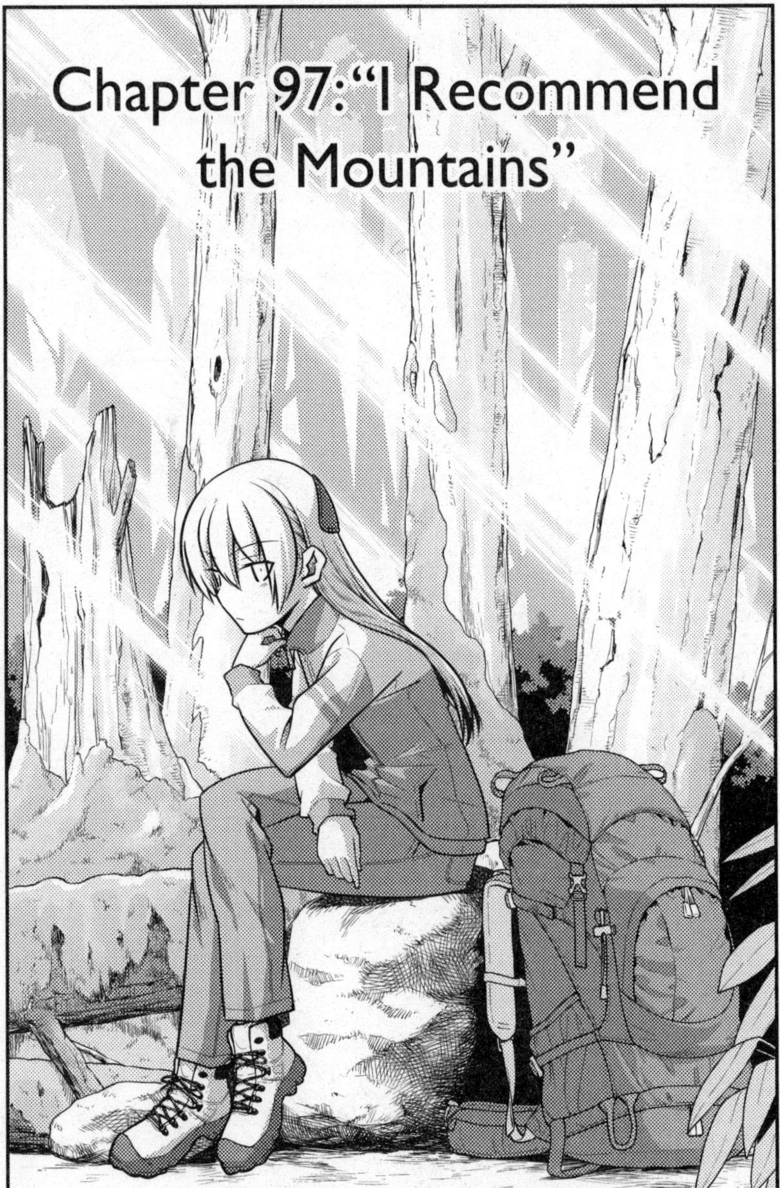
Chapter 97: "I Recommend the Mountains"

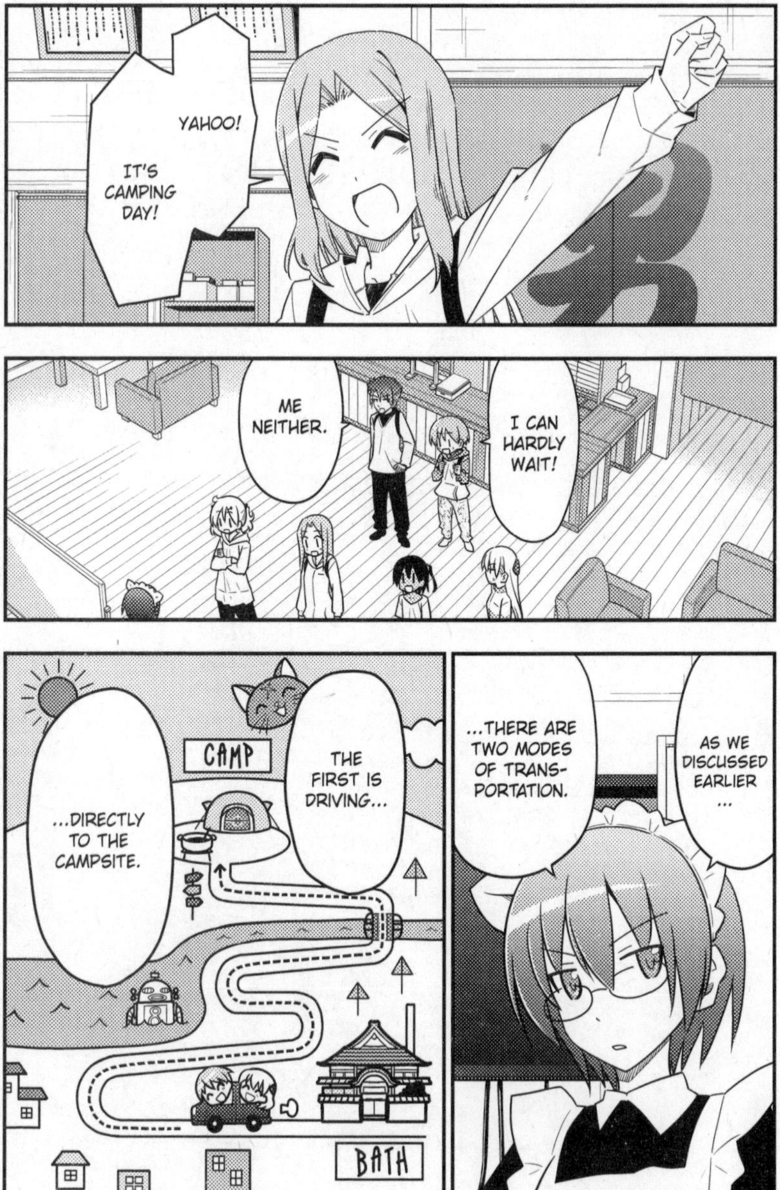
YAHOO!
IT'S CAMPING DAY!
I CAN HARDLY WAIT!
ME NEITHER.
AS WE DISCUSSED EARLIER ...
...THERE ARE TWO MODES OF TRANS-PORTATION.
THE FIRST IS DRIVING...
CAMP
BATH
...DIRECTLY TO THE CAMPSITE.

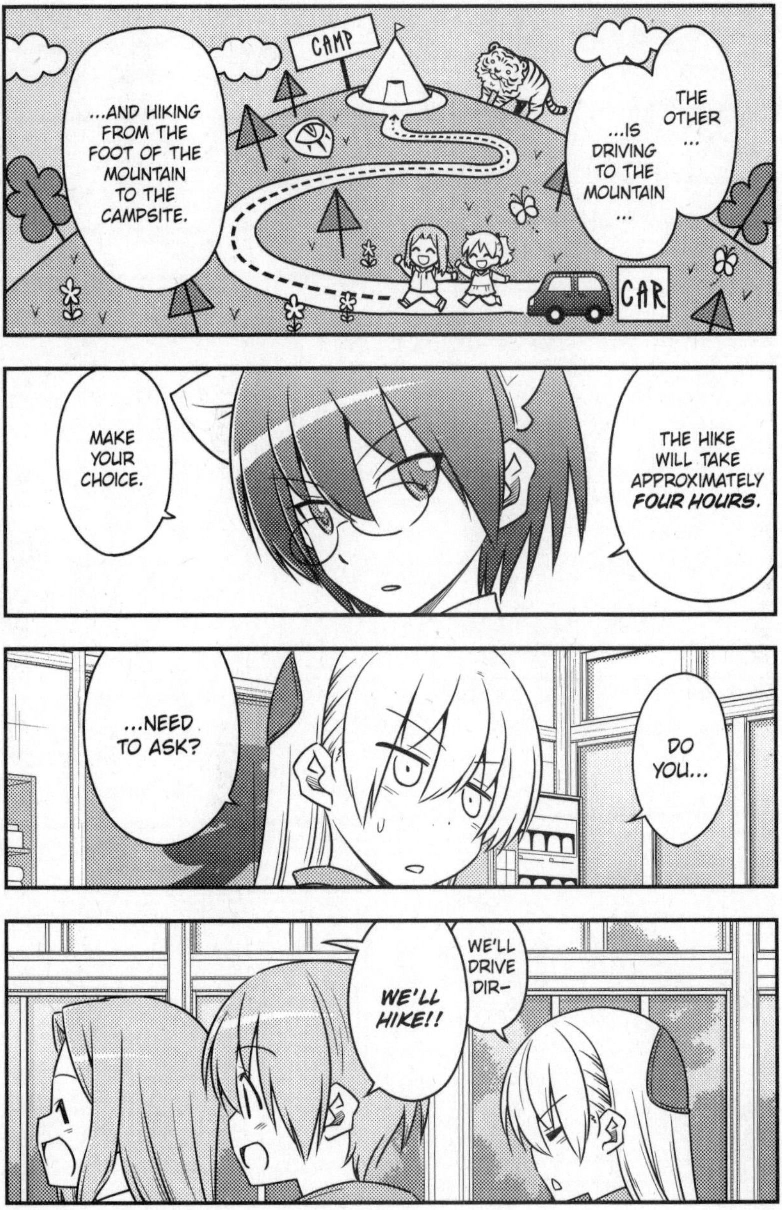
THE OTHER ...
...IS DRIVING TO THE MOUNTAIN ...
...AND HIKING FROM THE FOOT OF THE MOUNTAIN TO THE CAMPSITE.
CAMP
CAR
THE HIKE WILL TAKE APPROXIMATELY FOUR HOURS.
MAKE YOUR CHOICE.
DO YOU...
...NEED TO ASK?
WE'LL DRIVE DIR-
WE'LL HIKE!!

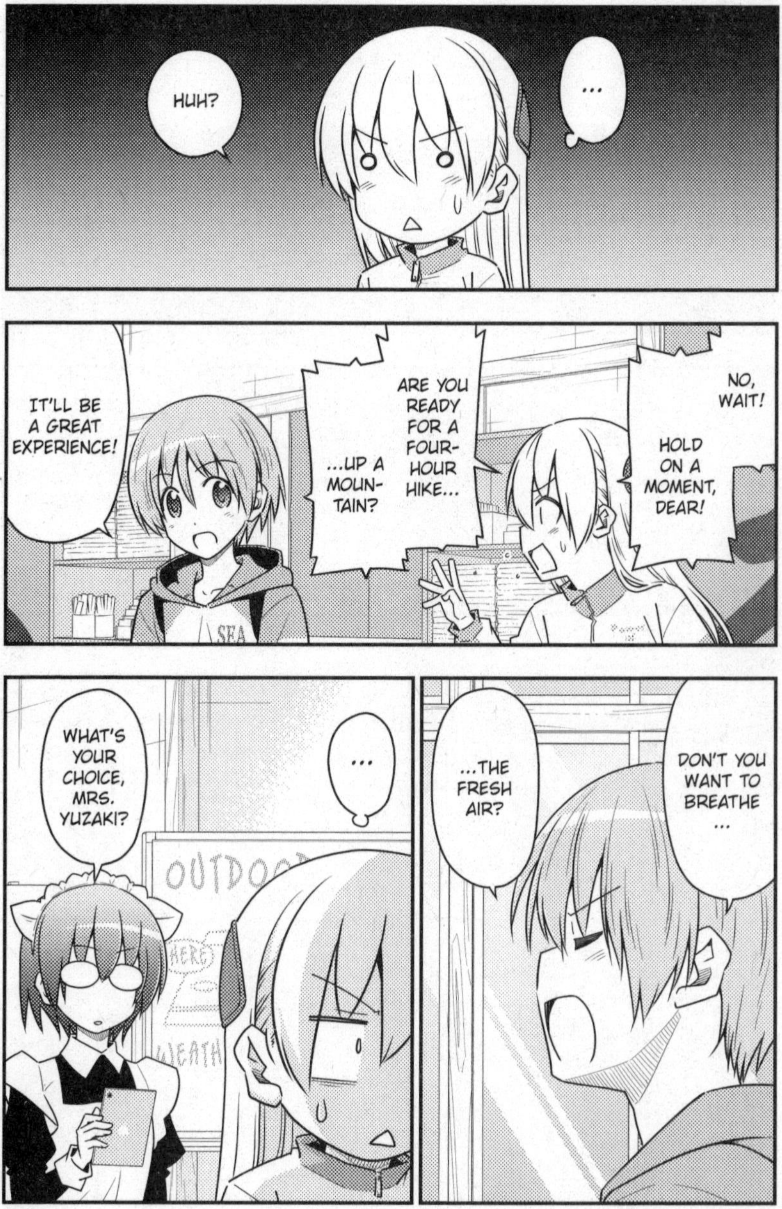
...
HUH?
NO, WAIT!
HOLD ON A MOMENT, DEAR!
ARE YOU READY FOR A FOUR-HOUR HIKE...
...UP A MOUN-TAIN?
IT'LL BE A GREAT EXPERIENCE!
DON'T YOU WANT TO BREATHE ...
...THE FRESH AIR?
...
WHAT'S YOUR CHOICE, MRS. YUZAKI?
HERE

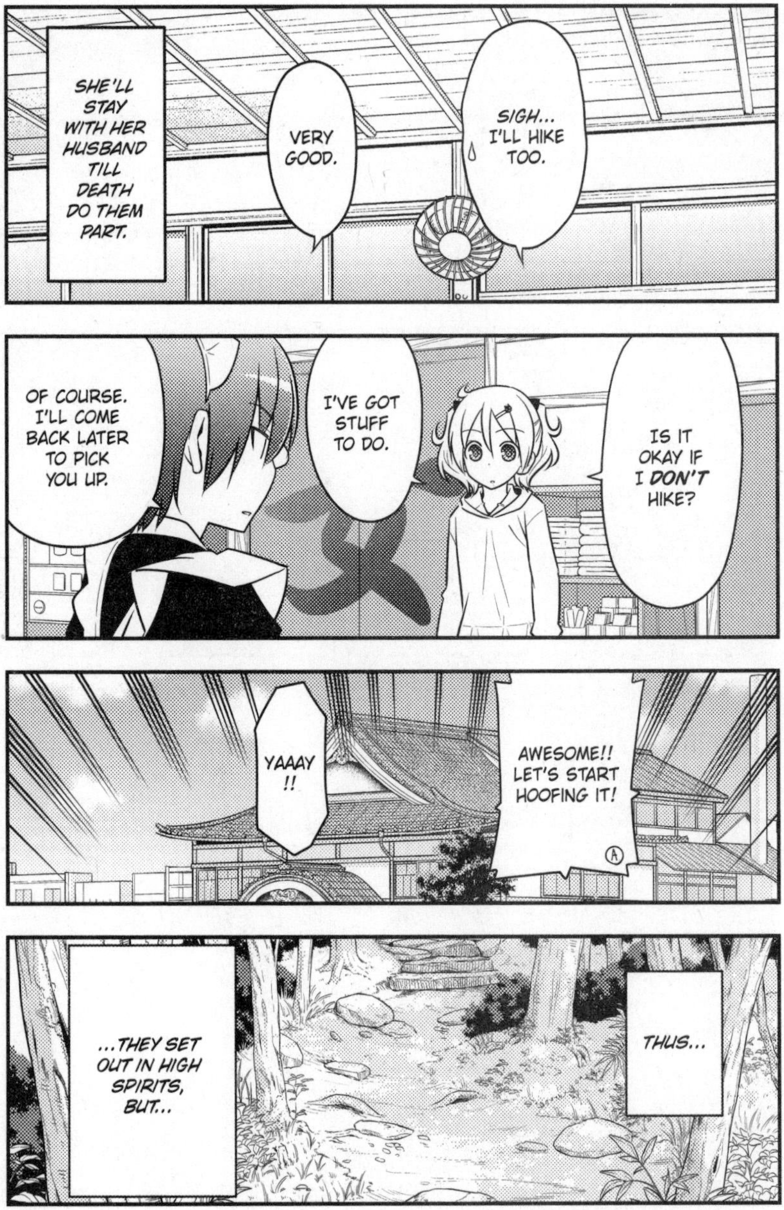
SIGH... I'LL HIKE TOO.
VERY GOOD.
SHE'LL STAY WITH HER HUSBAND TILL DEATH DO THEM PART.
IS IT OKAY IF I **DON'T** HIKE?
I'VE GOT STUFF TO DO.
OF COURSE. I'LL COME BACK LATER TO PICK YOU UP.
AWESOME!! LET'S START HOOFING IT!
YAAAY !!
THUS...
...THEY SET OUT IN HIGH SPIRITS, BUT...

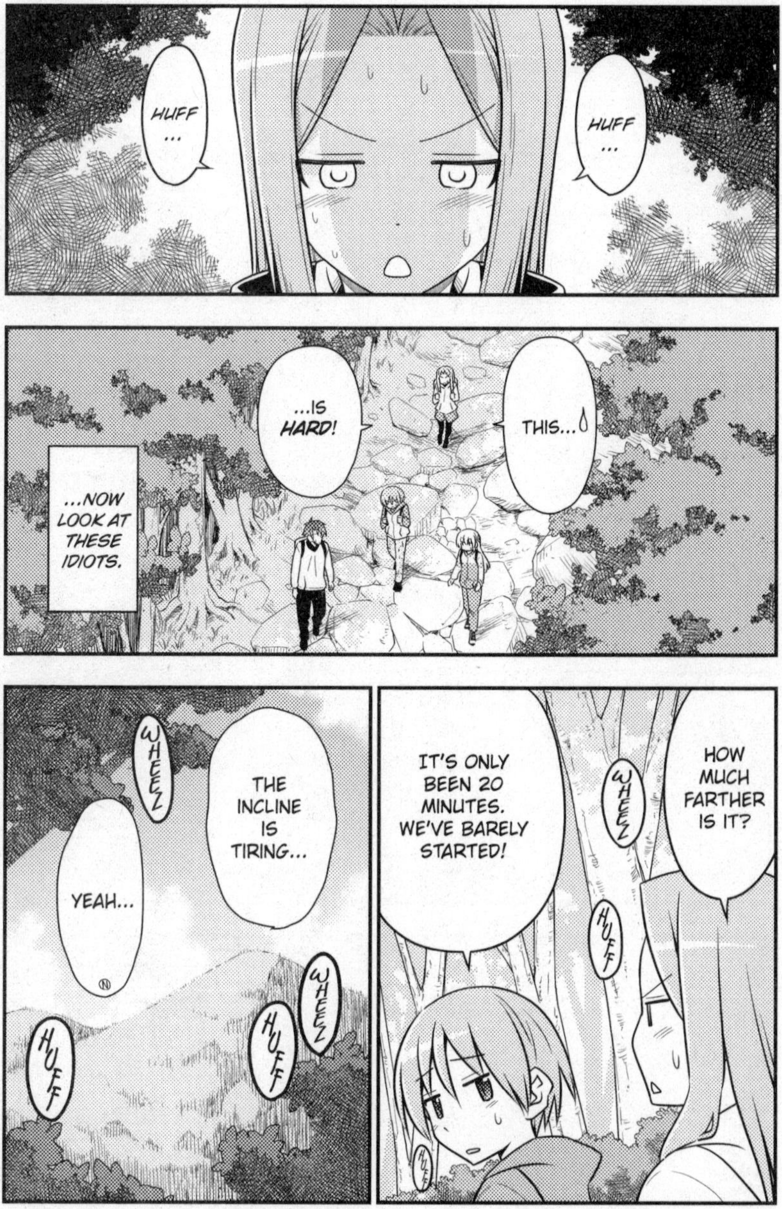
HUFF ...
HUFF ...
THIS...
...IS HARD!
...NOW LOOK AT THESE IDIOTS.
HOW MUCH FARTHER IS IT?
WHEEZ
IT'S ONLY BEEN 20 MINUTES. WE'VE BARELY STARTED!
HUFF
HUFF
WHEEZ
THE INCLINE IS TIRING...
YEAH...
WHEEZ
HUFF
HUFF

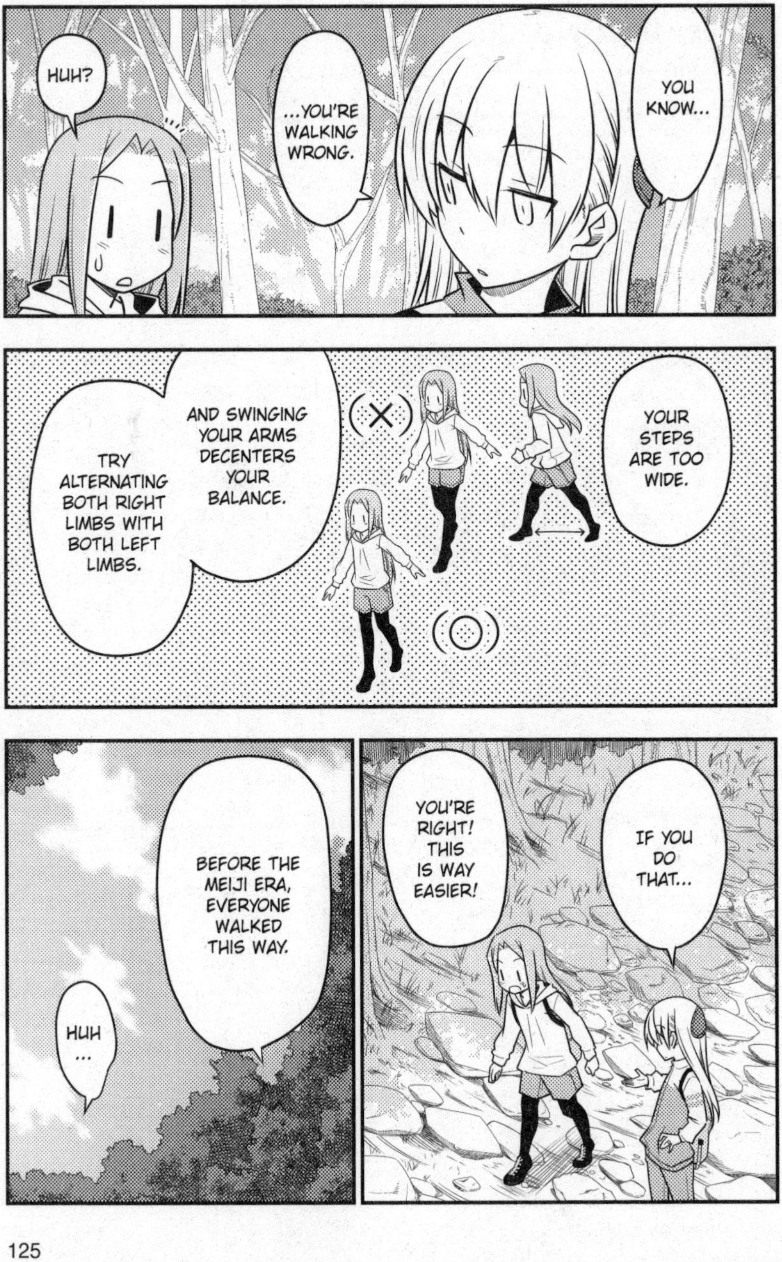
YOU KNOW...
...YOU'RE WALKING WRONG.
HUH?
YOUR STEPS ARE TOO WIDE.
AND SWINGING YOUR ARMS DECENTERS YOUR BALANCE.
TRY ALTERNATING BOTH RIGHT LIMBS WITH BOTH LEFT LIMBS.
IF YOU DO THAT...
YOU'RE RIGHT! THIS IS WAY EASIER!
BEFORE THE MEIJI ERA, EVERYONE WALKED THIS WAY.
HUH ...

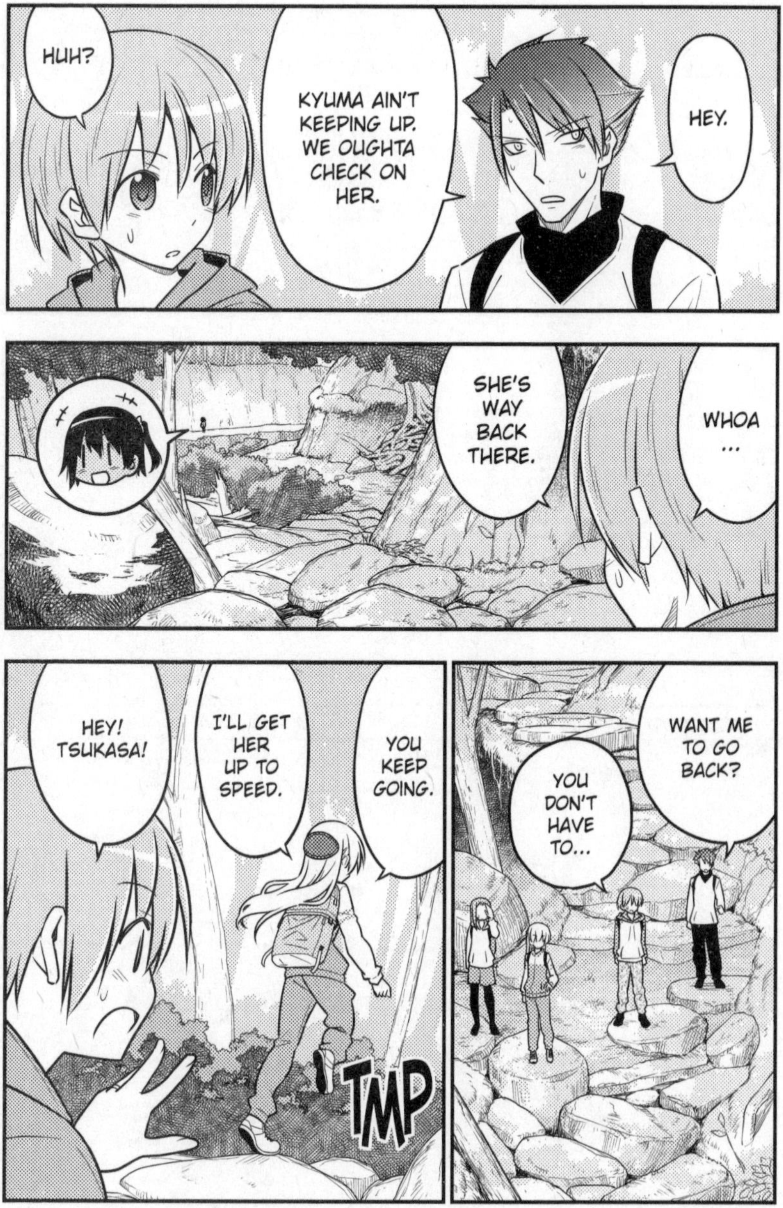
HEY.
KYUMA AIN'T KEEPING UP. WE OUGHTA CHECK ON HER.
HUH?
WHOA ...
SHE'S WAY BACK THERE.
WANT ME TO GO BACK?
YOU DON'T HAVE TO...
YOU KEEP GOING.
I'LL GET HER UP TO SPEED.
HEY! TSUKASA!
TMP

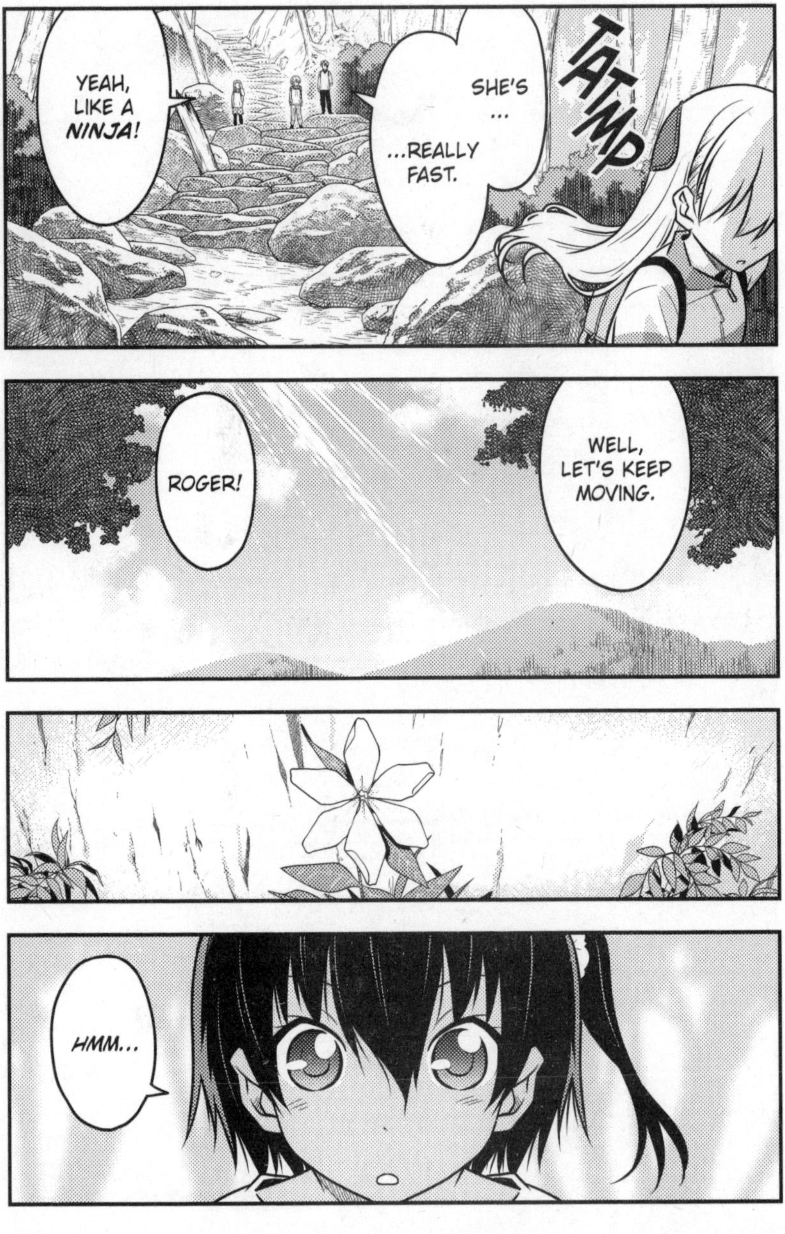
TATMP
SHE'S ... ...REALLY FAST.
YEAH, LIKE A *NINJA!*
WELL, LET'S KEEP MOVING.
ROGER!
HMM...

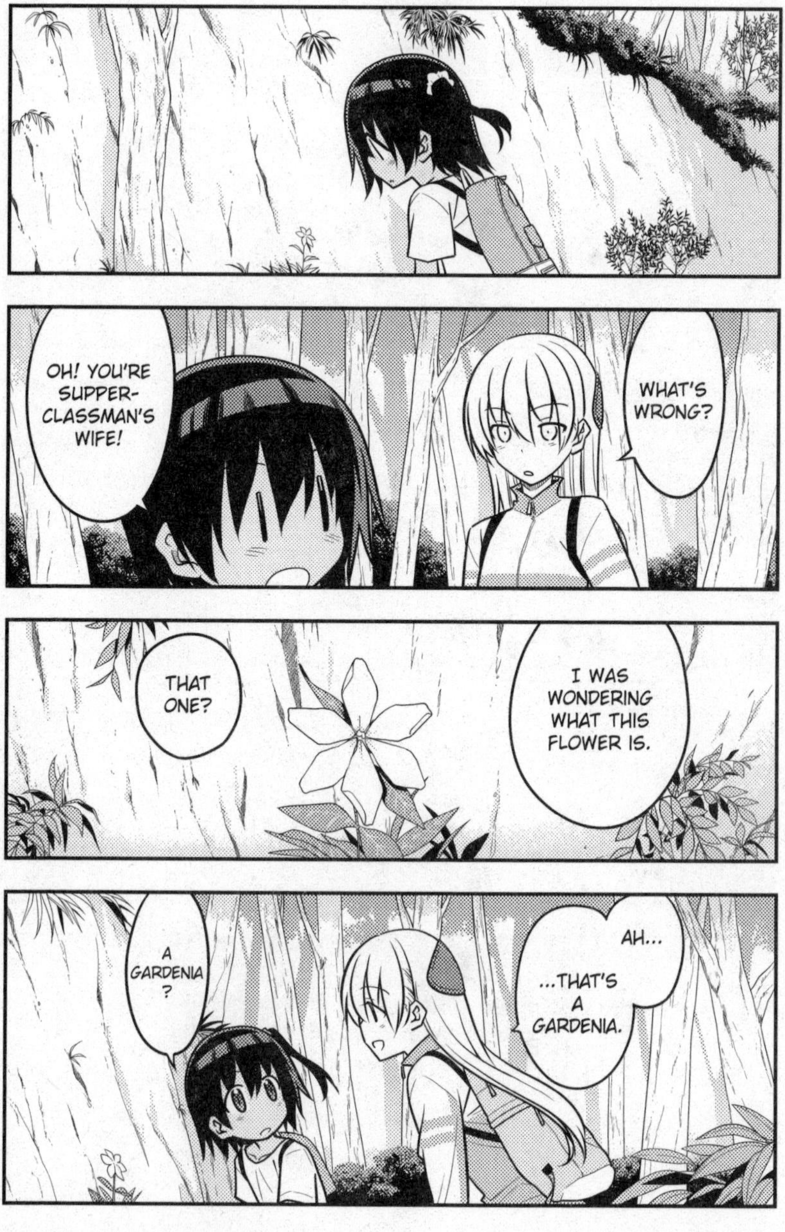
WHAT'S WRONG?
OH! YOU'RE SUPPER-CLASSMAN'S WIFE!
I WAS WONDERING WHAT THIS FLOWER IS.
THAT ONE?
AH...
...THAT'S A GARDENIA.
A GARDENIA ?

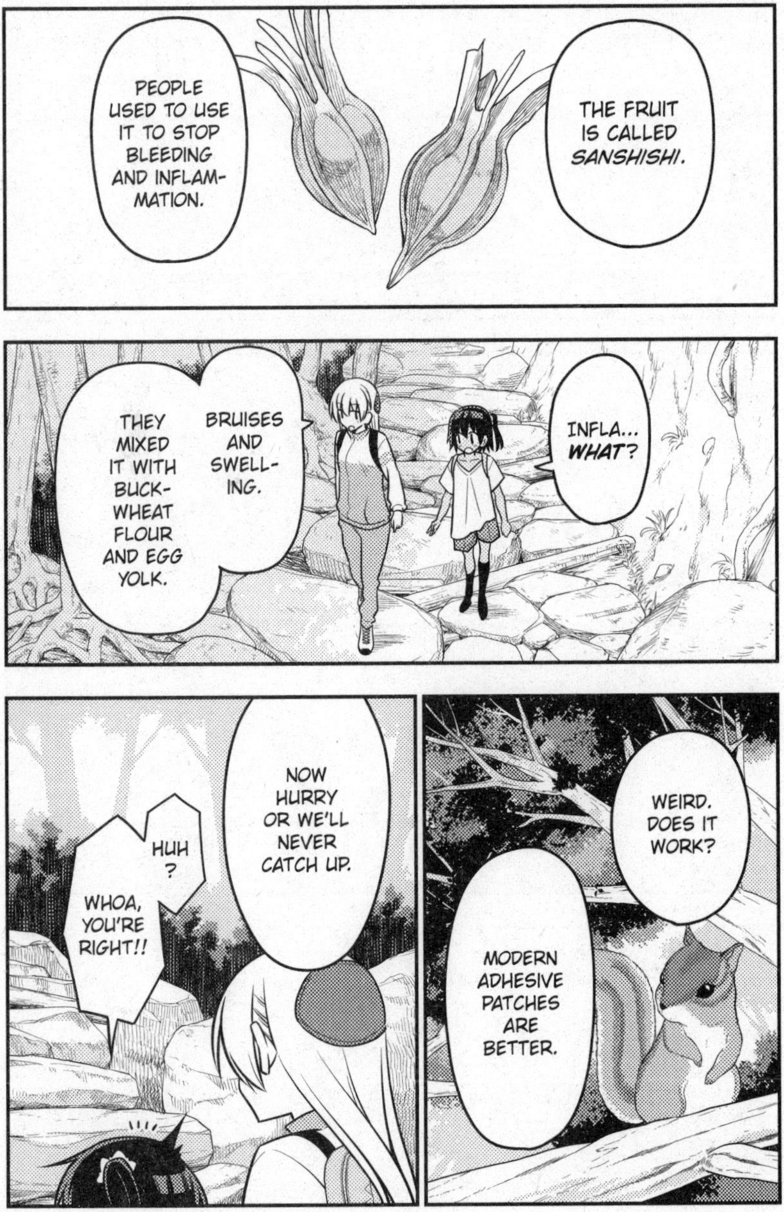
THE FRUIT IS CALLED *SANSHISHI*.
PEOPLE USED TO USE IT TO STOP BLEEDING AND INFLAMMATION.
INFLA... **WHAT**?
BRUISES AND SWELLING.
THEY MIXED IT WITH BUCKWHEAT FLOUR AND EGG YOLK.
WEIRD. DOES IT WORK?
MODERN ADHESIVE PATCHES ARE BETTER.
NOW HURRY OR WE'LL NEVER CATCH UP.
HUH?
WHOA, YOU'RE RIGHT!!

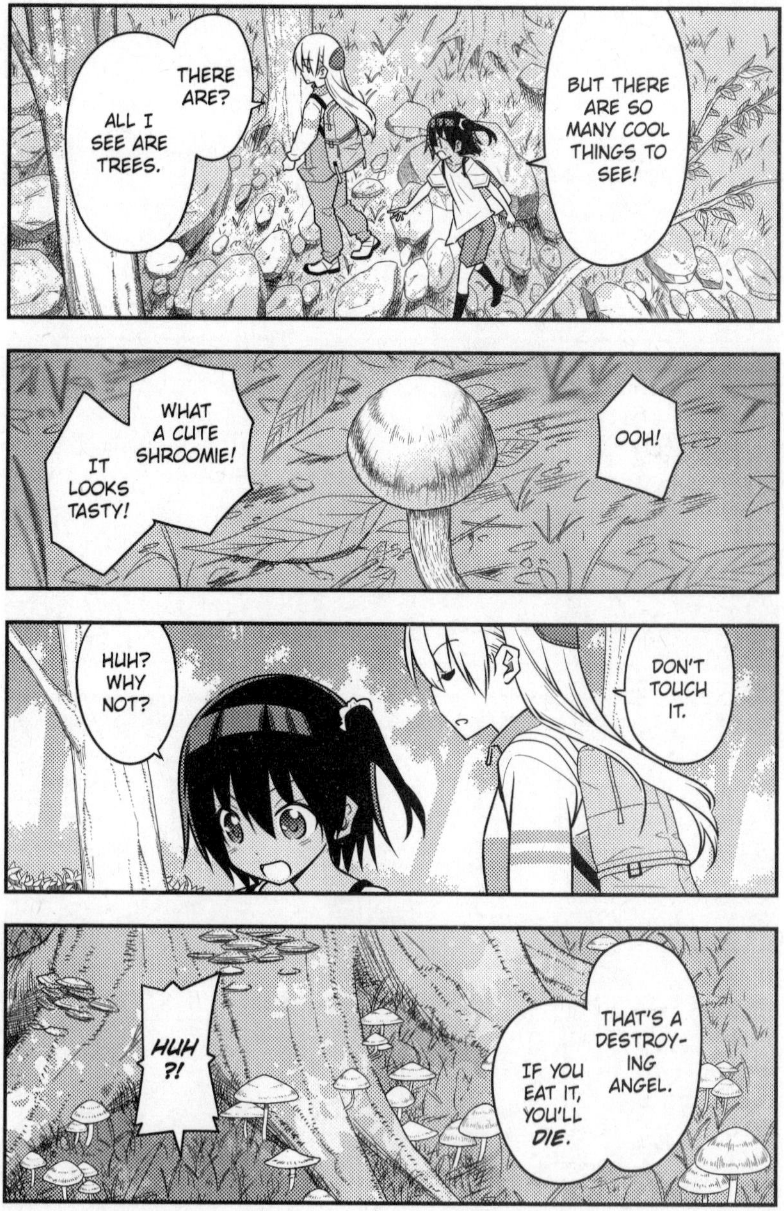
BUT THERE ARE SO MANY COOL THINGS TO SEE!
THERE ARE?
ALL I SEE ARE TREES.
OOH!
WHAT A CUTE SHROOMIE!
IT LOOKS TASTY!
DON'T TOUCH IT.
HUH? WHY NOT?
THAT'S A DESTROYING ANGEL.
IF YOU EAT IT, YOU'LL *DIE*.
HUH ?!

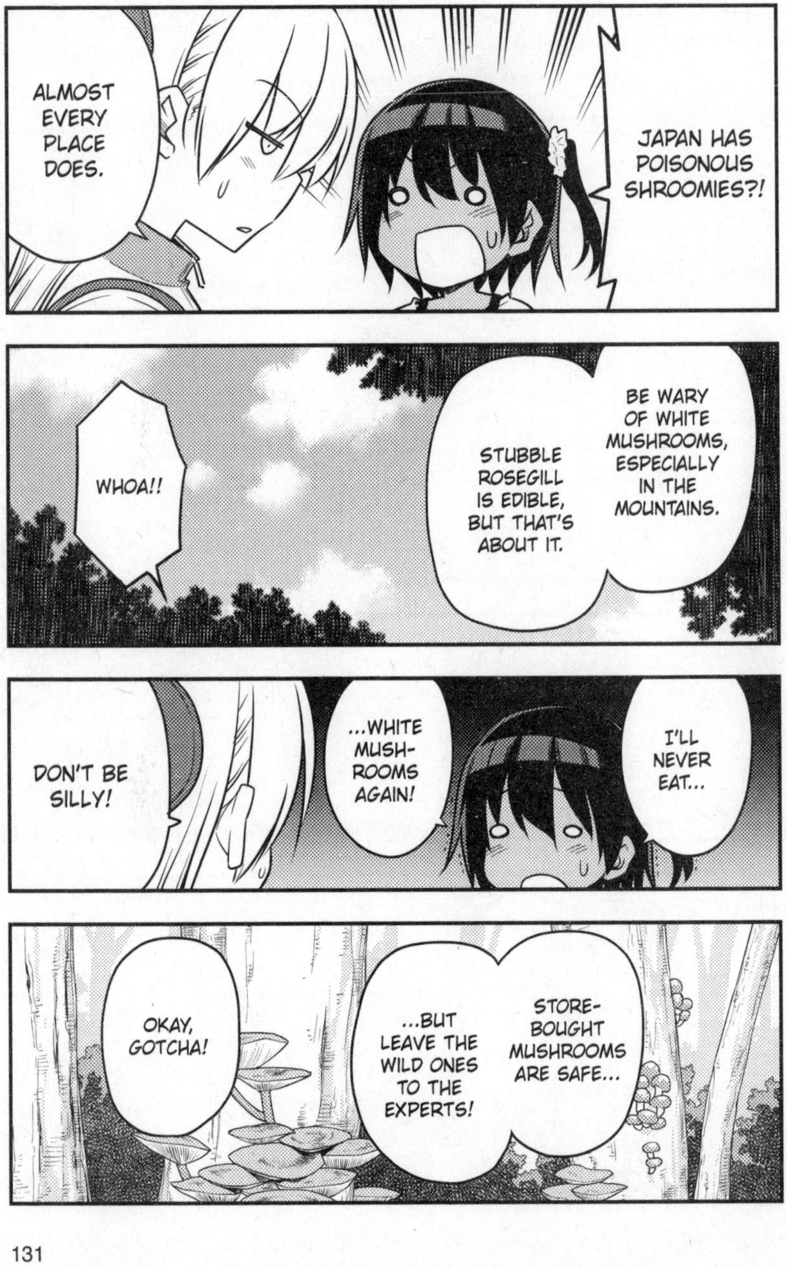
JAPAN HAS POISONOUS SHROOMIES?!
ALMOST EVERY PLACE DOES.
BE WARY OF WHITE MUSHROOMS, ESPECIALLY IN THE MOUNTAINS.
STUBBLE ROSEGILL IS EDIBLE, BUT THAT'S ABOUT IT.
WHOA!!
I'LL NEVER EAT...
...WHITE MUSH-ROOMS AGAIN!
DON'T BE SILLY!
STORE-BOUGHT MUSHROOMS ARE SAFE...
...BUT LEAVE THE WILD ONES TO THE EXPERTS!
OKAY, GOTCHA!

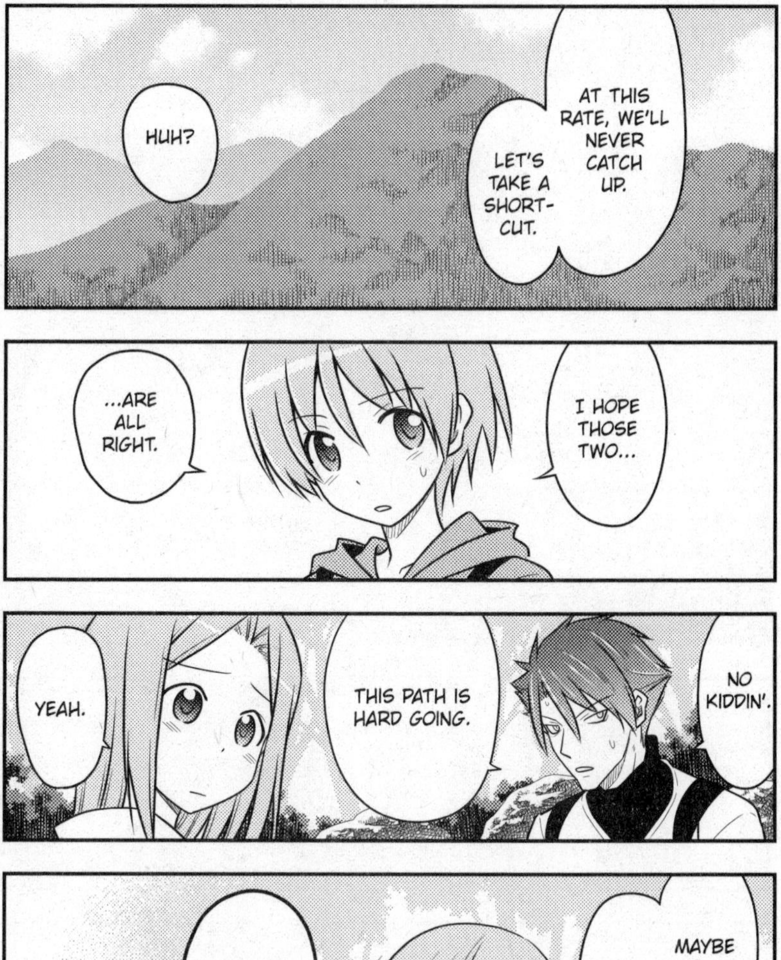
AT THIS RATE, WE'LL NEVER CATCH UP.
LET'S TAKE A SHORT-CUT.
HUH?
I HOPE THOSE TWO...
...ARE ALL RIGHT.
NO KIDDIN'.
THIS PATH IS HARD GOING.
YEAH.
MAYBE I...
...SHOULD GO BACK AND CHECK.
DON'T EVEN THINK ABOUT IT.

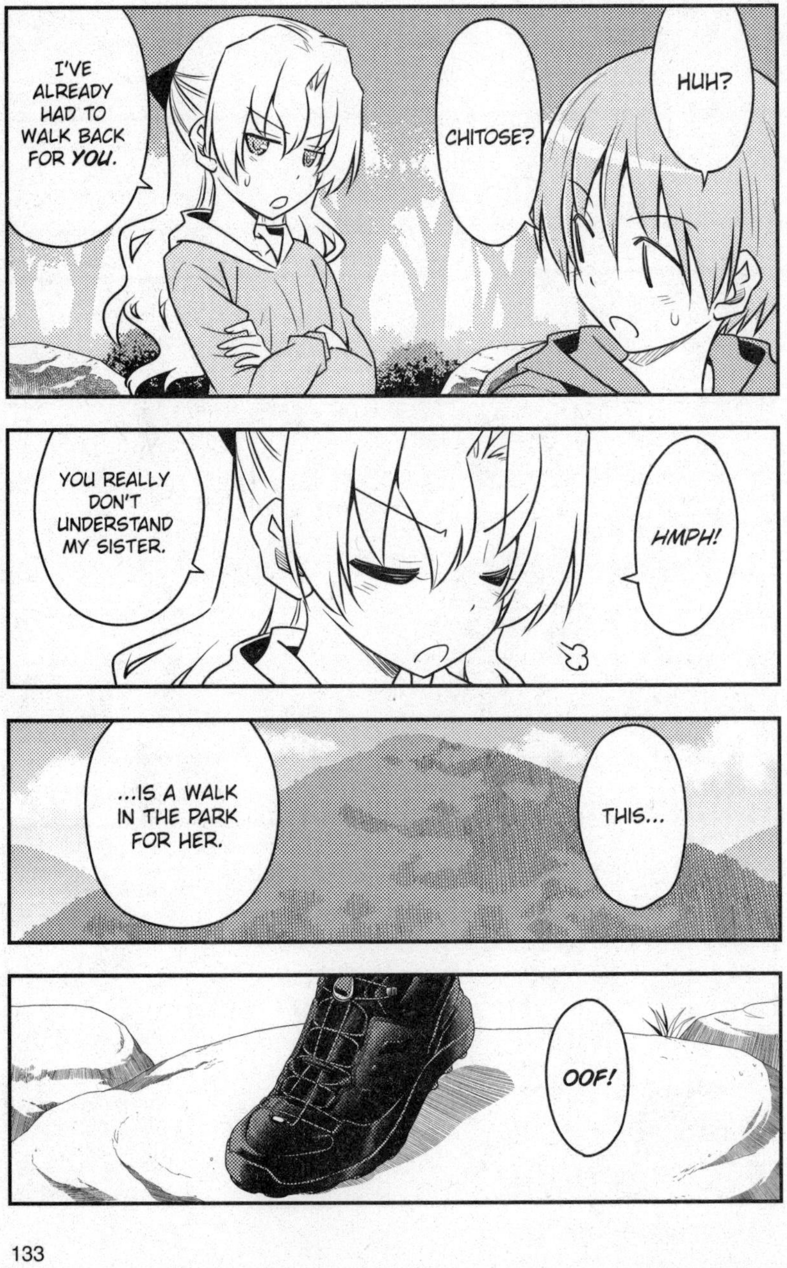
HUH?
CHITOSE?
I'VE ALREADY HAD TO WALK BACK FOR *YOU*.
HMPH!
YOU REALLY DON'T UNDERSTAND MY SISTER.
THIS...
...IS A WALK IN THE PARK FOR HER.
OOF!

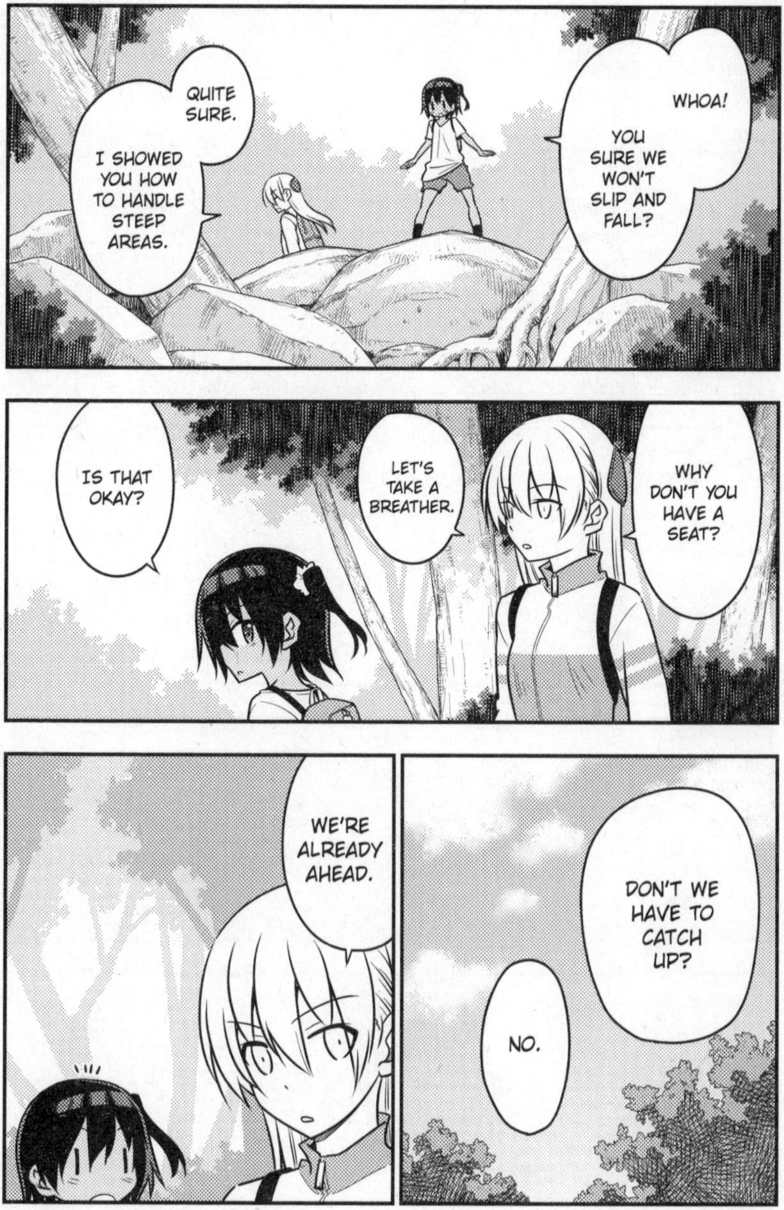
WHOA!
YOU SURE WE WON'T SLIP AND FALL?
QUITE SURE.
I SHOWED YOU HOW TO HANDLE STEEP AREAS.
WHY DON'T YOU HAVE A SEAT?
LET'S TAKE A BREATHER.
IS THAT OKAY?
DON'T WE HAVE TO CATCH UP?
NO.
WE'RE ALREADY AHEAD.

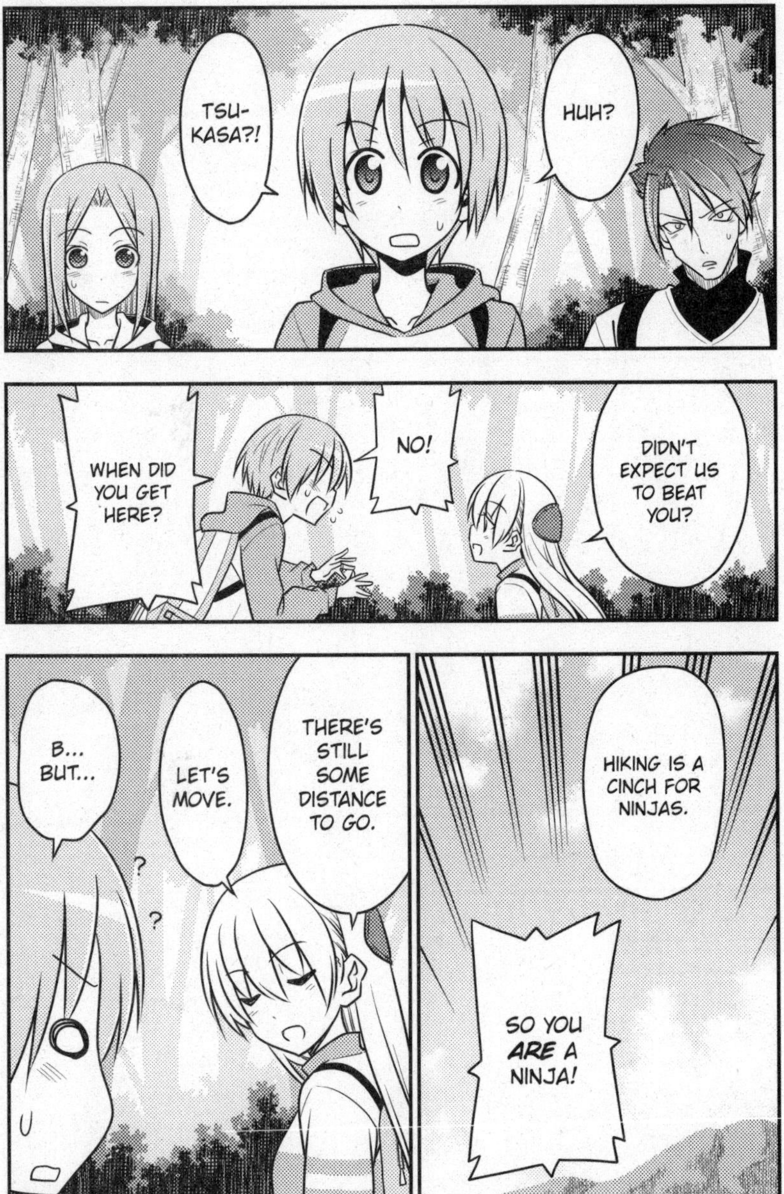
HUH?
TSU-KASA?!
DIDN'T EXPECT US TO BEAT YOU?
NO!
WHEN DID YOU GET HERE?
HIKING IS A CINCH FOR NINJAS.
SO YOU **ARE** A NINJA!
THERE'S STILL SOME DISTANCE TO GO.
LET'S MOVE.
B... BUT...
? ?

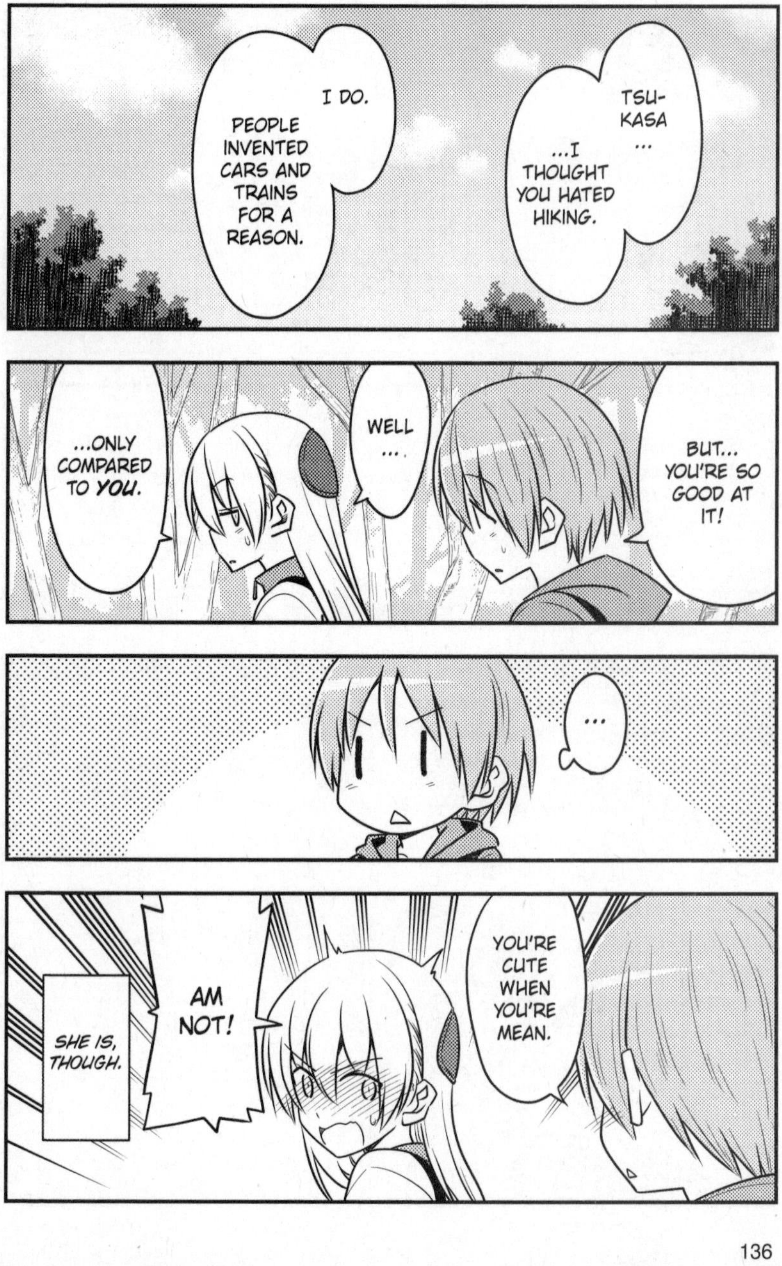
TSU-KASA ... ...I THOUGHT YOU HATED HIKING.
I DO.
PEOPLE INVENTED CARS AND TRAINS FOR A REASON.
BUT... YOU'RE SO GOOD AT IT!
WELL ....
...ONLY COMPARED TO *YOU*.
...
YOU'RE CUTE WHEN YOU'RE MEAN.
AM NOT!
SHE IS, THOUGH.

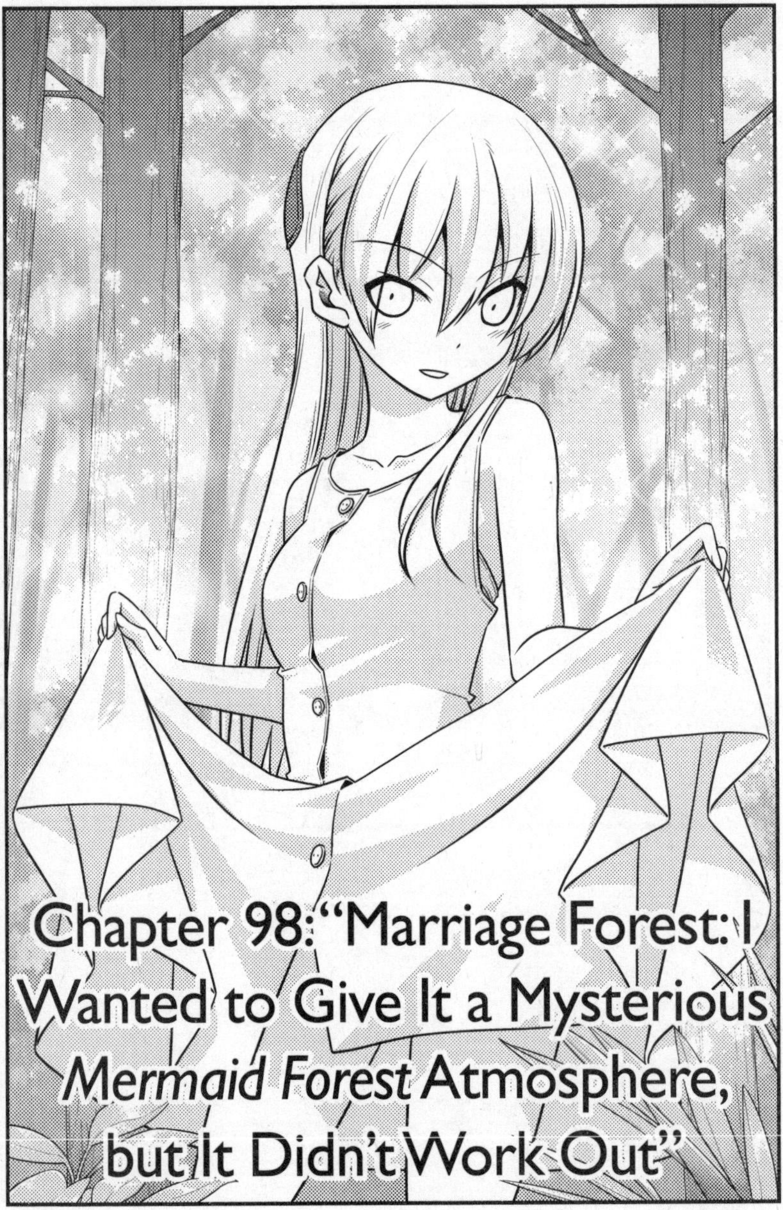
Chapter 98: "Marriage Forest: I Wanted to Give It a Mysterious *Mermaid Forest* Atmosphere, but It Didn't Work Out"

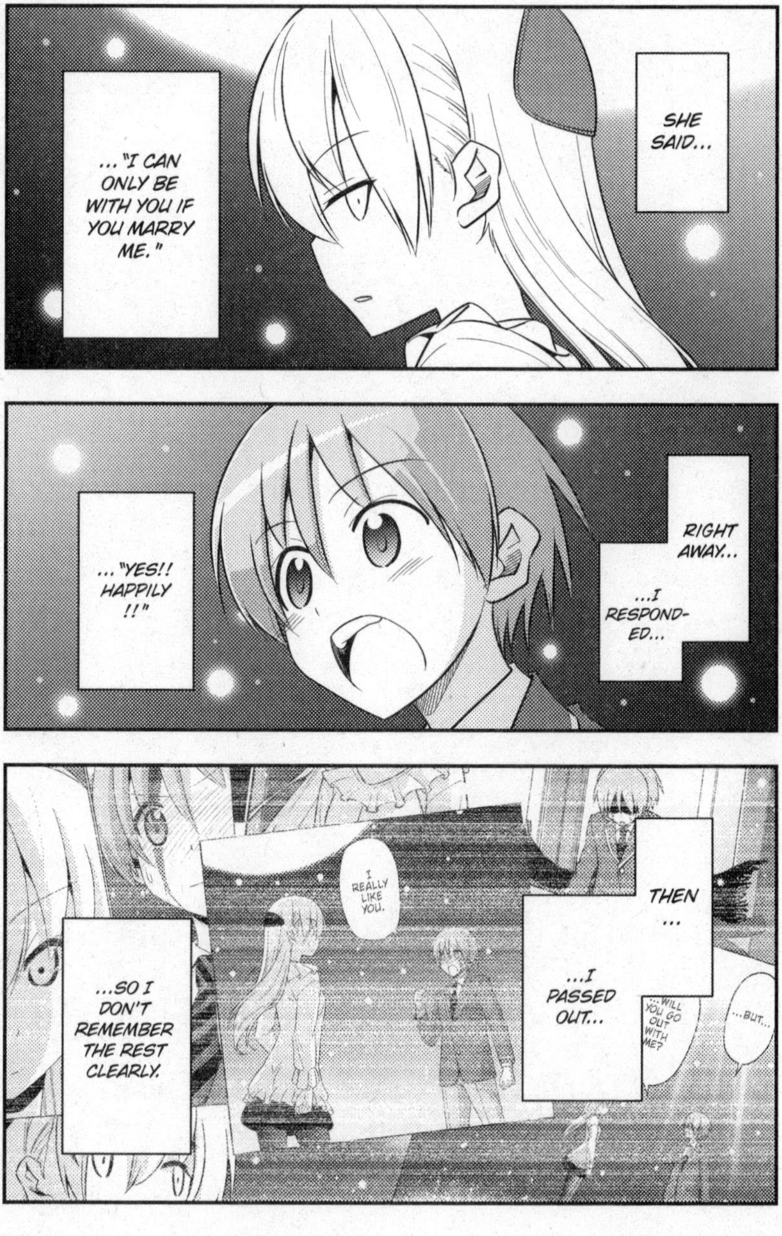
SHE SAID...
..."I CAN ONLY BE WITH YOU IF YOU MARRY ME."
RIGHT AWAY...
...I RESPOND-ED...
..."YES!! HAPPILY!!"
...BUT...
...WILL YOU GO OUT WITH ME?
THEN...
...I PASSED OUT...
I REALLY LIKE YOU.
...SO I DON'T REMEMBER THE REST CLEARLY.

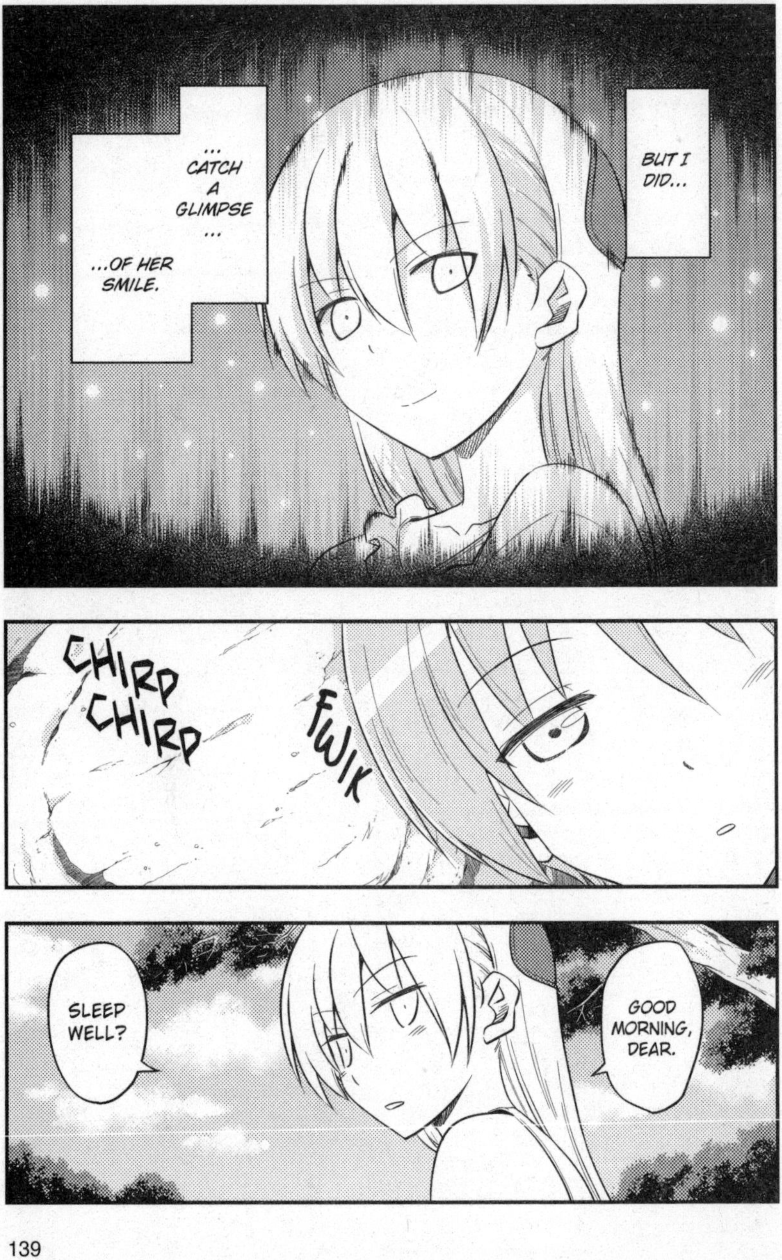
BUT I DID...
...CATCH A GLIMPSE ...
...OF HER SMILE.
FWIK
CHIRP CHIRP
GOOD MORNING, DEAR.
SLEEP WELL?

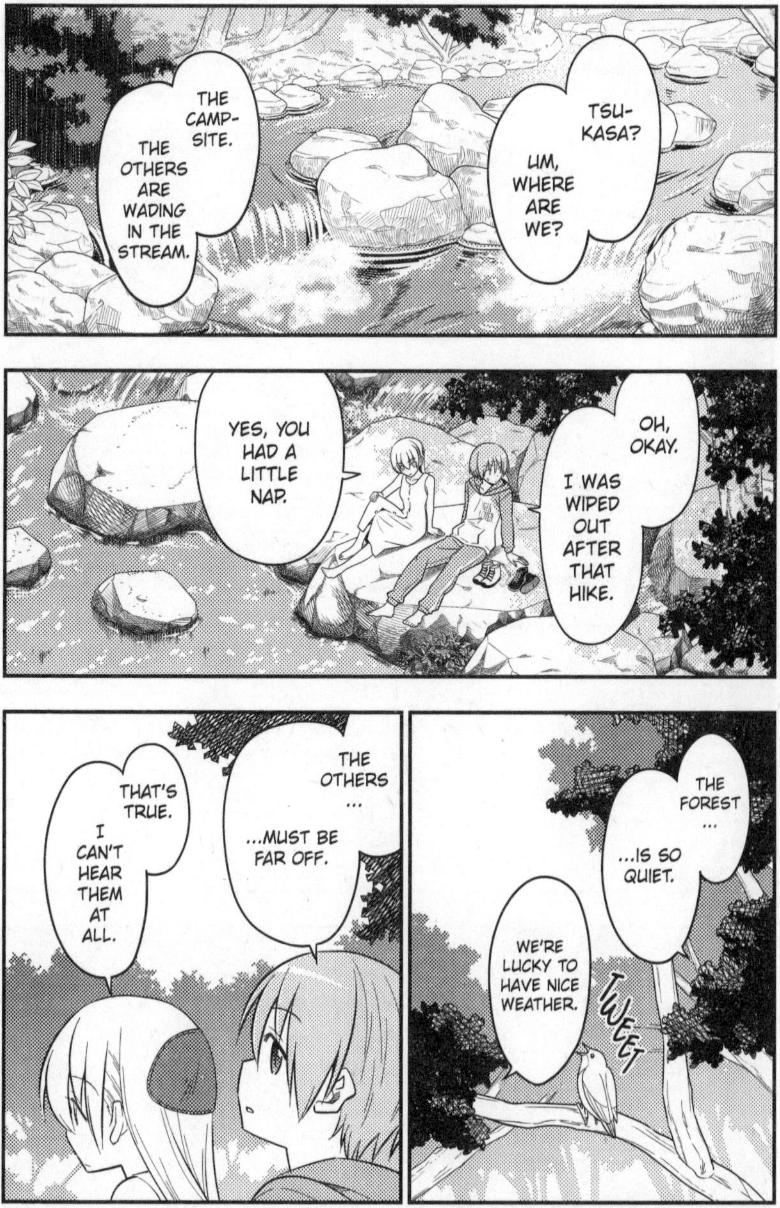
TSU-KASA?
UM, WHERE ARE WE?
THE CAMP-SITE.
THE OTHERS ARE WADING IN THE STREAM.
OH, OKAY.
I WAS WIPED OUT AFTER THAT HIKE.
YES, YOU HAD A LITTLE NAP.
THE FOREST...
...IS SO QUIET.
WE'RE LUCKY TO HAVE NICE WEATHER.
TWEET
THE OTHERS...
...MUST BE FAR OFF.
THAT'S TRUE.
I CAN'T HEAR THEM AT ALL.

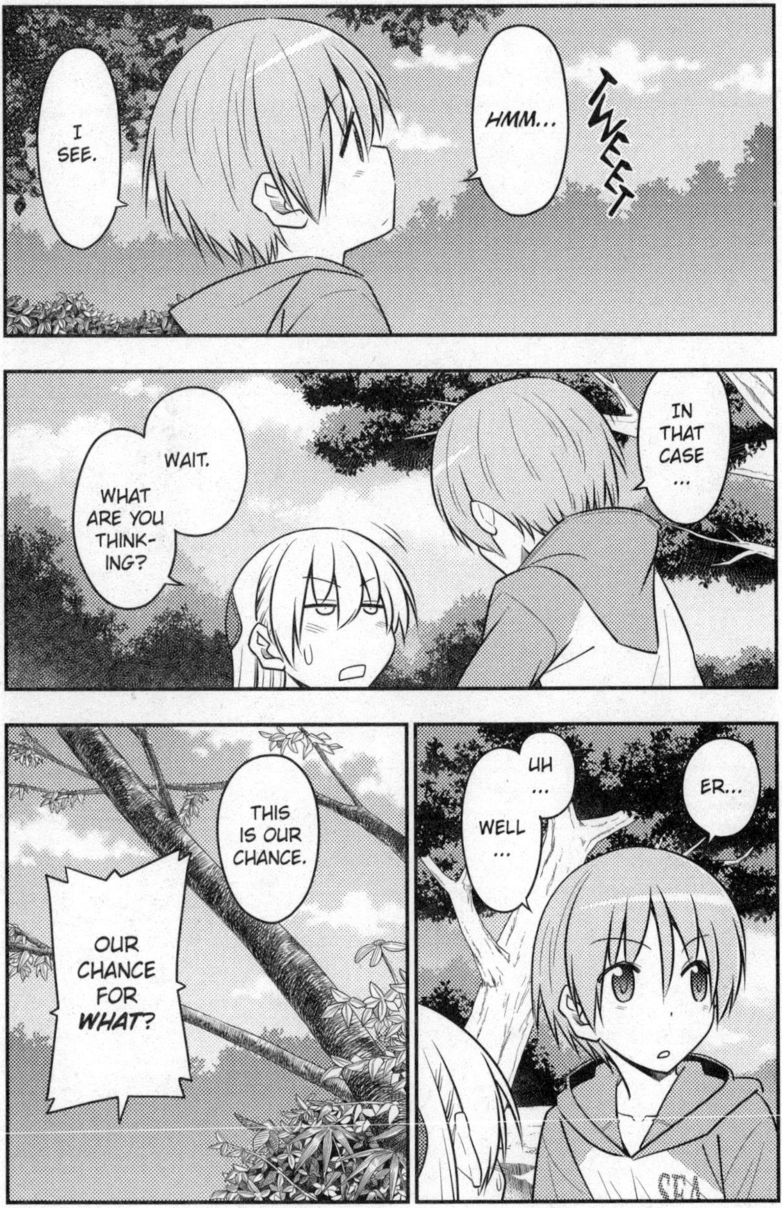
TWEET
HMM...
I SEE.
IN THAT CASE ...
WAIT.
WHAT ARE YOU THINK-ING?
ER...
UH ...
WELL ...
THIS IS OUR CHANCE.
OUR CHANCE FOR **WHAT?**

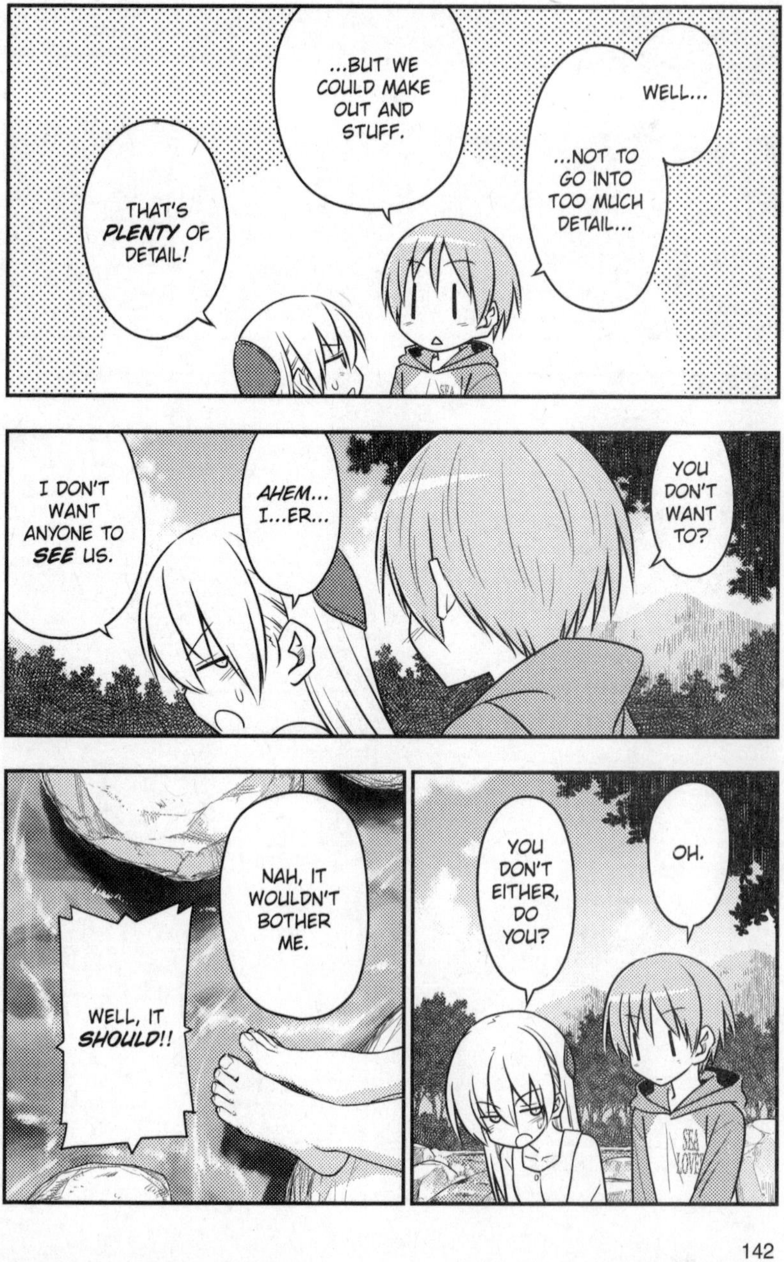
WELL...
...NOT TO GO INTO TOO MUCH DETAIL...
...BUT WE COULD MAKE OUT AND STUFF.
THAT'S **PLENTY** OF DETAIL!
YOU DON'T WANT TO?
AHEM... I...ER...
I DON'T WANT ANYONE TO **SEE** US.
OH.
YOU DON'T EITHER, DO YOU?
NAH, IT WOULDN'T BOTHER ME.
WELL, IT **SHOULD**!!

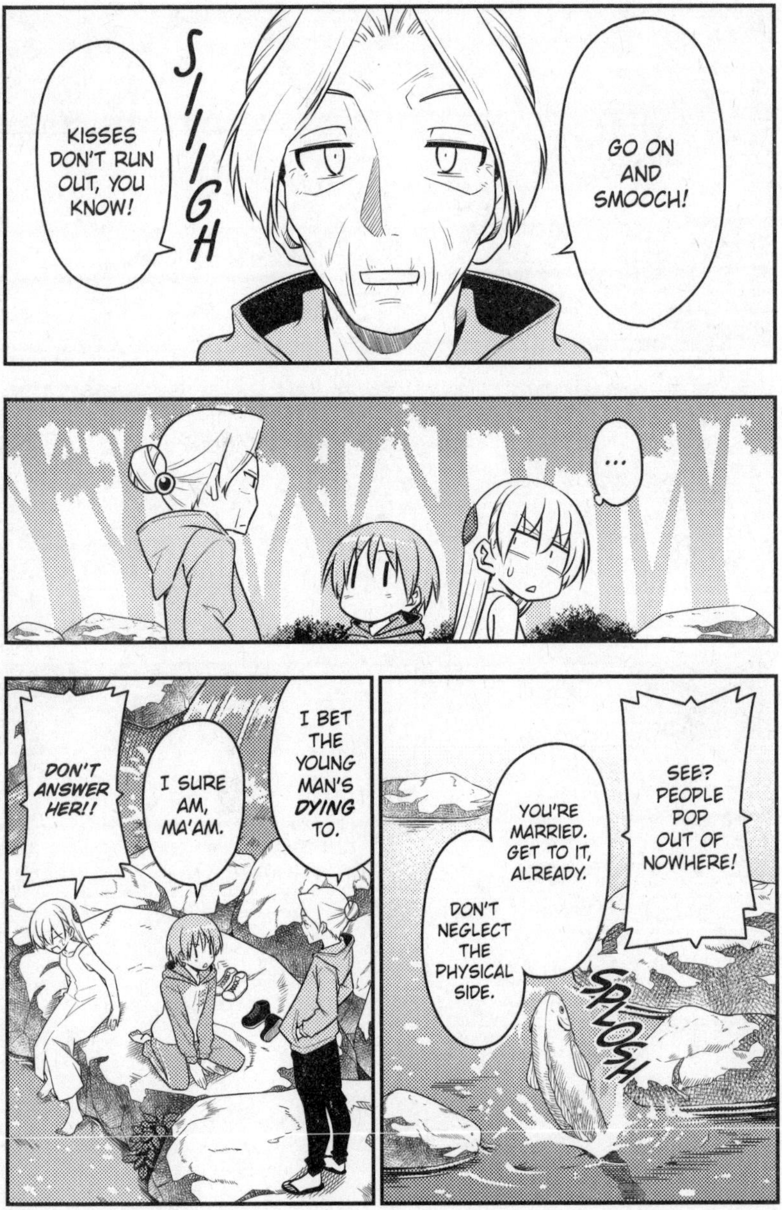
GO ON AND SMOOCH!
SIIIGH
KISSES DON'T RUN OUT, YOU KNOW!
...
SEE? PEOPLE POP OUT OF NOWHERE!
YOU'RE MARRIED. GET TO IT, ALREADY.
DON'T NEGLECT THE PHYSICAL SIDE.
SPLOSH
I BET THE YOUNG MAN'S DYING TO.
I SURE AM, MA'AM.
DON'T ANSWER HER!!

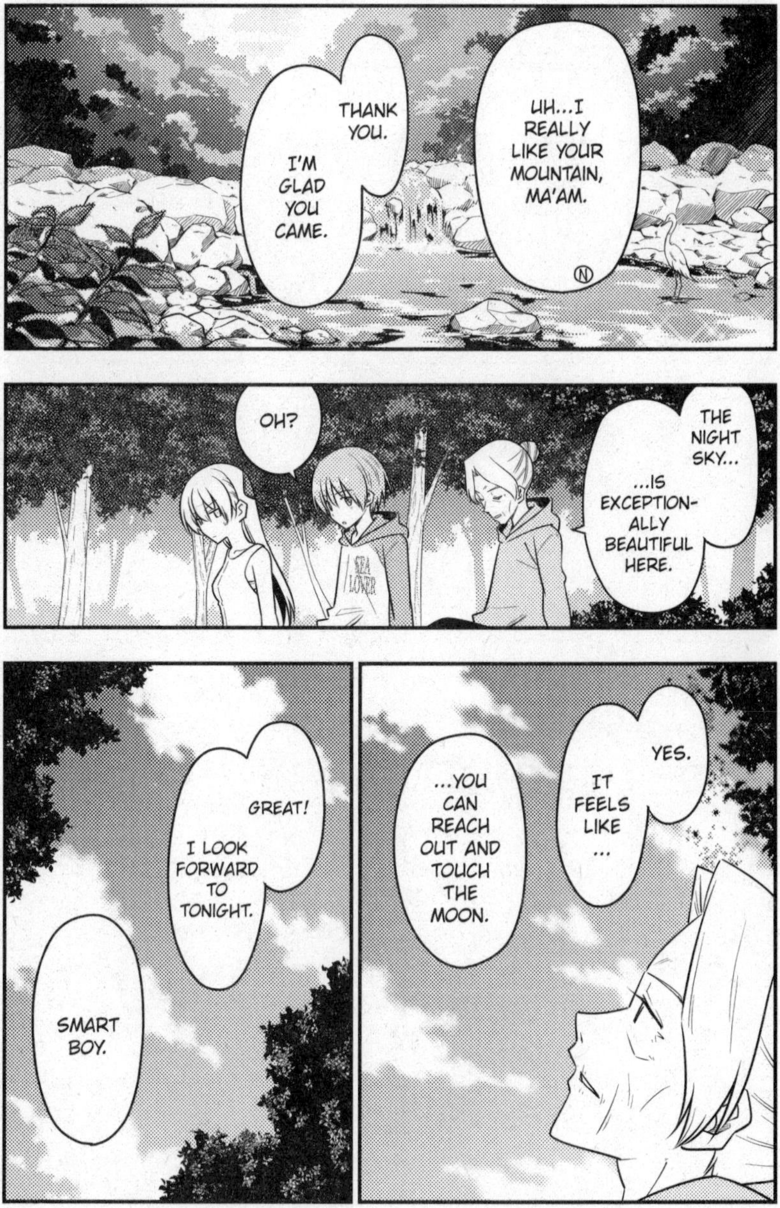
UH...I REALLY LIKE YOUR MOUNTAIN, MA'AM.
THANK YOU.
I'M GLAD YOU CAME.
THE NIGHT SKY...
...IS EXCEPTION-ALLY BEAUTIFUL HERE.
OH?
YES.
IT FEELS LIKE ...
...YOU CAN REACH OUT AND TOUCH THE MOON.
GREAT!
I LOOK FORWARD TO TONIGHT.
SMART BOY.

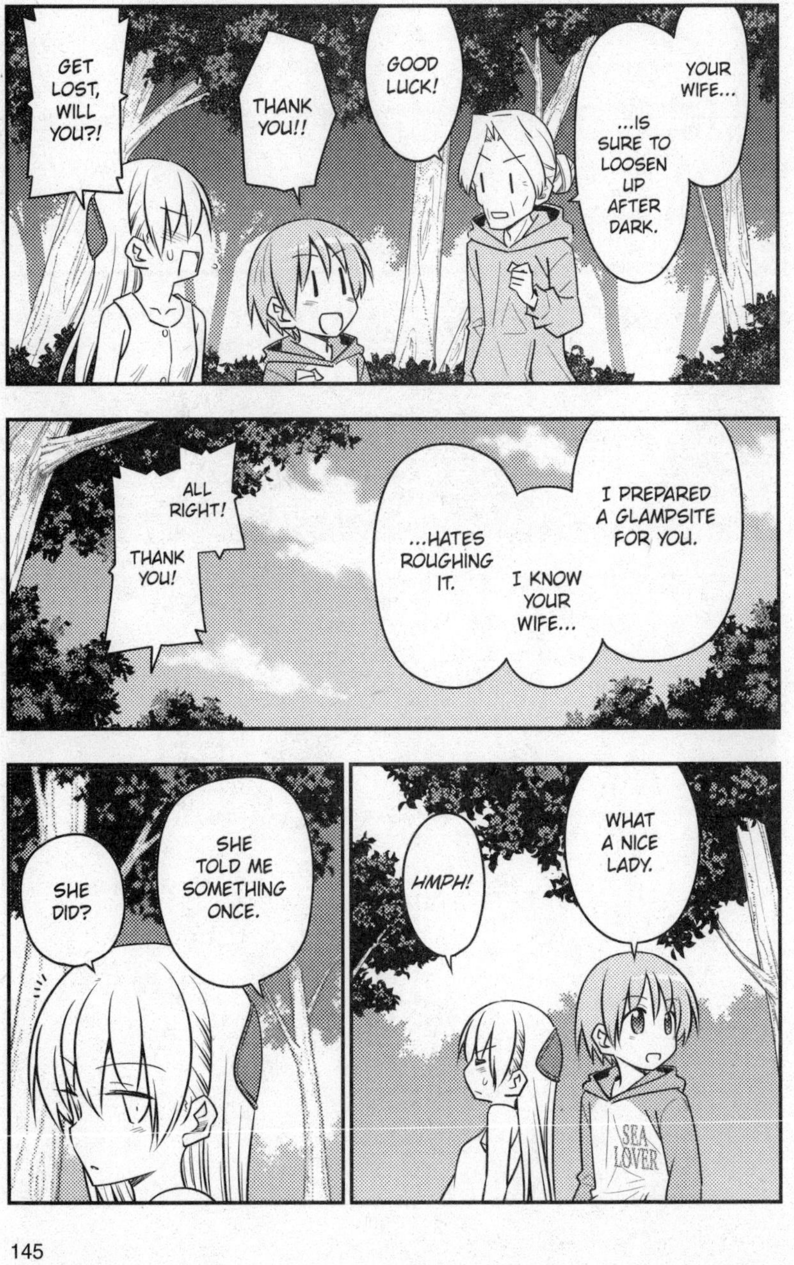
YOUR WIFE...
...IS SURE TO LOOSEN UP AFTER DARK.
GOOD LUCK!
THANK YOU!!
GET LOST, WILL YOU?!
I PREPARED A GLAMPSITE FOR YOU.
I KNOW YOUR WIFE...
...HATES ROUGHING IT.
ALL RIGHT!
THANK YOU!
WHAT A NICE LADY.
HMPH!
SHE TOLD ME SOMETHING ONCE.
SHE DID?
SEA LOVER

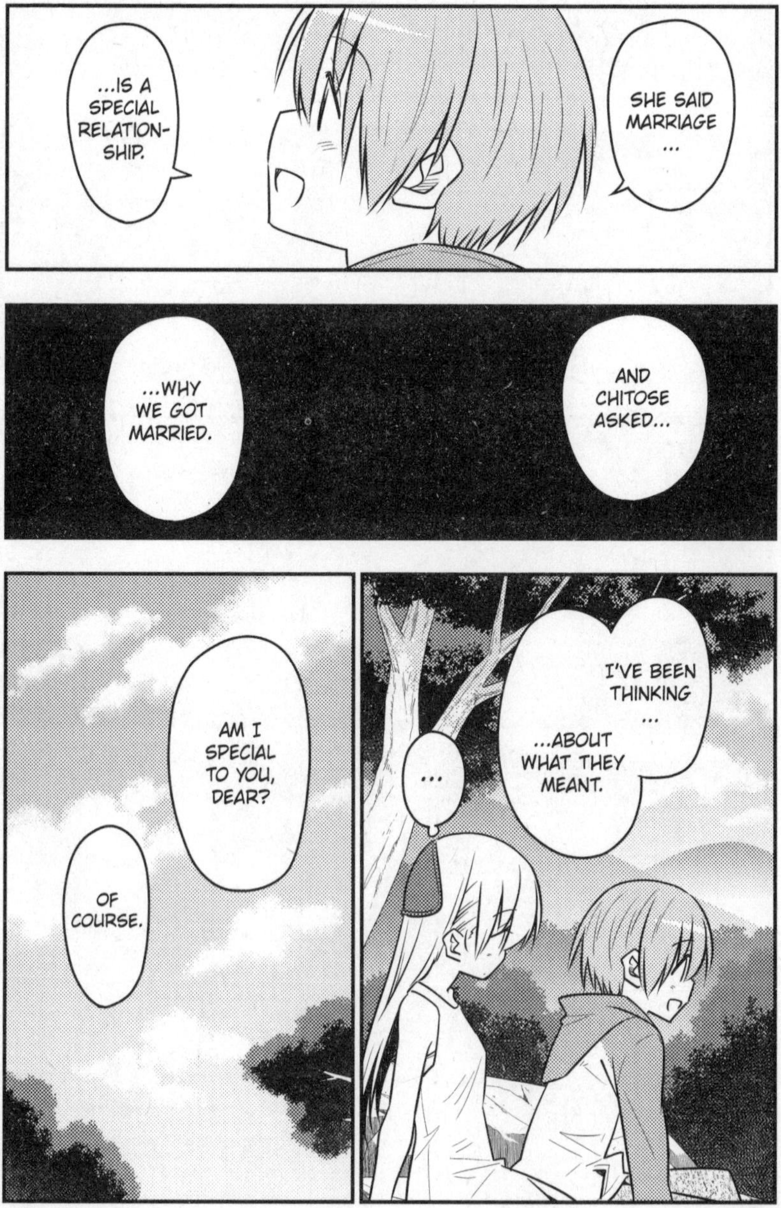
SHE SAID MARRIAGE ...
...IS A SPECIAL RELATION-SHIP.
AND CHITOSE ASKED...
...WHY WE GOT MARRIED.
I'VE BEEN THINKING ...
...ABOUT WHAT THEY MEANT.
...
AM I SPECIAL TO YOU, DEAR?
OF COURSE.

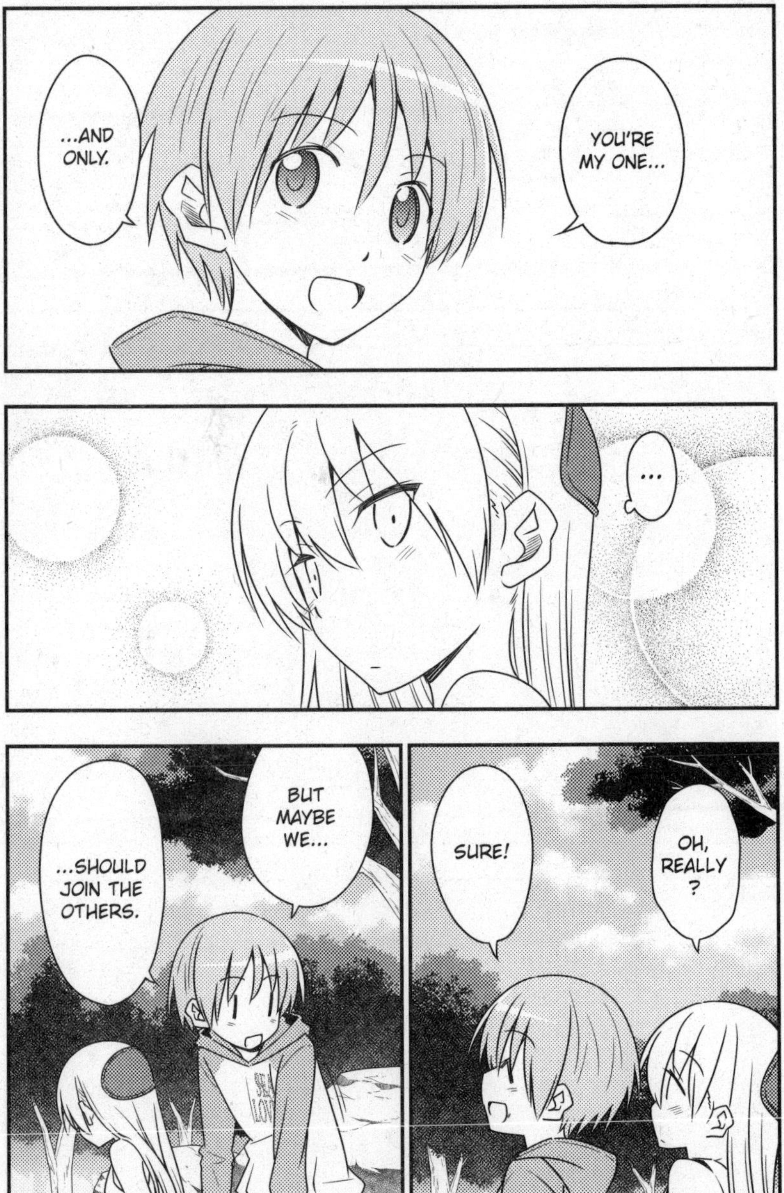
YOU'RE MY ONE...
...AND ONLY.
...
OH, REALLY?
SURE!
BUT MAYBE WE...
...SHOULD JOIN THE OTHERS.

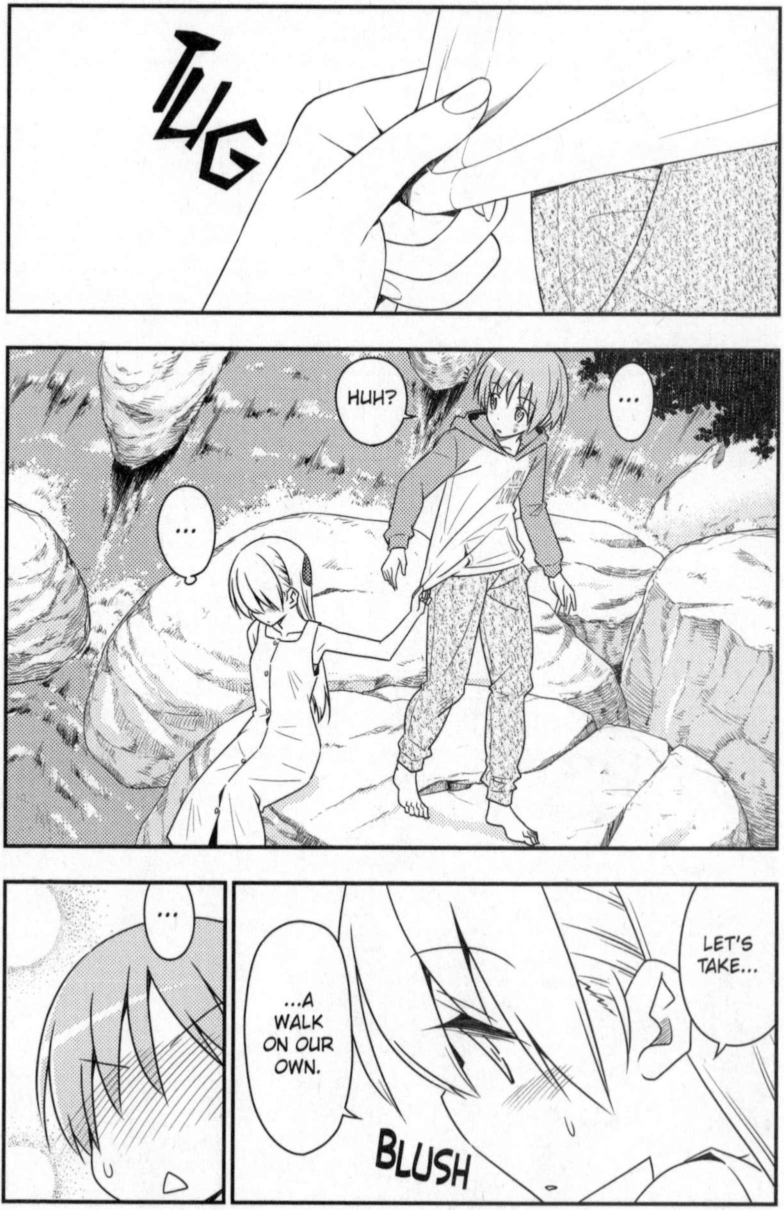
TUG
...
HUH?
...
LET'S TAKE...
...A WALK ON OUR OWN.
BLUSH
...

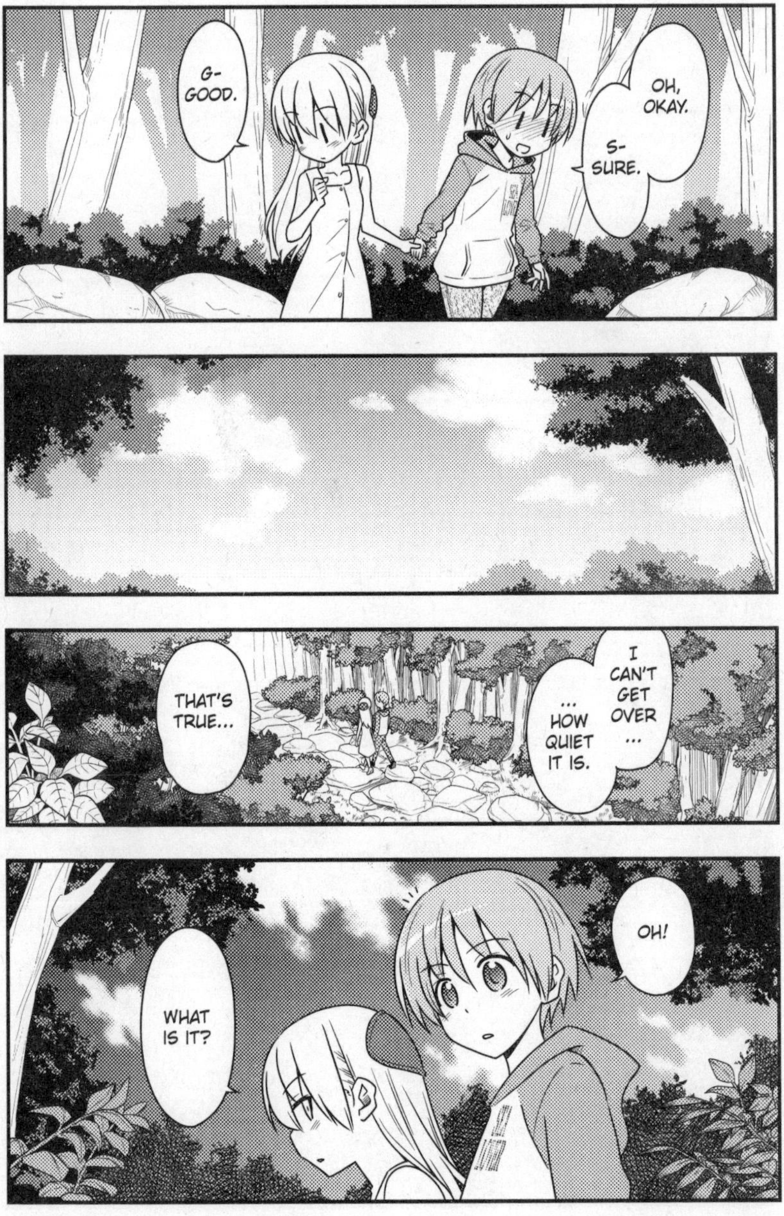
OH, OKAY.
S- SURE.
G- GOOD.
I CAN'T GET OVER ...
... HOW QUIET IT IS.
THAT'S TRUE...
OH!
WHAT IS IT?

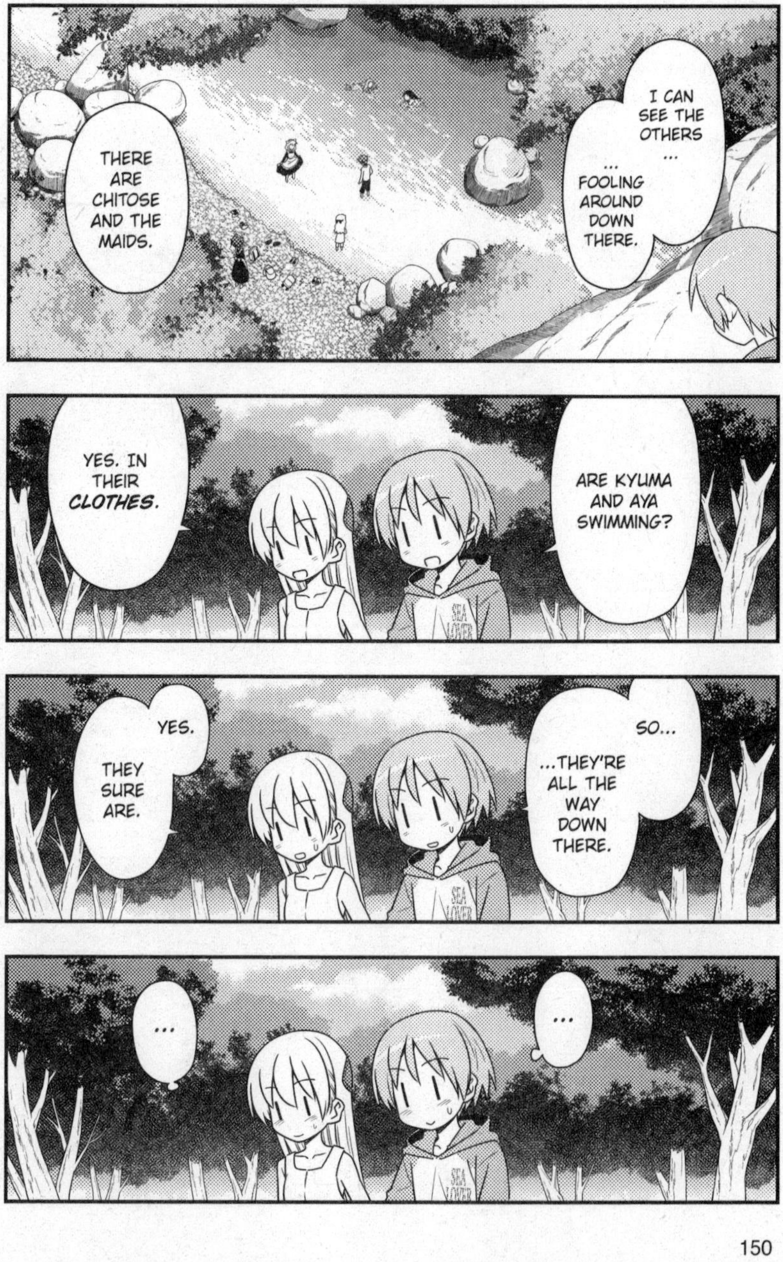
I CAN SEE THE OTHERS ... ... FOOLING AROUND DOWN THERE.
THERE ARE CHITOSE AND THE MAIDS.
ARE KYUMA AND AYA SWIMMING?
YES. IN THEIR *CLOTHES*.
SO... ...THEY'RE ALL THE WAY DOWN THERE.
YES. THEY SURE ARE.
...
...

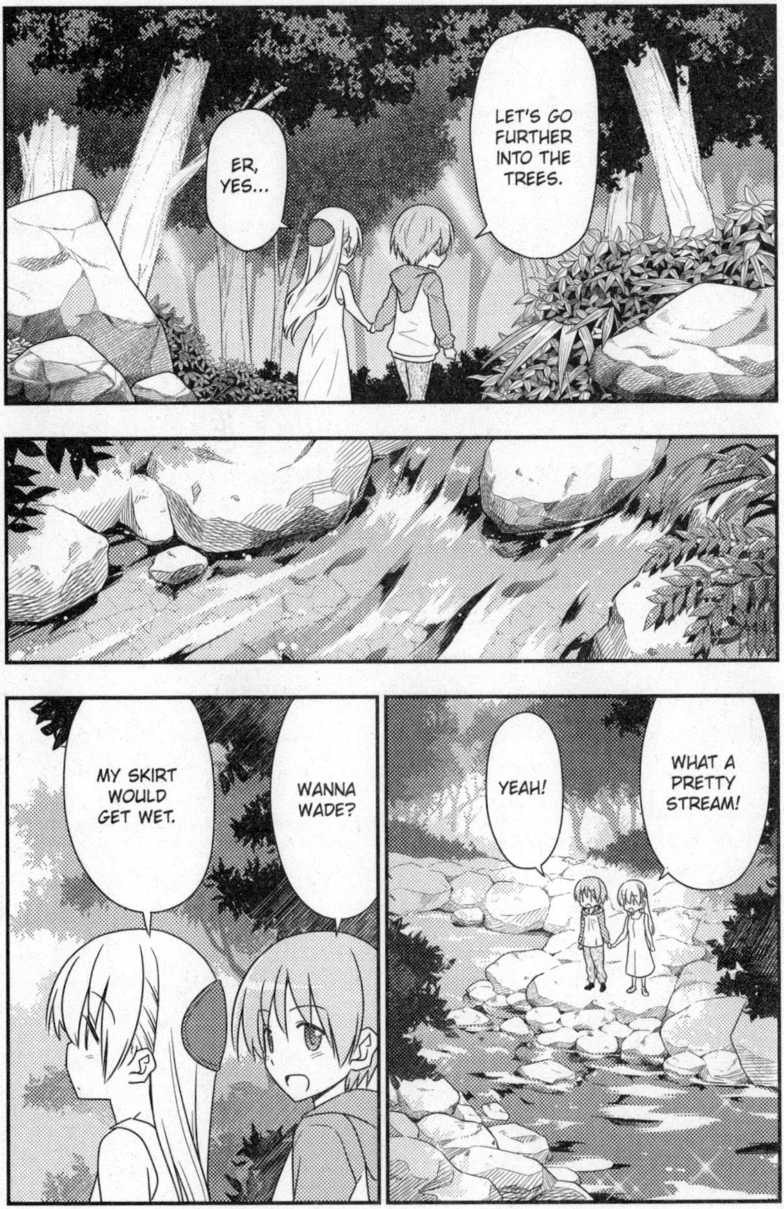
LET'S GO FURTHER INTO THE TREES.
ER, YES...
WHAT A PRETTY STREAM!
YEAH!
WANNA WADE?
MY SKIRT WOULD GET WET.

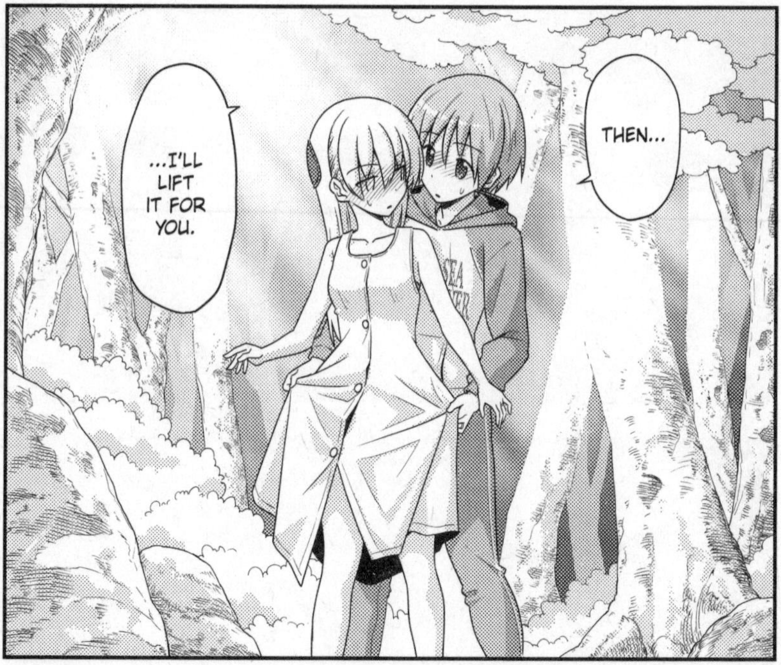
THEN...
...I'LL LIFT IT FOR YOU.
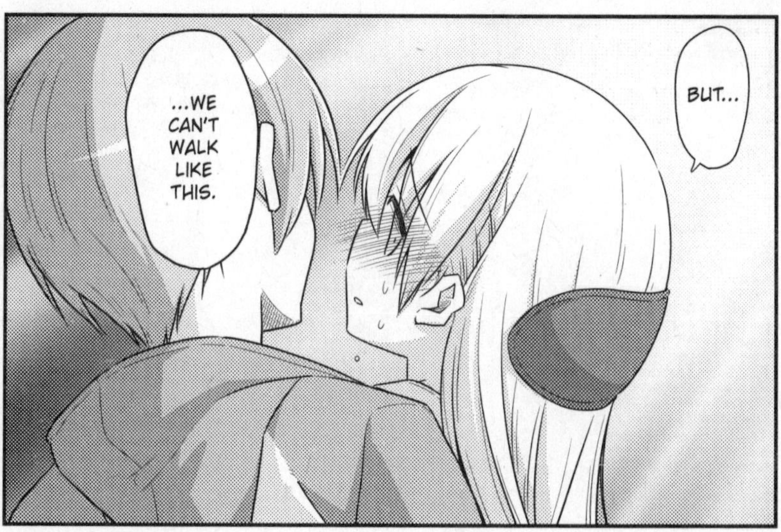
BUT...
...WE CAN'T WALK LIKE THIS.

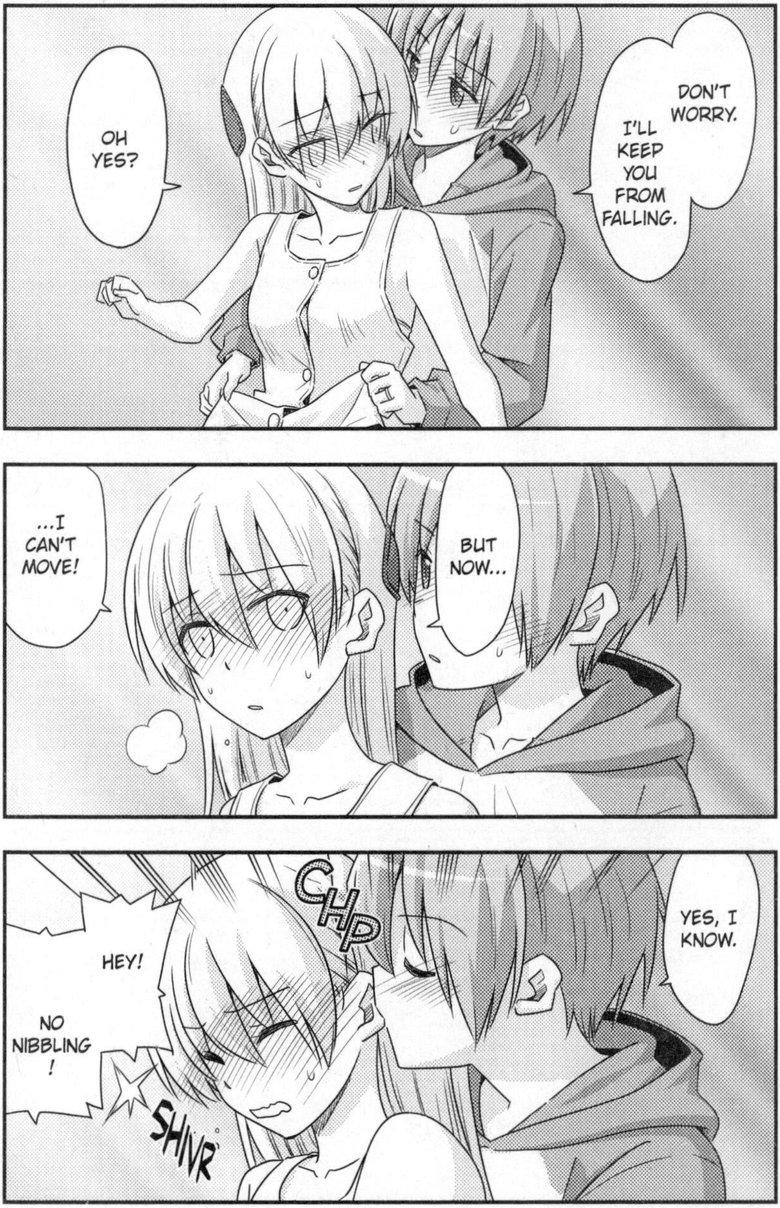
DON'T WORRY.
I'LL KEEP YOU FROM FALLING.
OH YES?
BUT NOW...
...I CAN'T MOVE!
YES, I KNOW.
CHP
HEY!
NO NIBBLING!
SHIVR

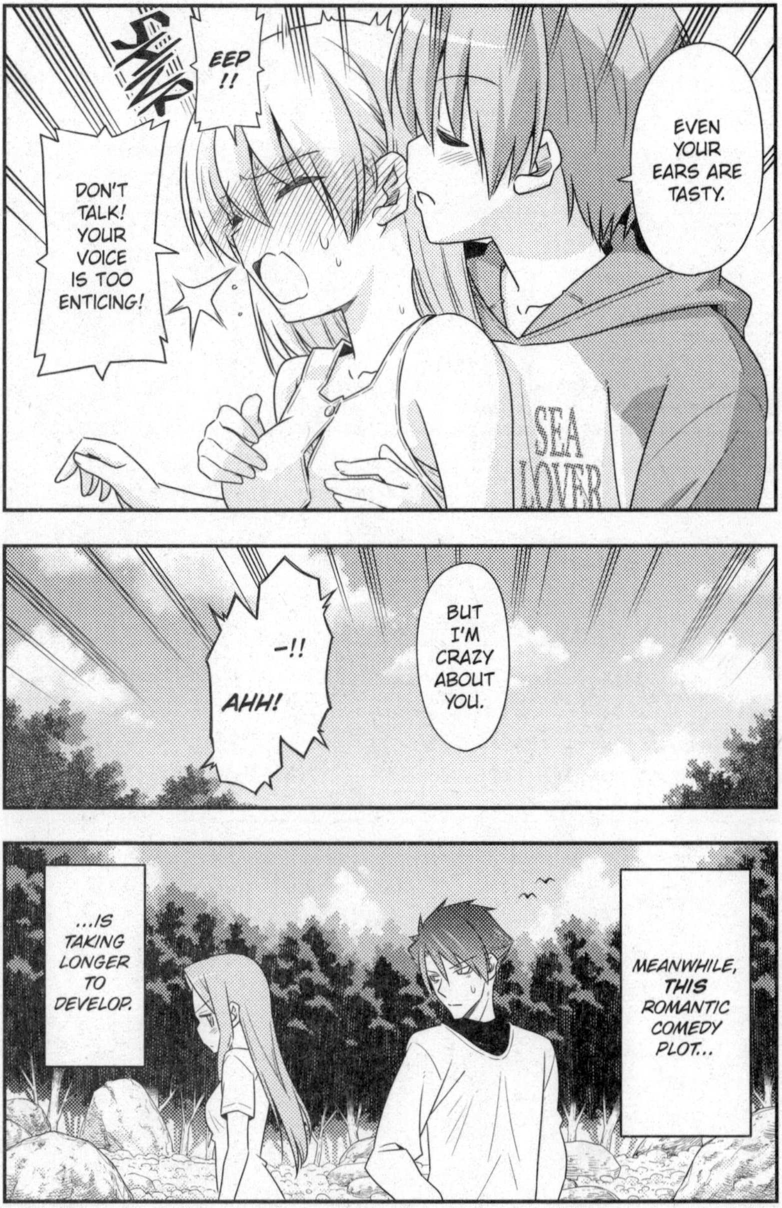
EVEN YOUR EARS ARE TASTY.
EEP !!
SHNK
DON'T TALK! YOUR VOICE IS TOO ENTICING!
BUT I'M CRAZY ABOUT YOU.
—!! AHH!
MEANWHILE, THIS ROMANTIC COMEDY PLOT...
...IS TAKING LONGER TO DEVELOP.

Chapter 99: "Thank You"

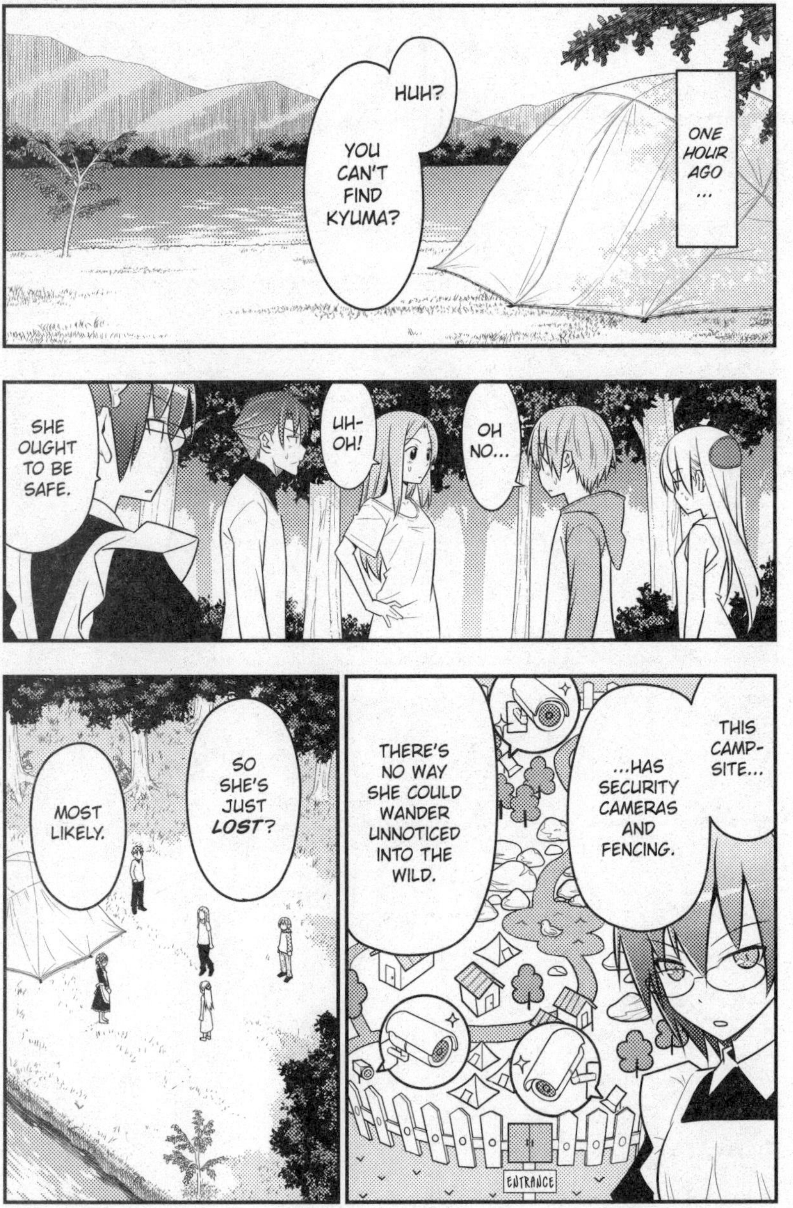
ONE HOUR AGO ...
HUH?
YOU CAN'T FIND KYUMA?
SHE OUGHT TO BE SAFE.
UH-OH!
OH NO...
THIS CAMP-SITE...
...HAS SECURITY CAMERAS AND FENCING.
THERE'S NO WAY SHE COULD WANDER UNNOTICED INTO THE WILD.
ENTRANCE
SO SHE'S JUST LOST?
MOST LIKELY.

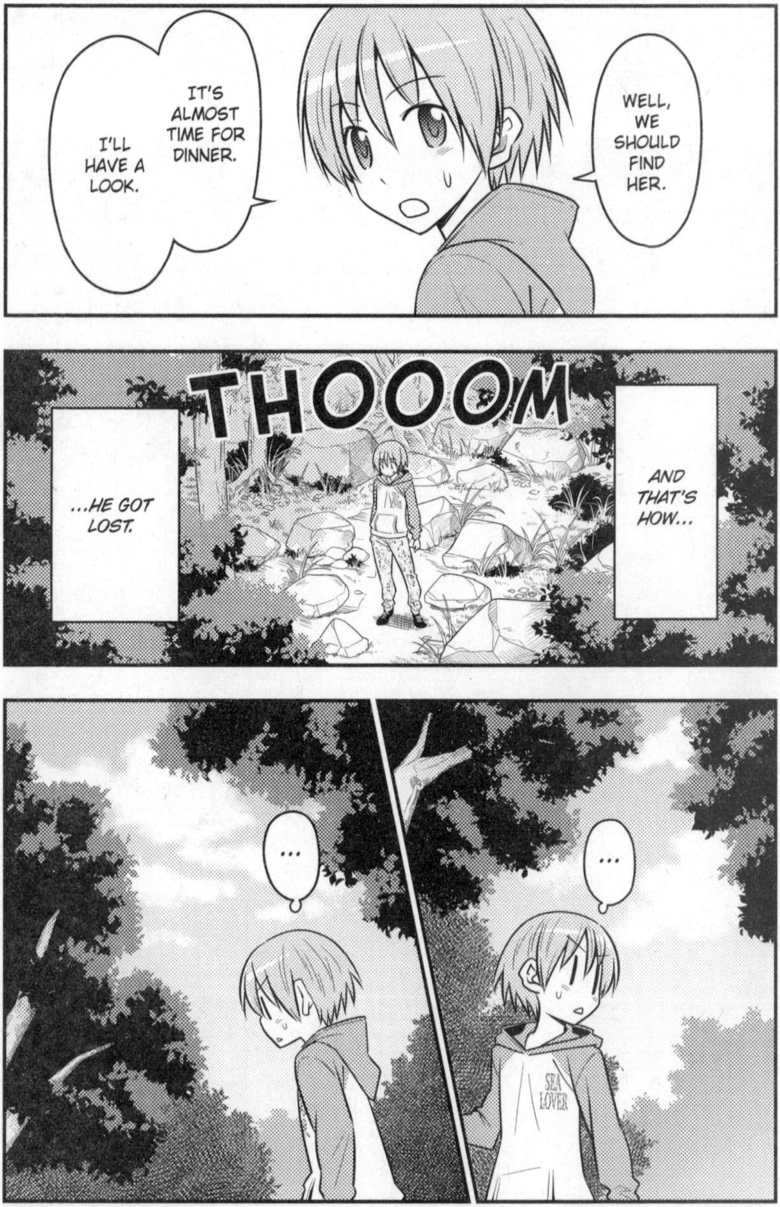
WELL, WE SHOULD FIND HER.
IT'S ALMOST TIME FOR DINNER.
I'LL HAVE A LOOK.
AND THAT'S HOW...
THOOOM
...HE GOT LOST.
SEA LOVER
...
...

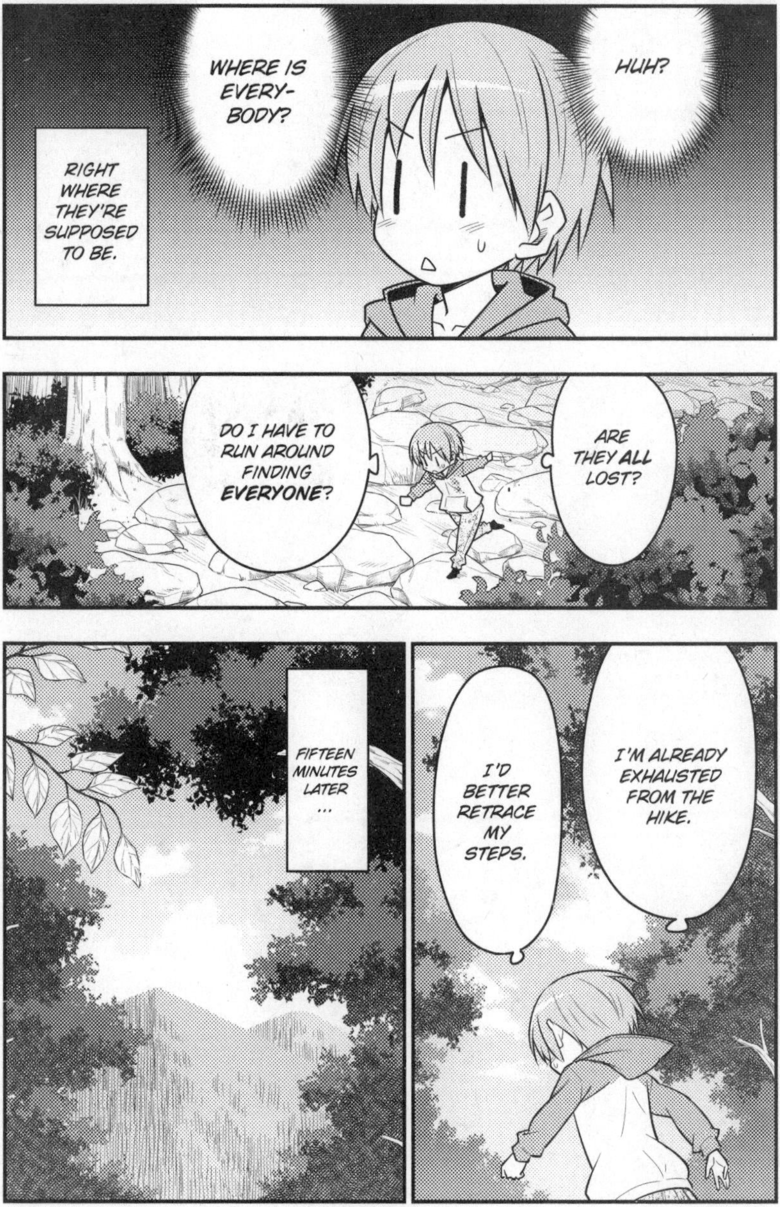
HUH?
WHERE IS EVERY-BODY?
RIGHT WHERE THEY'RE SUPPOSED TO BE.
ARE THEY ALL LOST?
DO I HAVE TO RUN AROUND FINDING EVERYONE?
I'M ALREADY EXHAUSTED FROM THE HIKE.
I'D BETTER RETRACE MY STEPS.
FIFTEEN MINUTES LATER ...

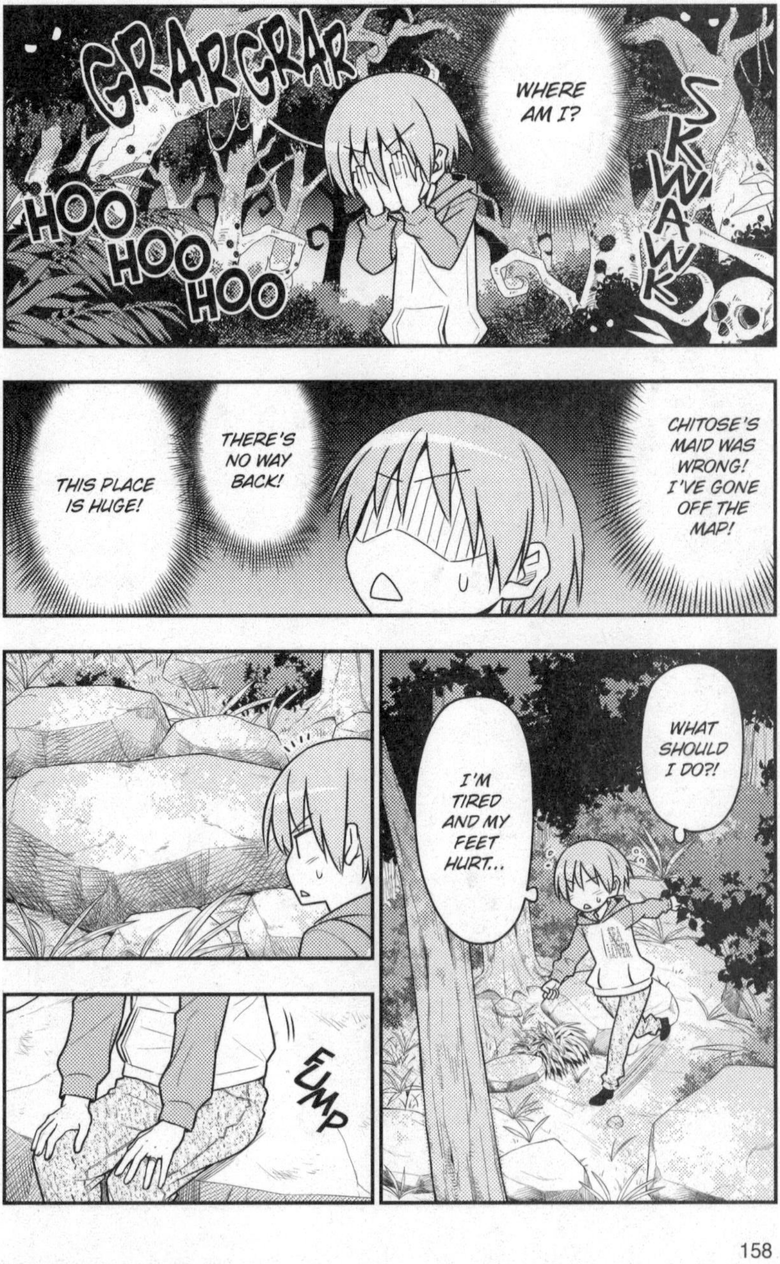
SKWAWK
WHERE AM I?
GRAR GRAR
HOO HOO HOO
CHITOSE'S MAID WAS WRONG! I'VE GONE OFF THE MAP!
THERE'S NO WAY BACK!
THIS PLACE IS HUGE!
WHAT SHOULD I DO?!
I'M TIRED AND MY FEET HURT...
FUMP

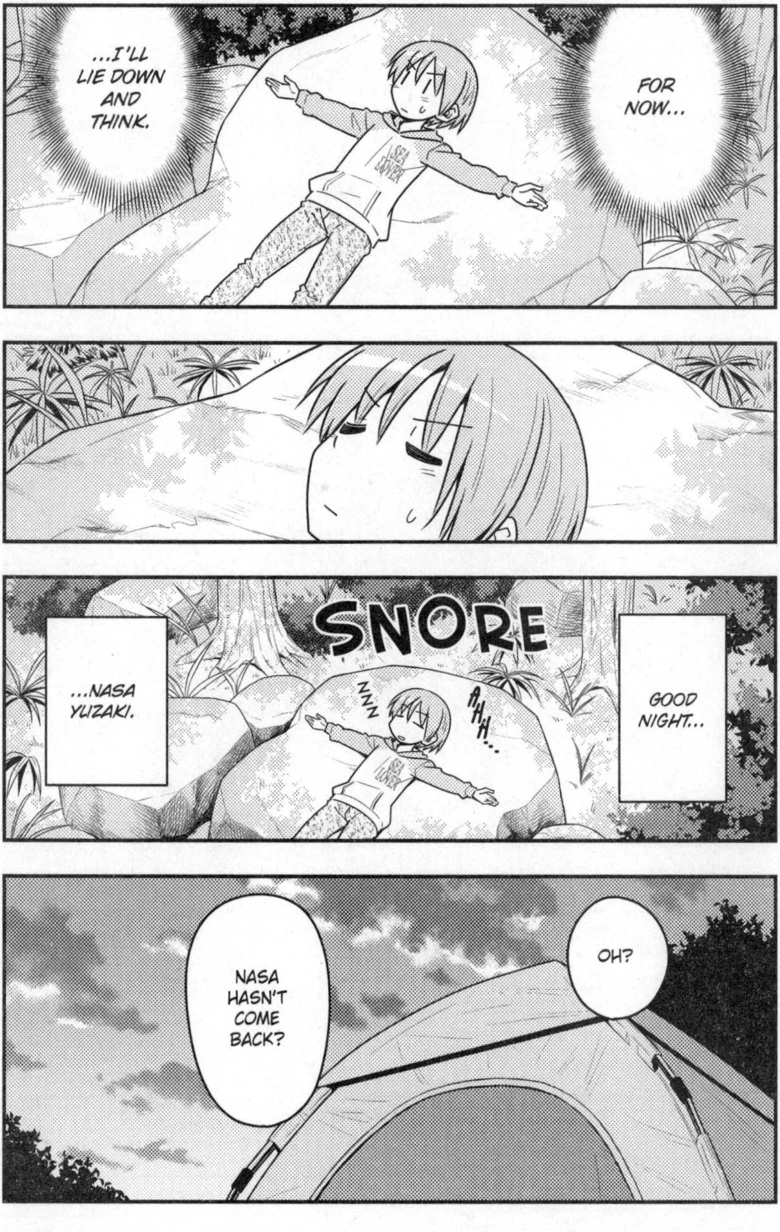
FOR NOW...
...I'LL LIE DOWN AND THINK.
GOOD NIGHT...
SNORE
AHH...
ZZZ
...NASA YUZAKI.
OH?
NASA HASN'T COME BACK?

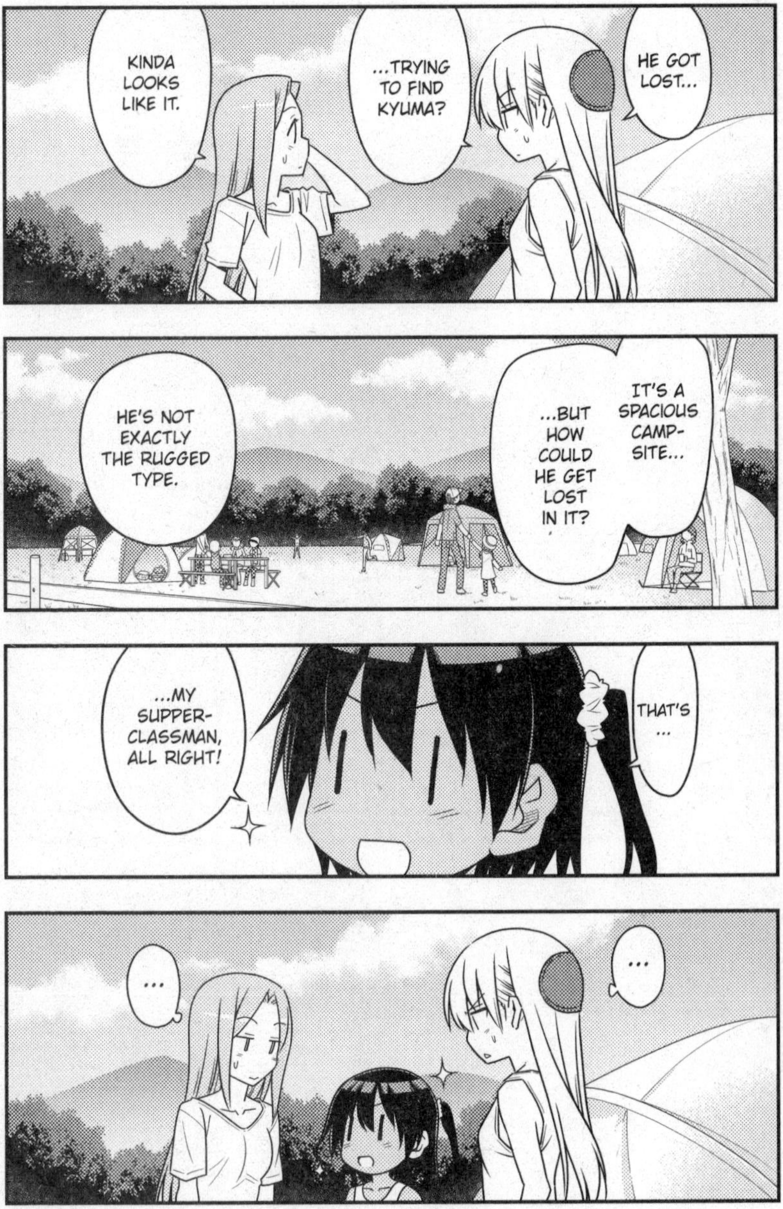
HE GOT LOST...
...TRYING TO FIND KYUMA?
KINDA LOOKS LIKE IT.
IT'S A SPACIOUS CAMP-SITE...
...BUT HOW COULD HE GET LOST IN IT?
HE'S NOT EXACTLY THE RUGGED TYPE.
THAT'S ...
...MY SUPPER-CLASSMAN, ALL RIGHT!
...
...

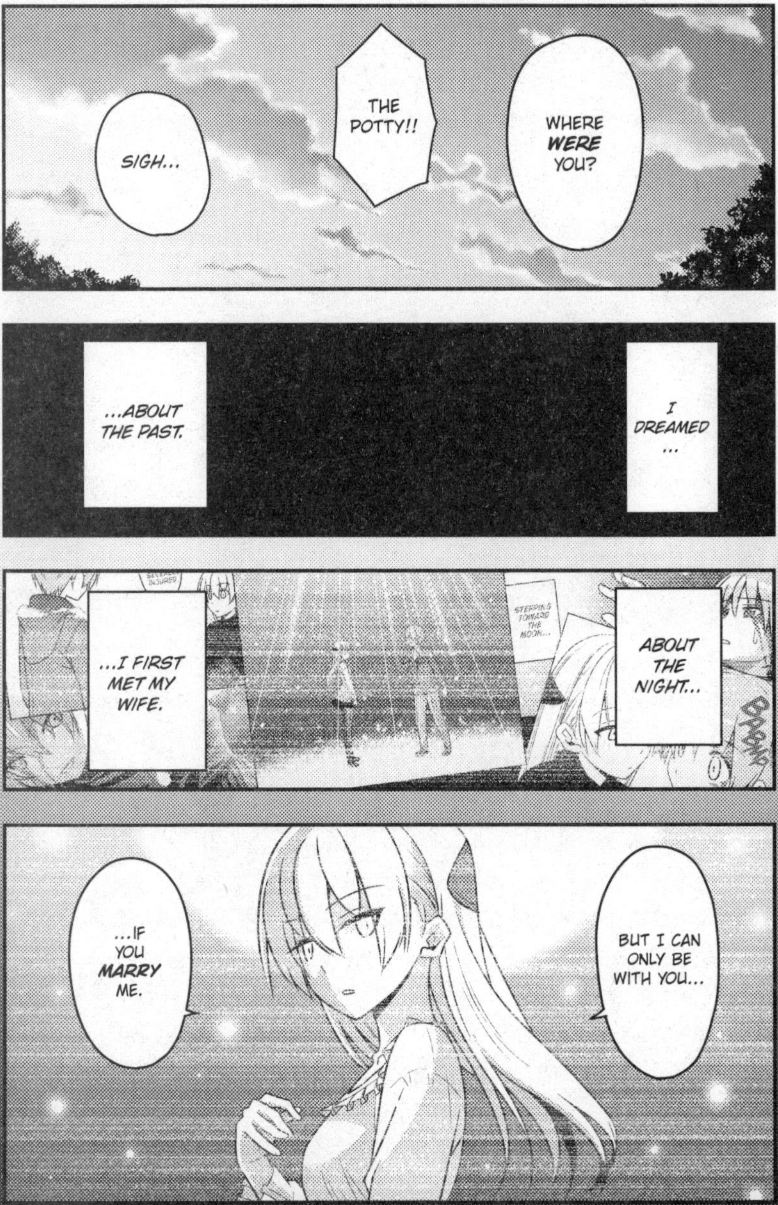
WHERE WERE YOU?
THE POTTY!!
SIGH...
I DREAMED...
...ABOUT THE PAST.
ABOUT THE NIGHT...
STEPPING TOWARD THE MOON...
SEVERELY INJURED
...I FIRST MET MY WIFE.
BUT I CAN ONLY BE WITH YOU...
...IF YOU MARRY ME.

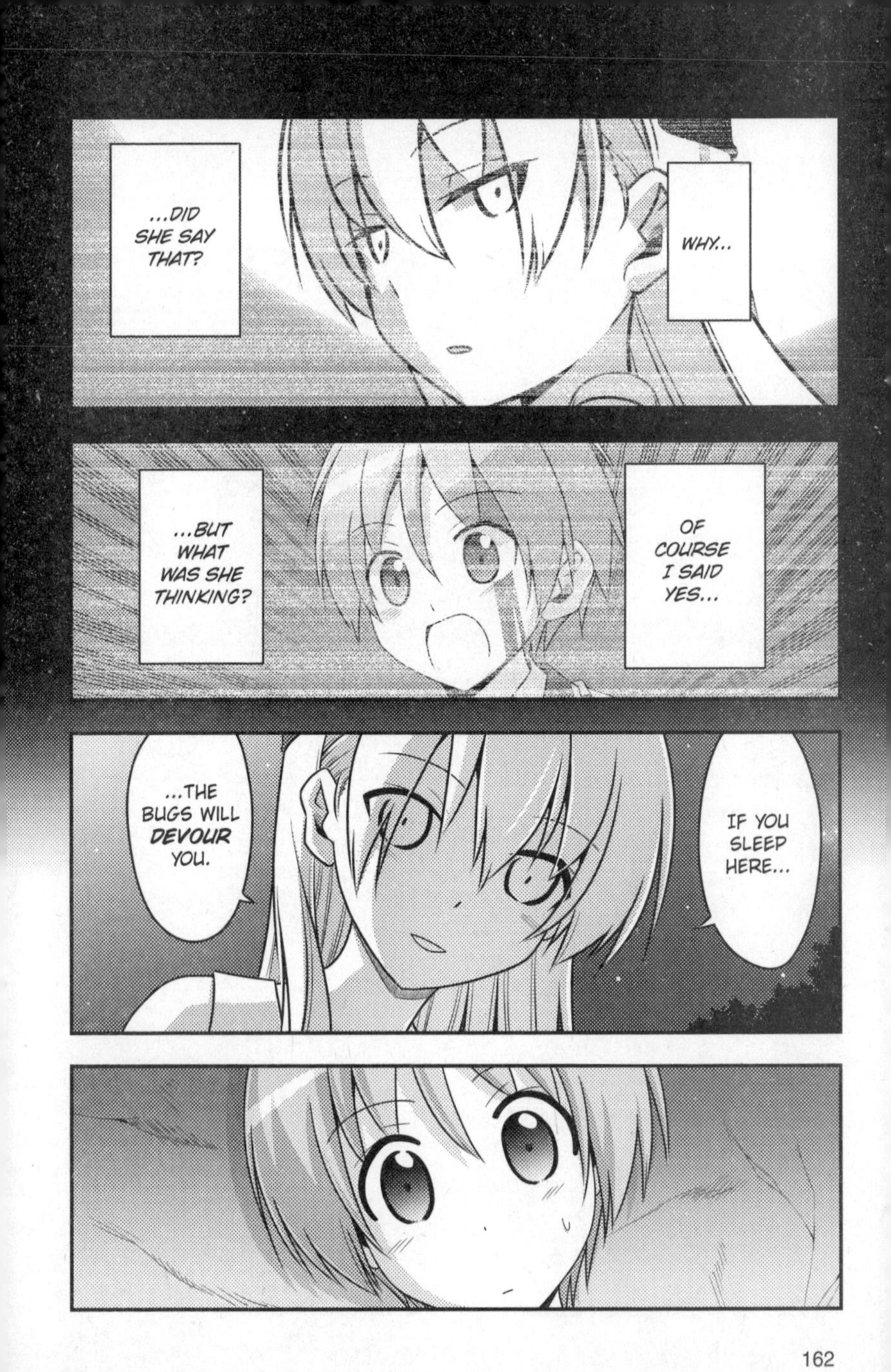
WHY...
...DID SHE SAY THAT?
OF COURSE I SAID YES...
...BUT WHAT WAS SHE THINKING?
IF YOU SLEEP HERE...
...THE BUGS WILL **DEVOUR** YOU.

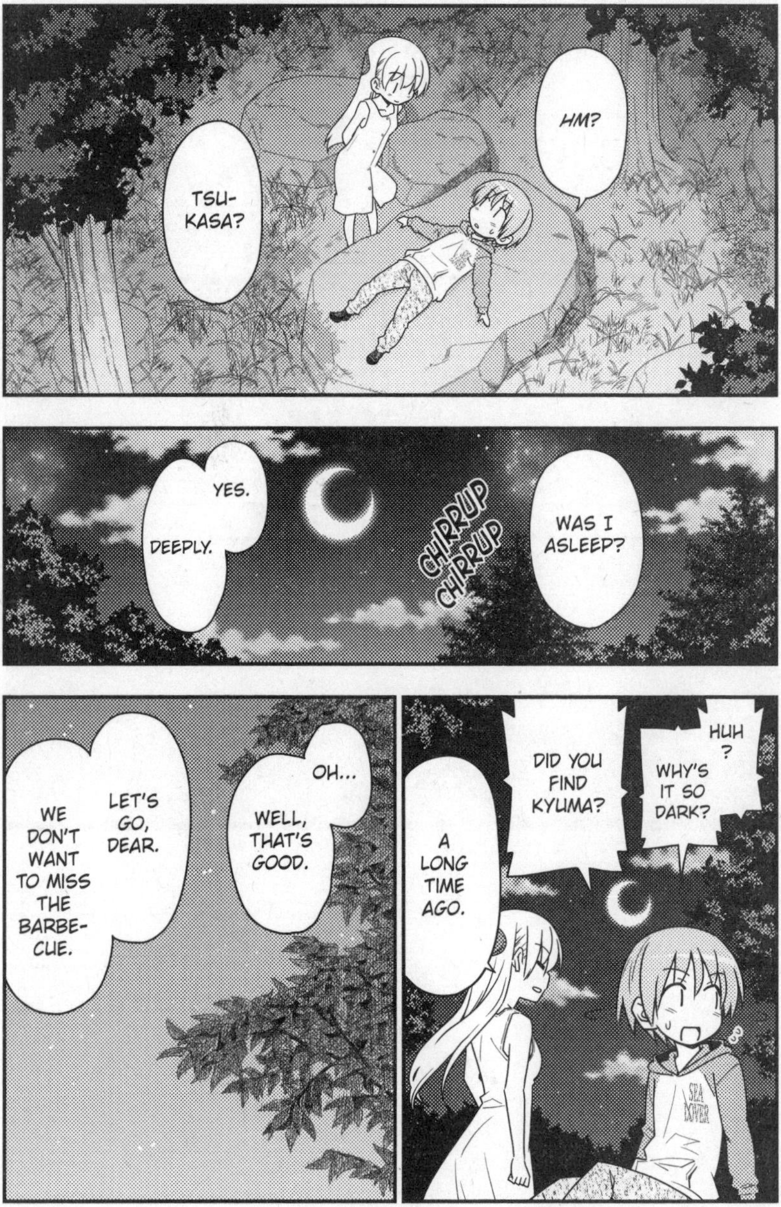
HM?
TSU-KASA?
WAS I ASLEEP?
CHIRRUP CHIRRUP
YES.
DEEPLY.
HUH? WHY'S IT SO DARK?
DID YOU FIND KYUMA?
A LONG TIME AGO.
OH...
WELL, THAT'S GOOD.
LET'S GO, DEAR.
WE DON'T WANT TO MISS THE BARBE-CUE.

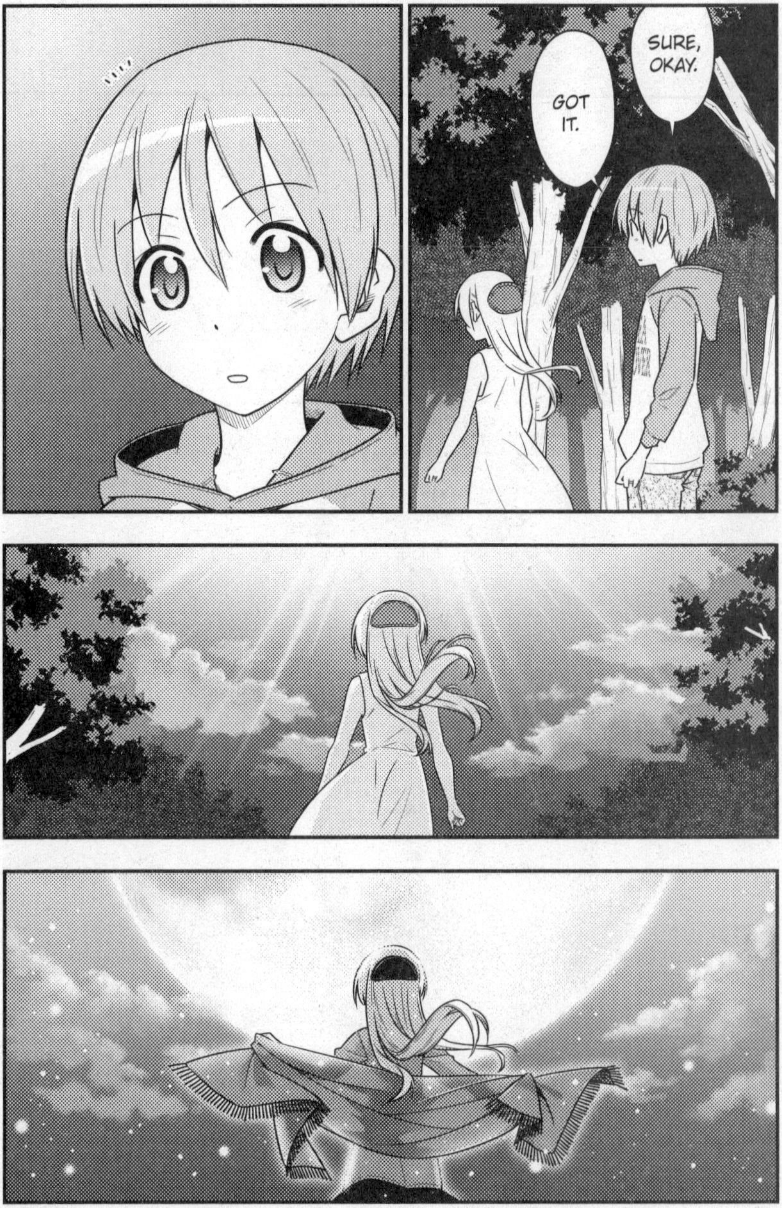
SURE, OKAY.
GOT IT.

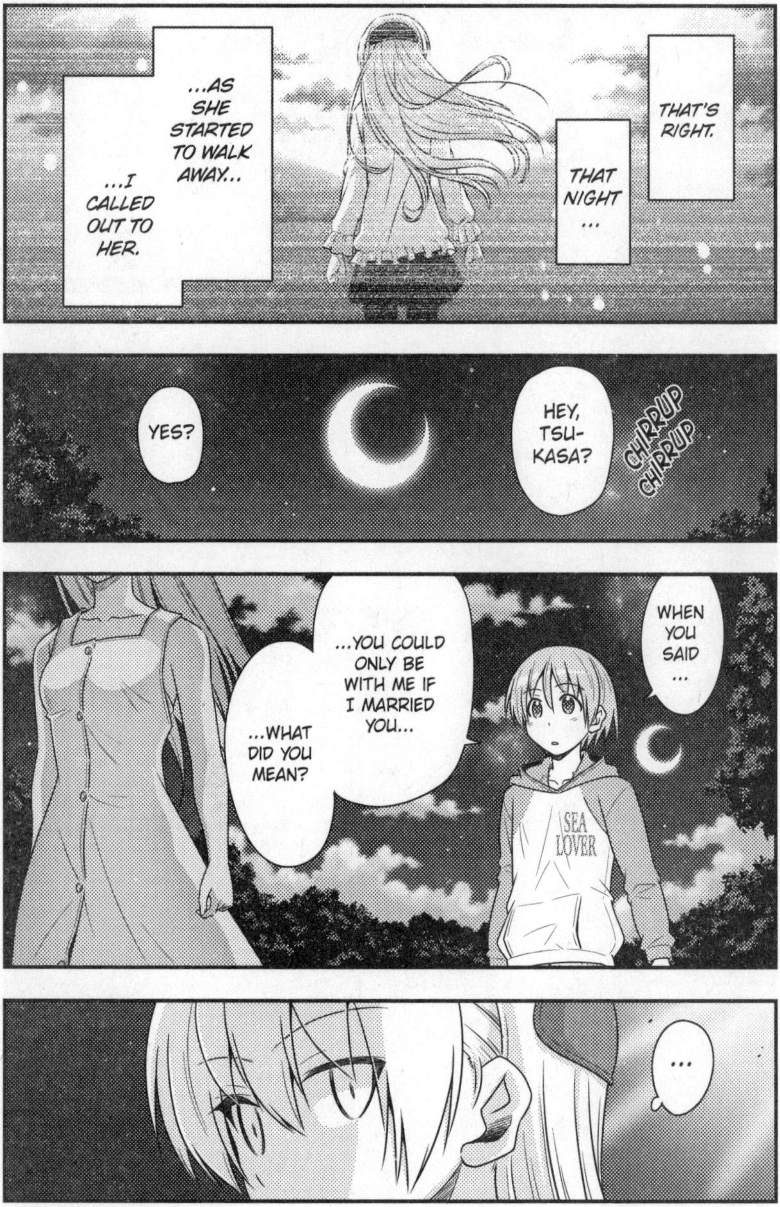
THAT'S RIGHT.
THAT NIGHT ...
...AS SHE STARTED TO WALK AWAY...
...I CALLED OUT TO HER.
HEY, TSU-KASA?
CHRRUP CHRRUP
YES?
WHEN YOU SAID ...
...YOU COULD ONLY BE WITH ME IF I MARRIED YOU...
...WHAT DID YOU MEAN?
SEA LOVER
...

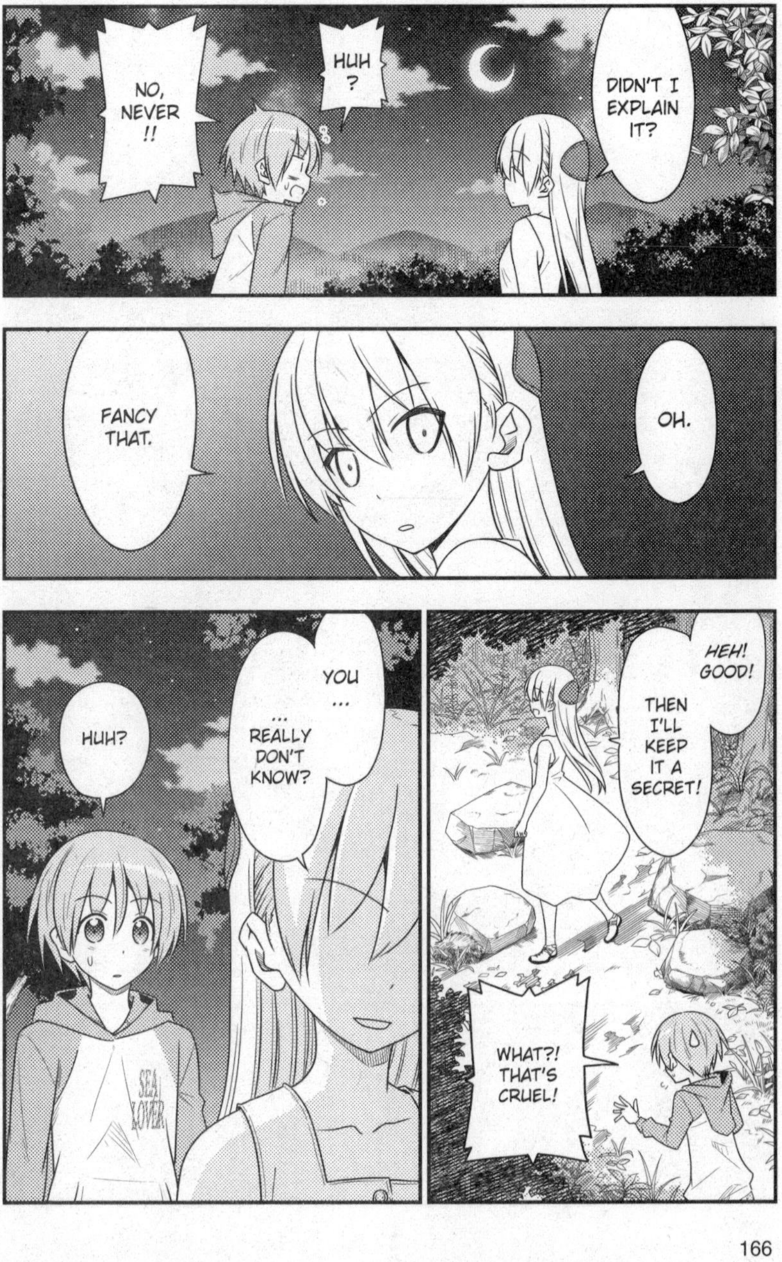
DIDN'T I EXPLAIN IT?
HUH ?
NO, NEVER !!
OH.
FANCY THAT.
HEH! GOOD!
THEN I'LL KEEP IT A SECRET!
WHAT?! THAT'S CRUEL!
YOU ...
... REALLY DON'T KNOW?
HUH?
SEA LOVER

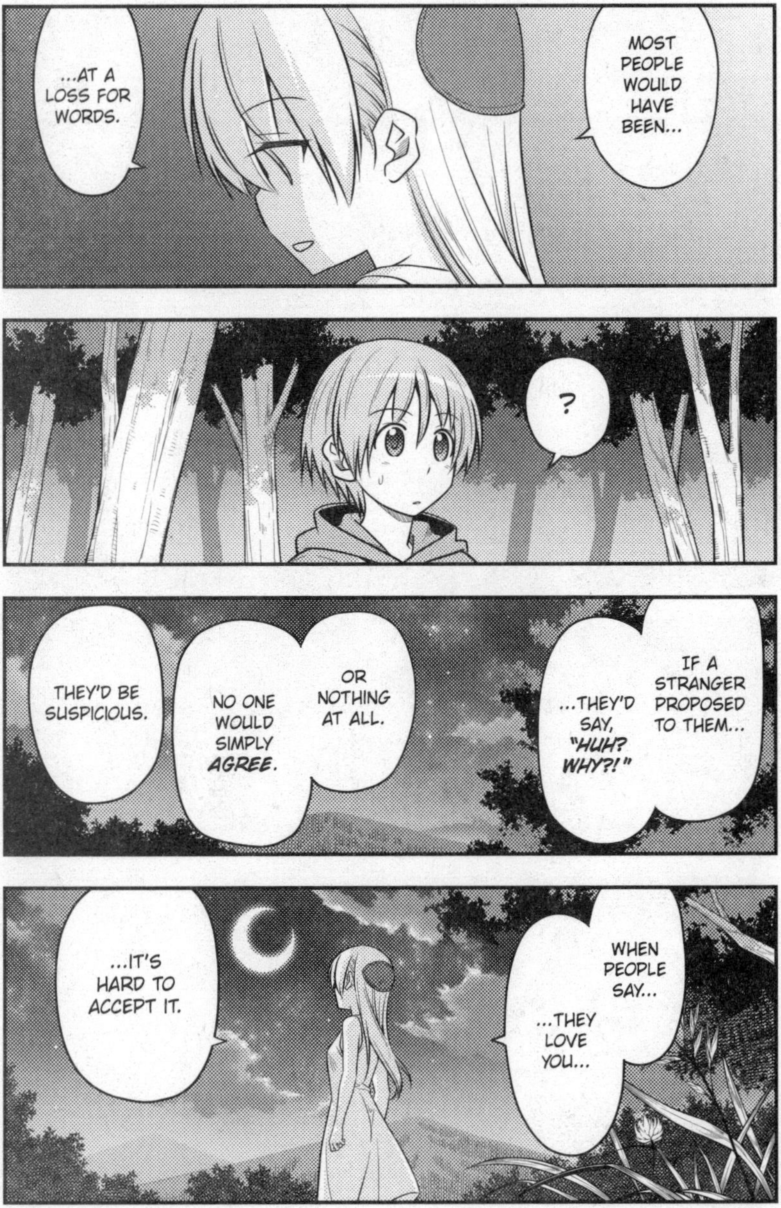
MOST PEOPLE WOULD HAVE BEEN...
...AT A LOSS FOR WORDS.
?
IF A STRANGER PROPOSED TO THEM...
...THEY'D SAY, "HUH? WHY?!"
OR NOTHING AT ALL.
NO ONE WOULD SIMPLY AGREE.
THEY'D BE SUSPICIOUS.
WHEN PEOPLE SAY...
...THEY LOVE YOU...
...IT'S HARD TO ACCEPT IT.

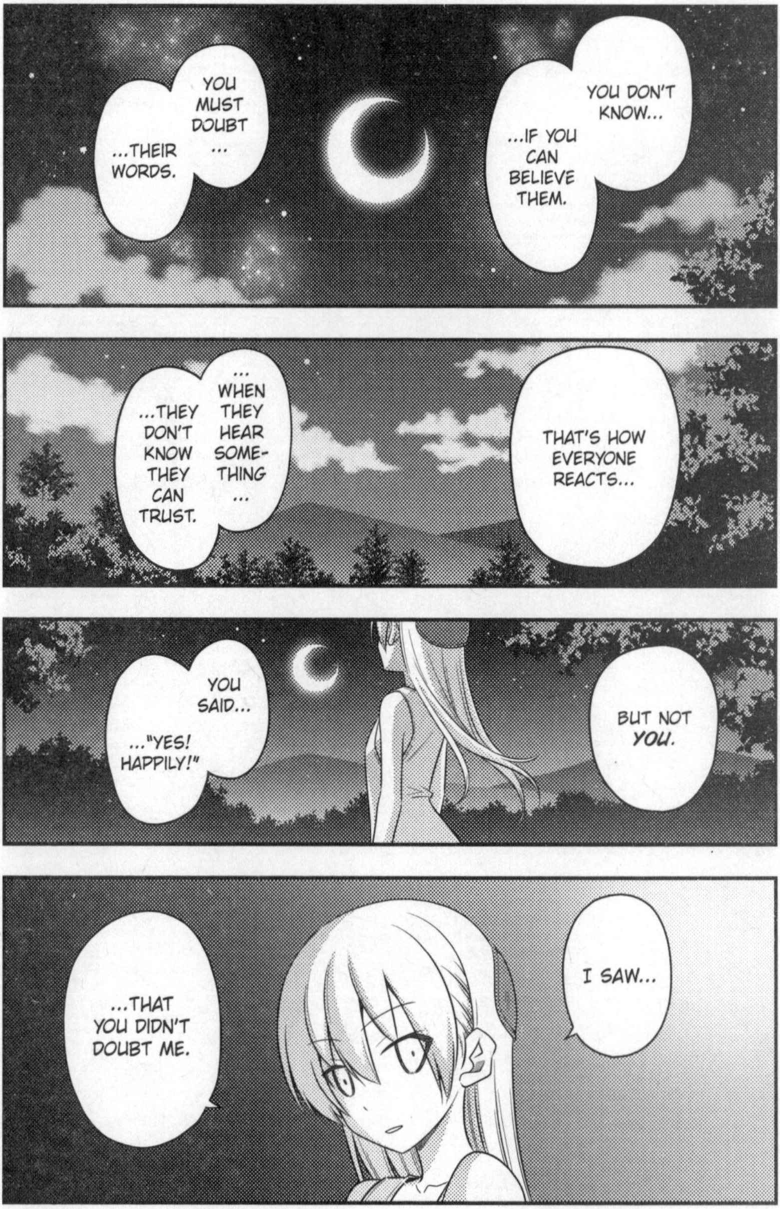
YOU DON'T KNOW...
...IF YOU CAN BELIEVE THEM.
YOU MUST DOUBT ...
...THEIR WORDS.
THAT'S HOW EVERYONE REACTS...
... WHEN THEY HEAR SOME-THING ...
...THEY DON'T KNOW THEY CAN TRUST.
BUT NOT *YOU*.
YOU SAID...
..."YES! HAPPILY!"
I SAW...
...THAT YOU DIDN'T DOUBT ME.

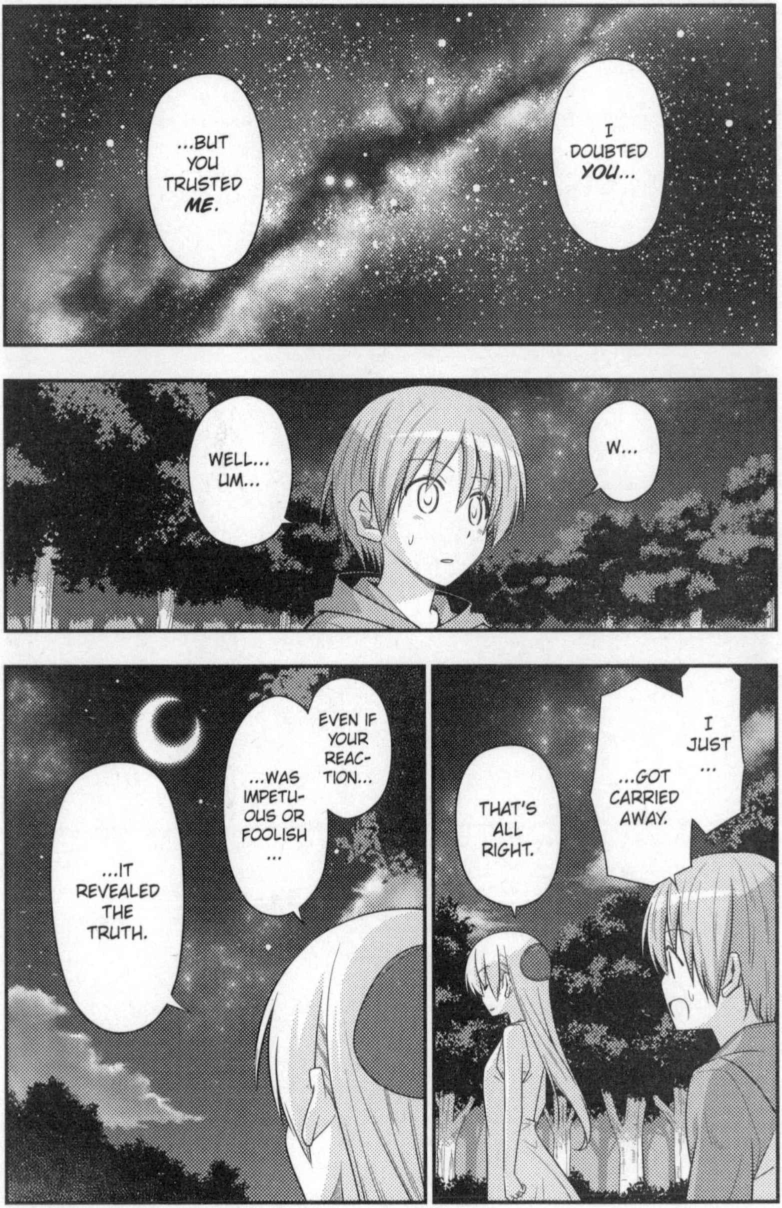
I DOUBTED *YOU*...
...BUT YOU TRUSTED *ME*.
W...
WELL... UM...
I JUST ...
...GOT CARRIED AWAY.
THAT'S ALL RIGHT.
EVEN IF YOUR REACTION...
...WAS IMPETUOUS OR FOOLISH ...
...IT REVEALED THE TRUTH.

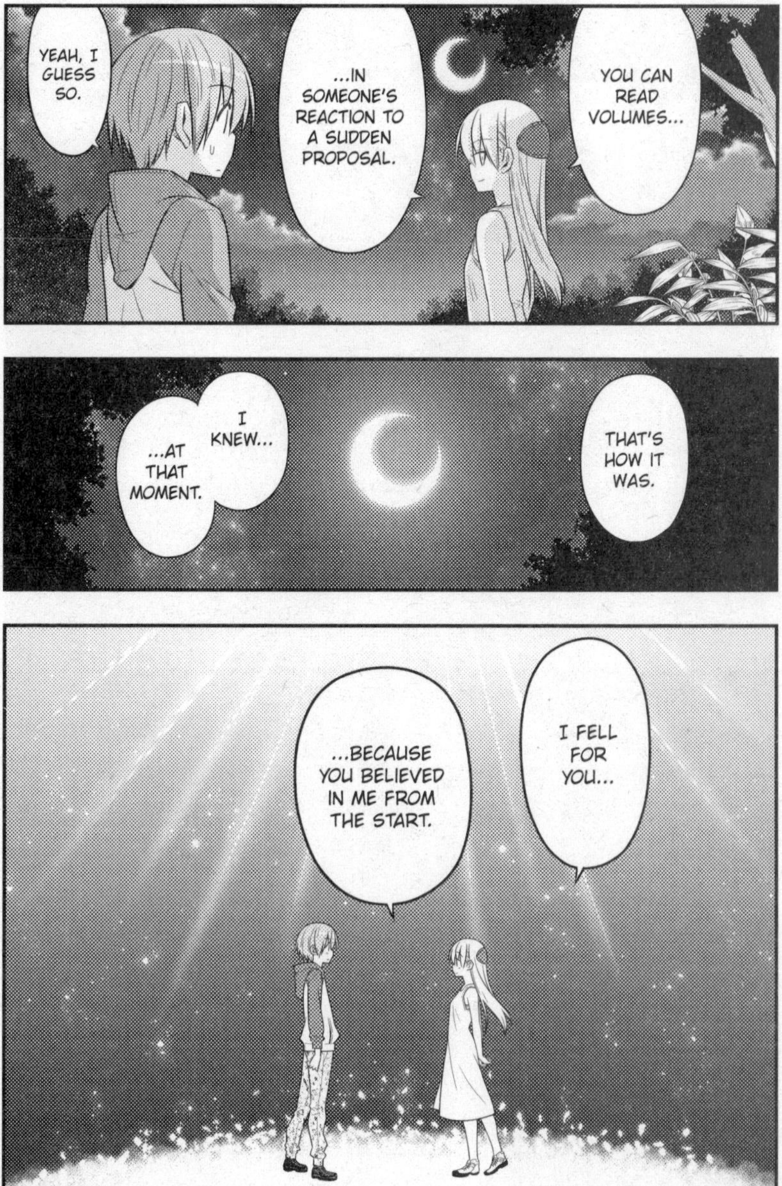
YOU CAN READ VOLUMES...
...IN SOMEONE'S REACTION TO A SUDDEN PROPOSAL.
YEAH, I GUESS SO.
THAT'S HOW IT WAS.
I KNEW...
...AT THAT MOMENT.
I FELL FOR YOU...
...BECAUSE YOU BELIEVED IN ME FROM THE START.

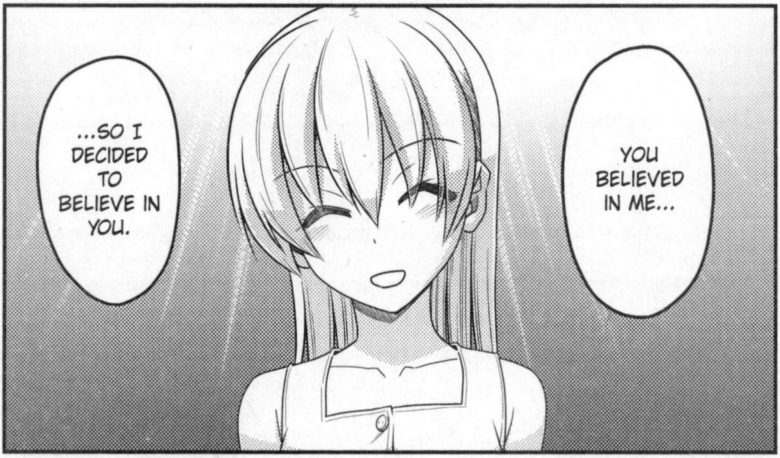
YOU BELIEVED IN ME...
...SO I DECIDED TO BELIEVE IN YOU.

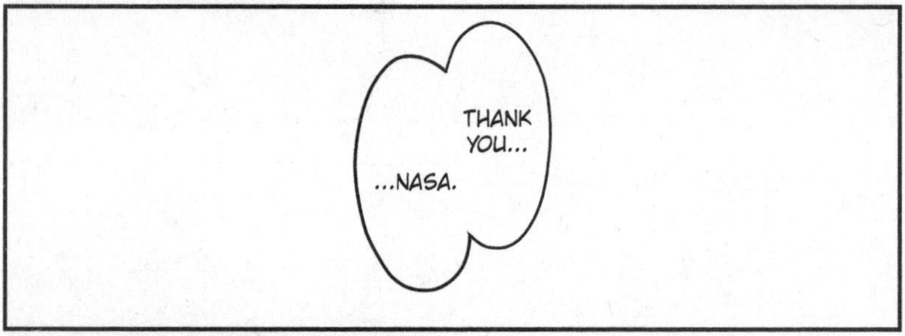
THANK YOU...
...NASA.

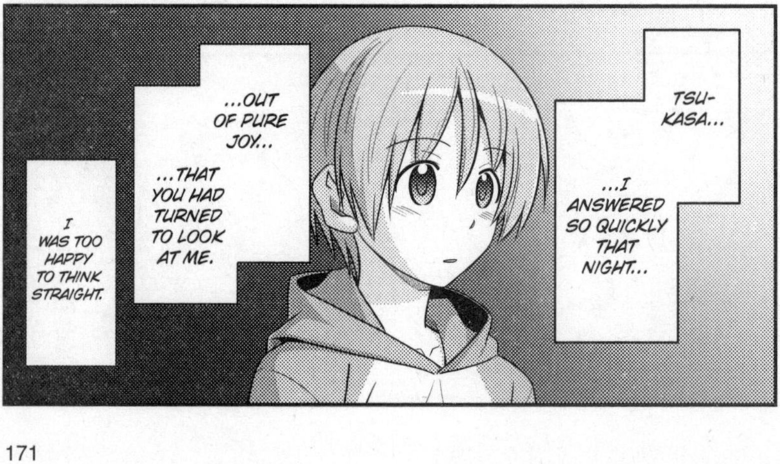
TSU-KASA...
...I ANSWERED SO QUICKLY THAT NIGHT...
...OUT OF PURE JOY...
...THAT YOU HAD TURNED TO LOOK AT ME.
I WAS TOO HAPPY TO THINK STRAIGHT.

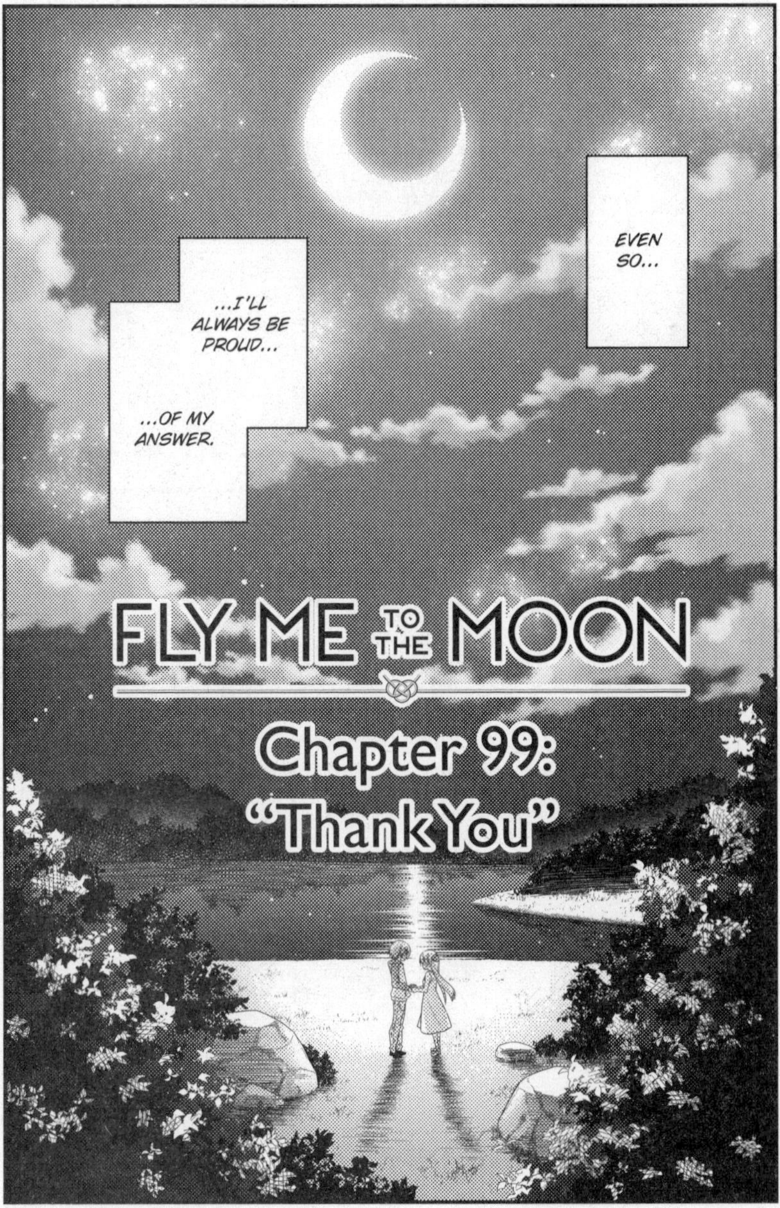
EVEN SO...
...I'LL ALWAYS BE PROUD...
...OF MY ANSWER.
FLY ME TO THE MOON
Chapter 99:
"Thank You"

—Fly Me to the Moon 10 / End—

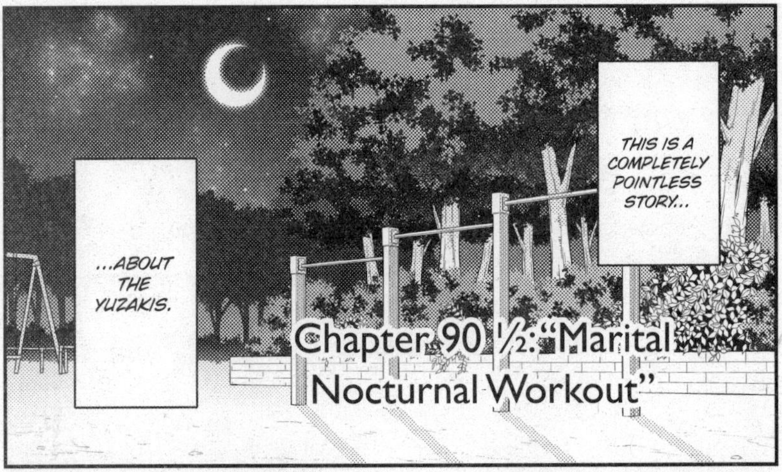
THIS IS A COMPLETELY POINTLESS STORY...
...ABOUT THE YUZAKIS.
Chapter 90 ½: "Marital Nocturnal Workout"
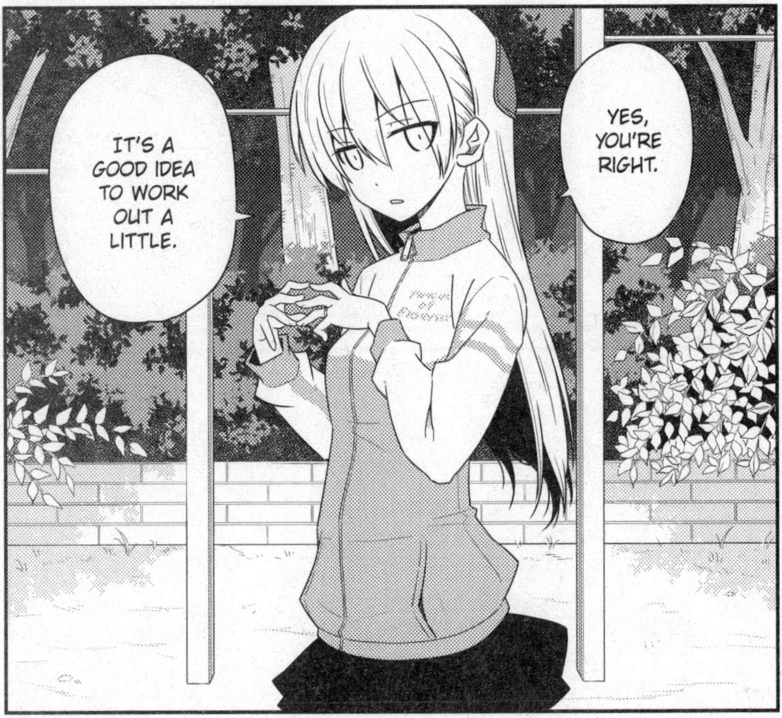
YES, YOU'RE RIGHT.
IT'S A GOOD IDEA TO WORK OUT A LITTLE.

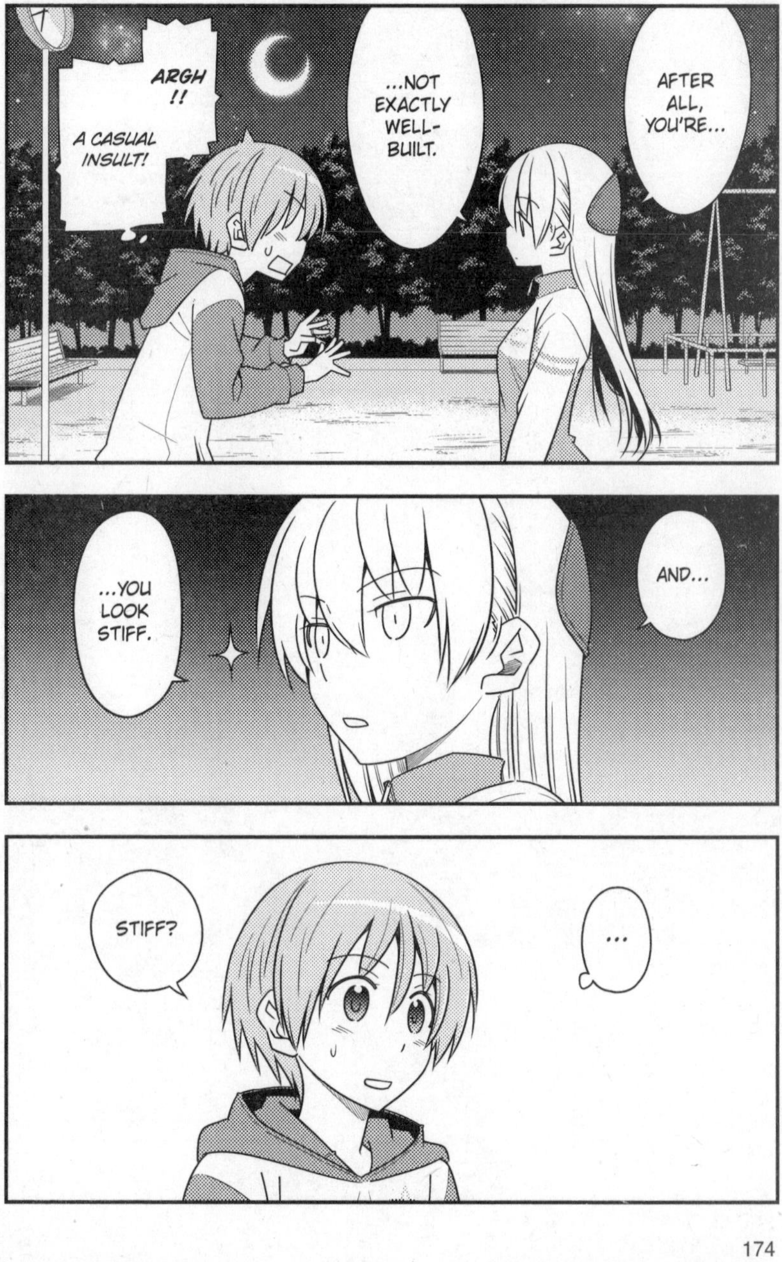
AFTER ALL, YOU'RE...
...NOT EXACTLY WELL-BUILT.
ARGH !!
A CASUAL INSULT!
AND...
...YOU LOOK STIFF.
...
STIFF?

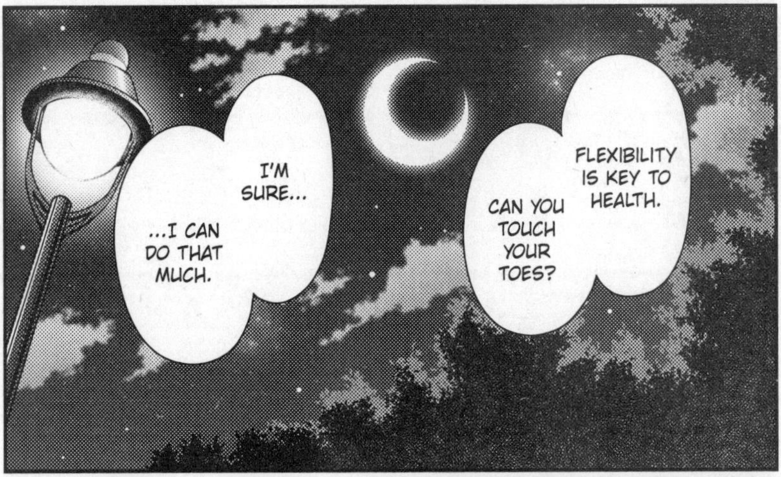
FLEXIBILITY IS KEY TO HEALTH.
CAN YOU TOUCH YOUR TOES?
I'M SURE...
...I CAN DO THAT MUCH.

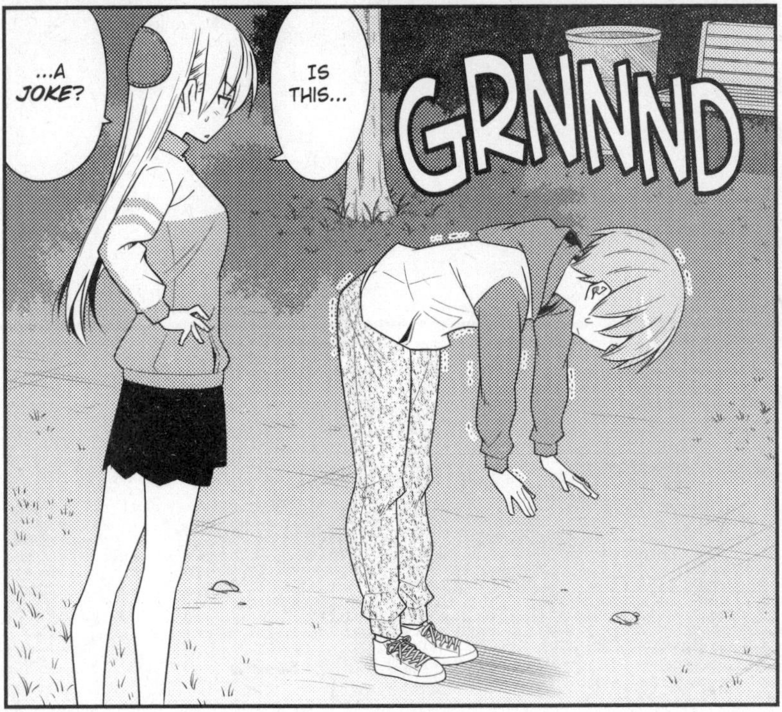
GRNNND
IS THIS...
...A JOKE?

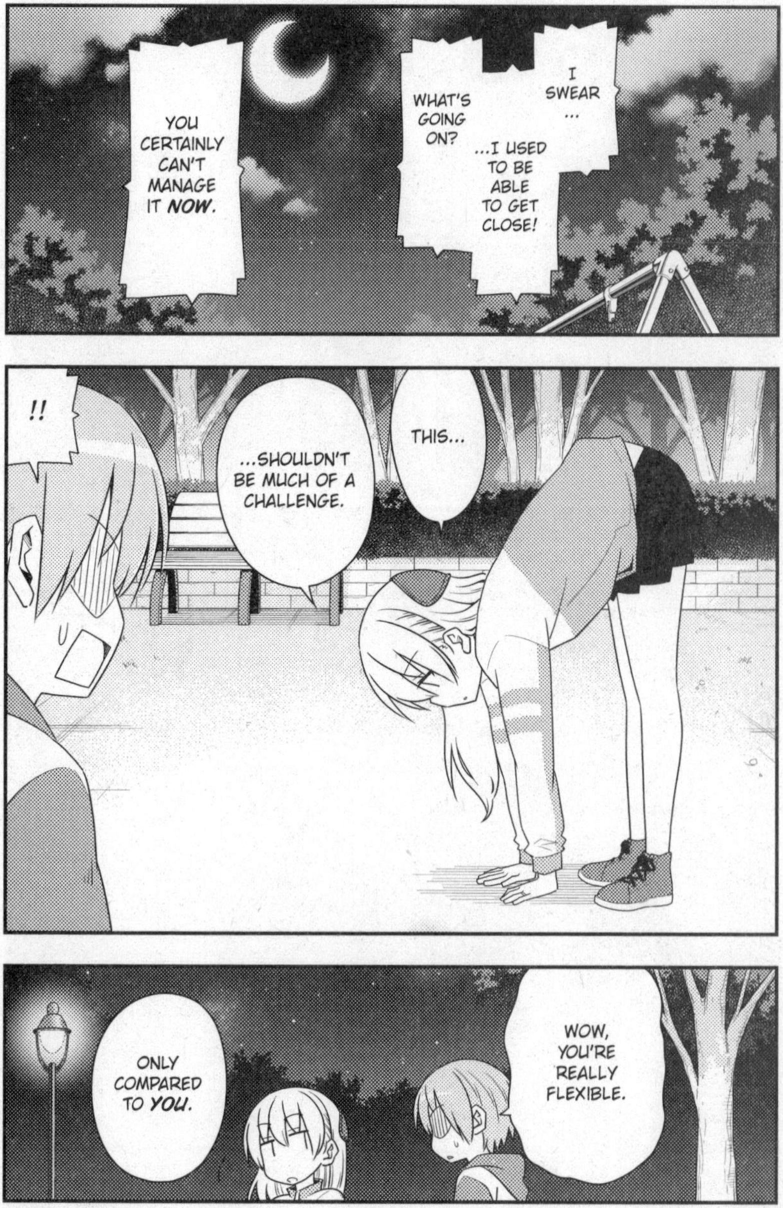
I SWEAR ...
...I USED TO BE ABLE TO GET CLOSE!
WHAT'S GOING ON?
YOU CERTAINLY CAN'T MANAGE IT *NOW*.
THIS...
...SHOULDN'T BE MUCH OF A CHALLENGE.
!!
WOW, YOU'RE REALLY FLEXIBLE.
ONLY COMPARED TO *YOU*.

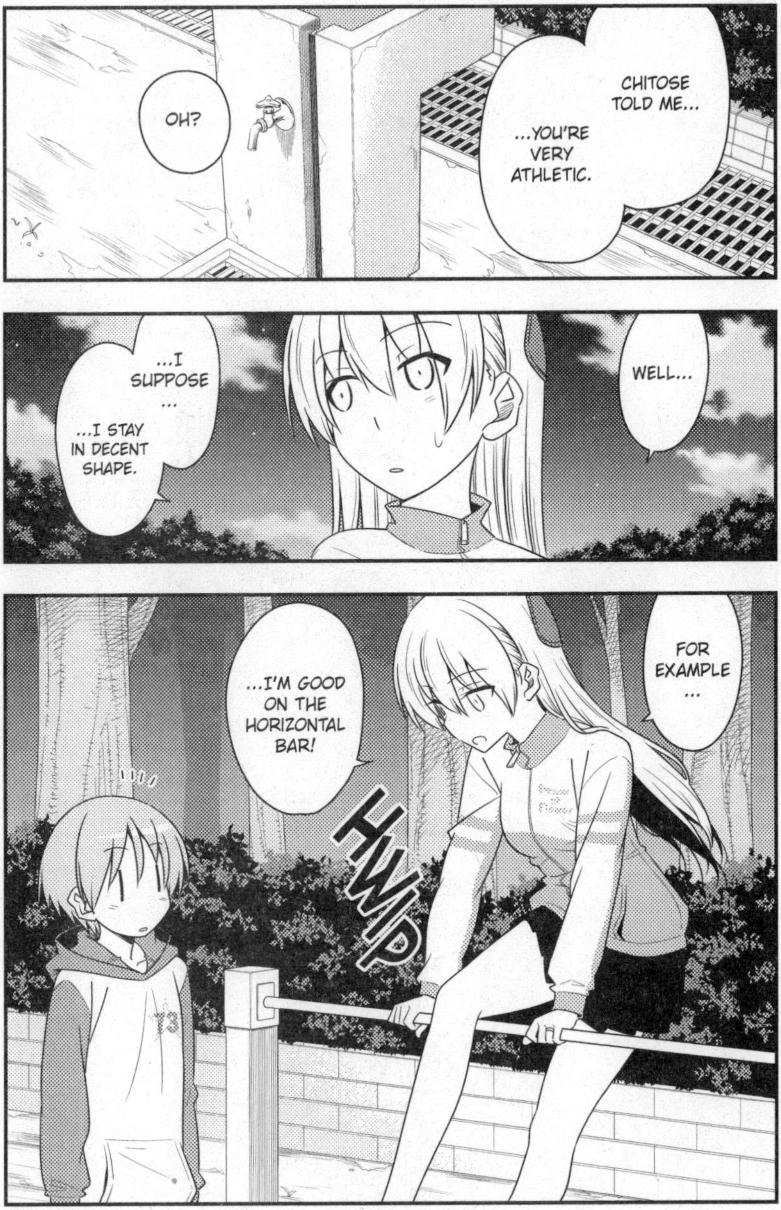
CHITOSE TOLD ME...
...YOU'RE VERY ATHLETIC.
OH?
WELL...
...I SUPPOSE ...
...I STAY IN DECENT SHAPE.
FOR EXAMPLE ...
...I'M GOOD ON THE HORIZONTAL BAR!
HWIP

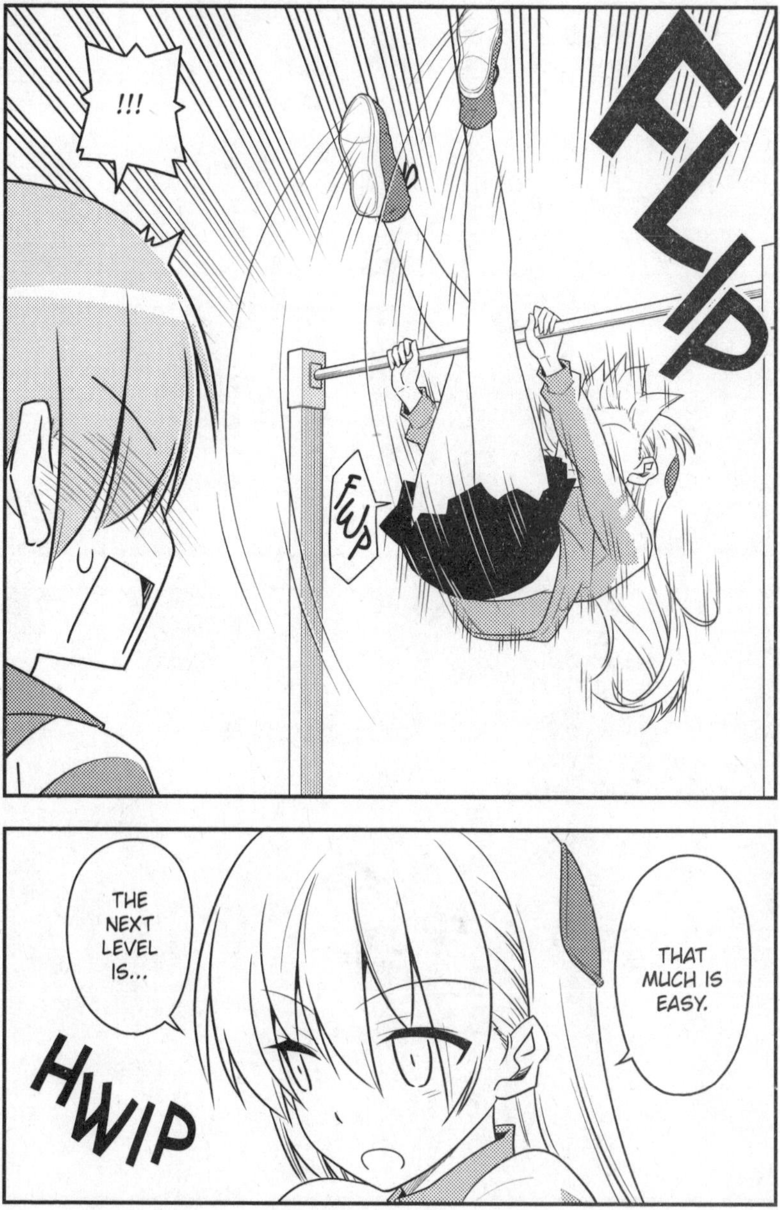
FLIP
FWP
!!!
THAT MUCH IS EASY.
THE NEXT LEVEL IS...
HWIP

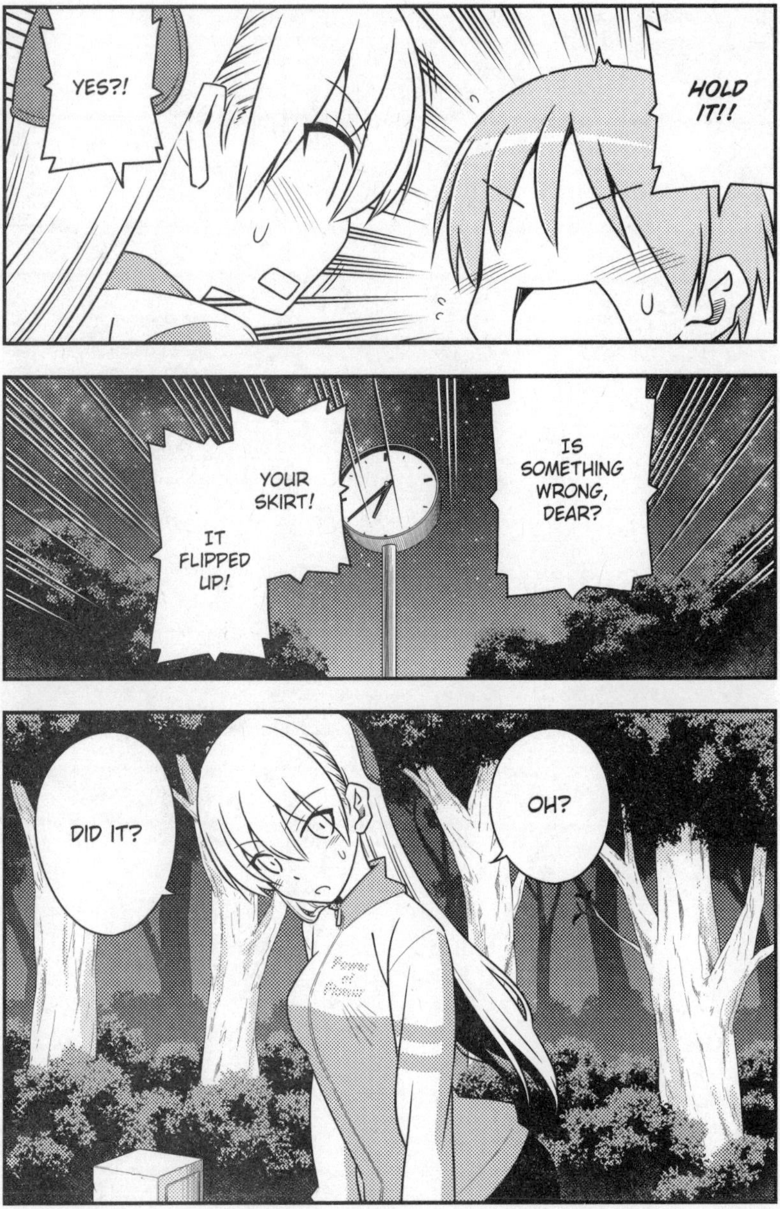
HOLD IT!!
YES?!
IS SOMETHING WRONG, DEAR?
YOUR SKIRT!
IT FLIPPED UP!
OH?
DID IT?

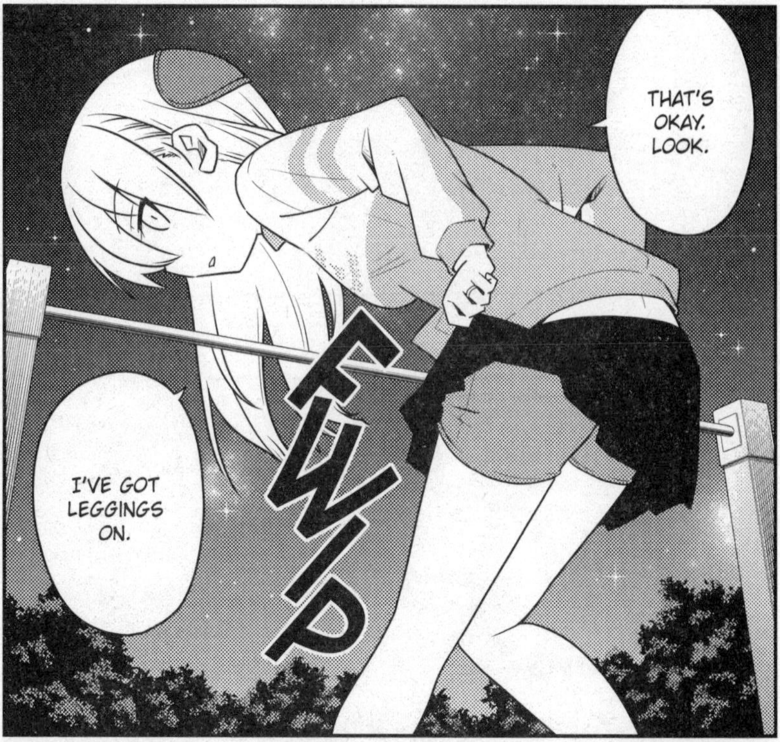
THAT'S OKAY. LOOK.
I'VE GOT LEGGINGS ON.
FWIP
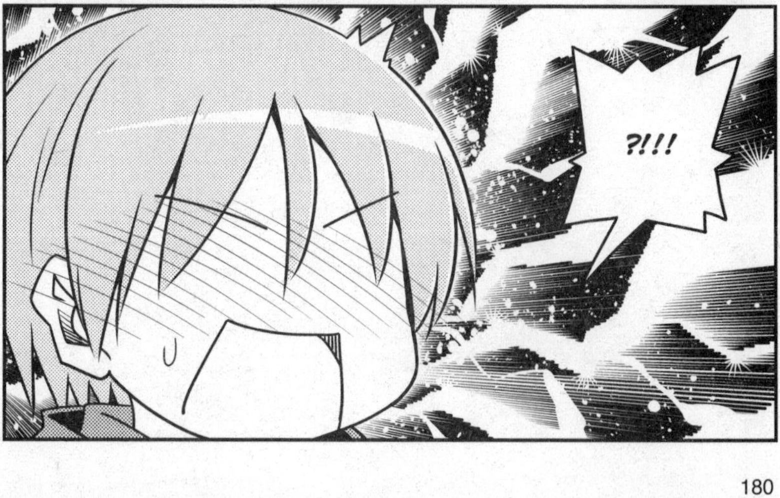
?!!!

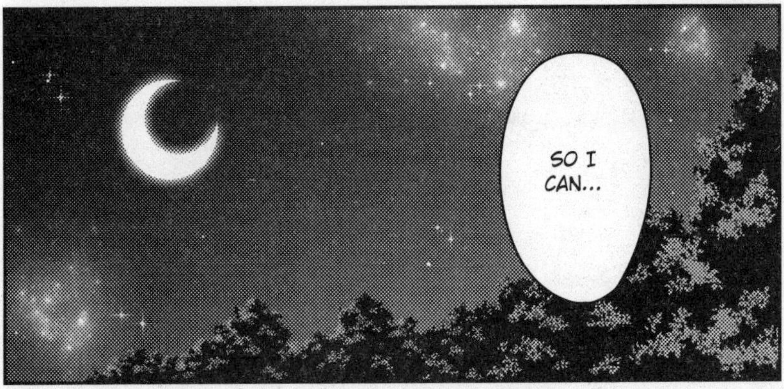
SO I CAN...

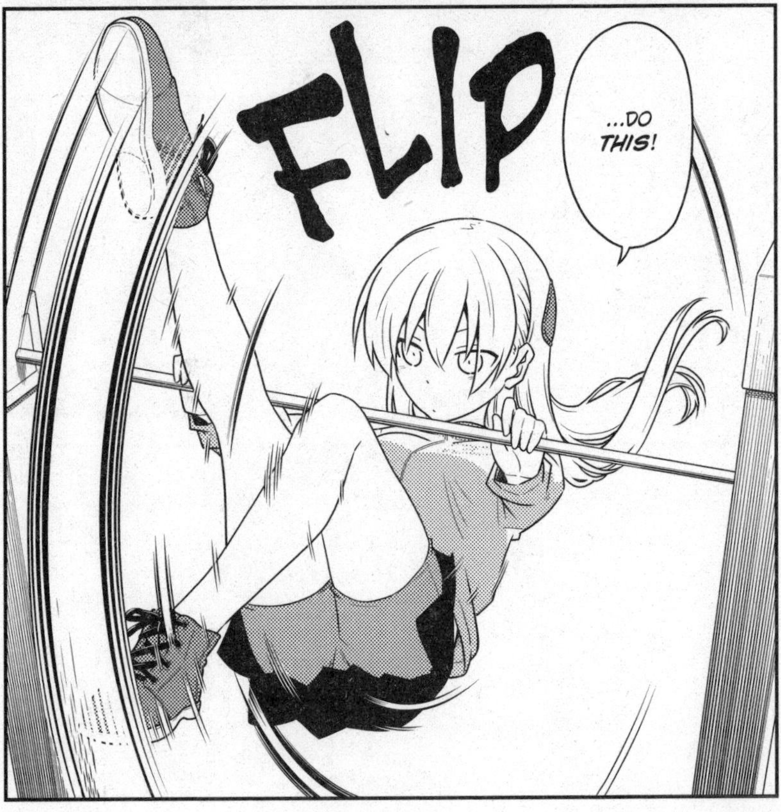
...DO THIS!
FLIP

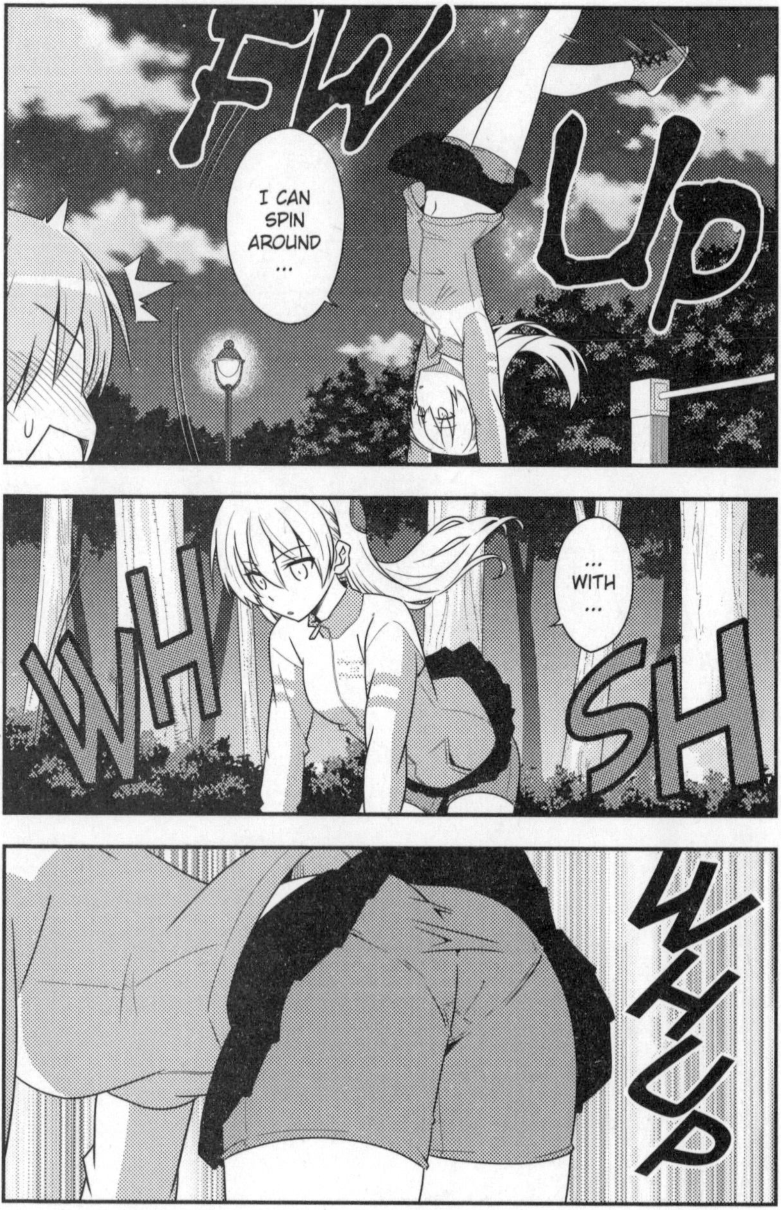
FW
UP
I CAN SPIN AROUND ...
WH
SH
... WITH ...
WHUP

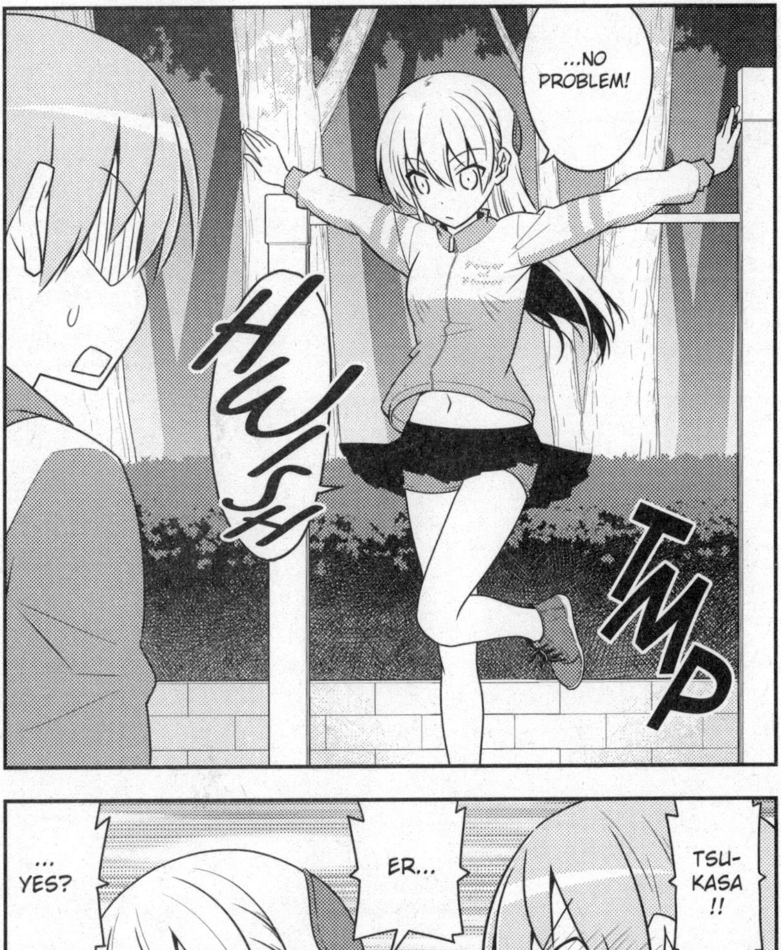
...NO PROBLEM!
TMP
HWISH
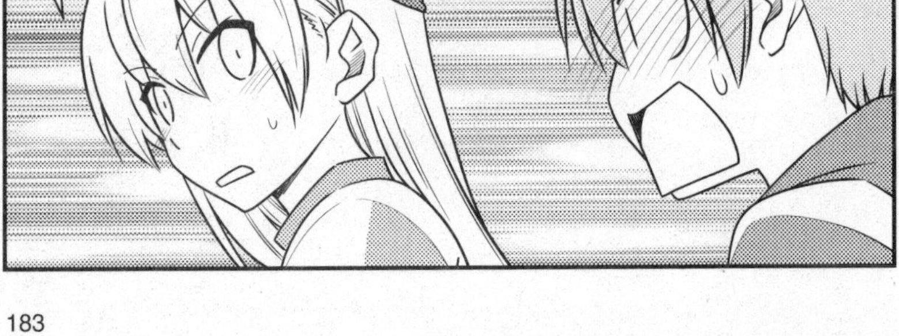
TSU-KASA !!
ER...
... YES?

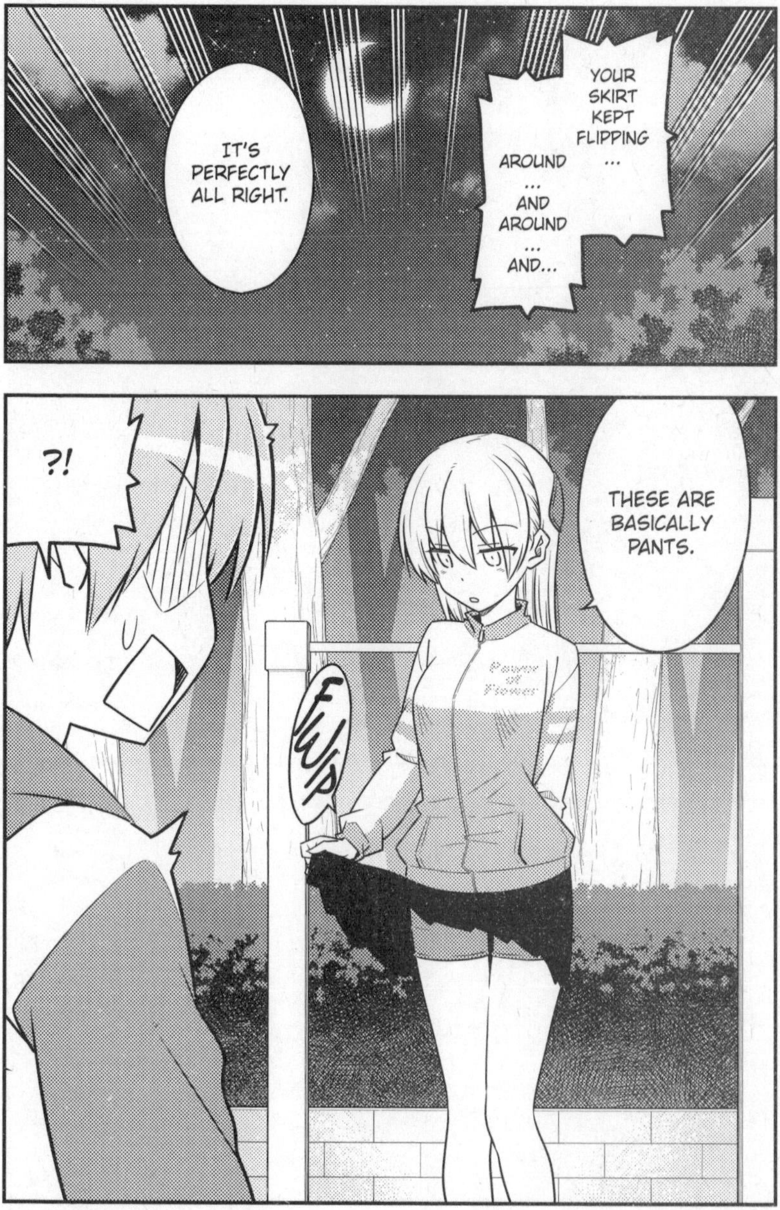
YOUR SKIRT KEPT FLIPPING ... AROUND ... AND AROUND ... AND...
IT'S PERFECTLY ALL RIGHT.
THESE ARE BASICALLY PANTS.
FWIP
?!
Power of Flower

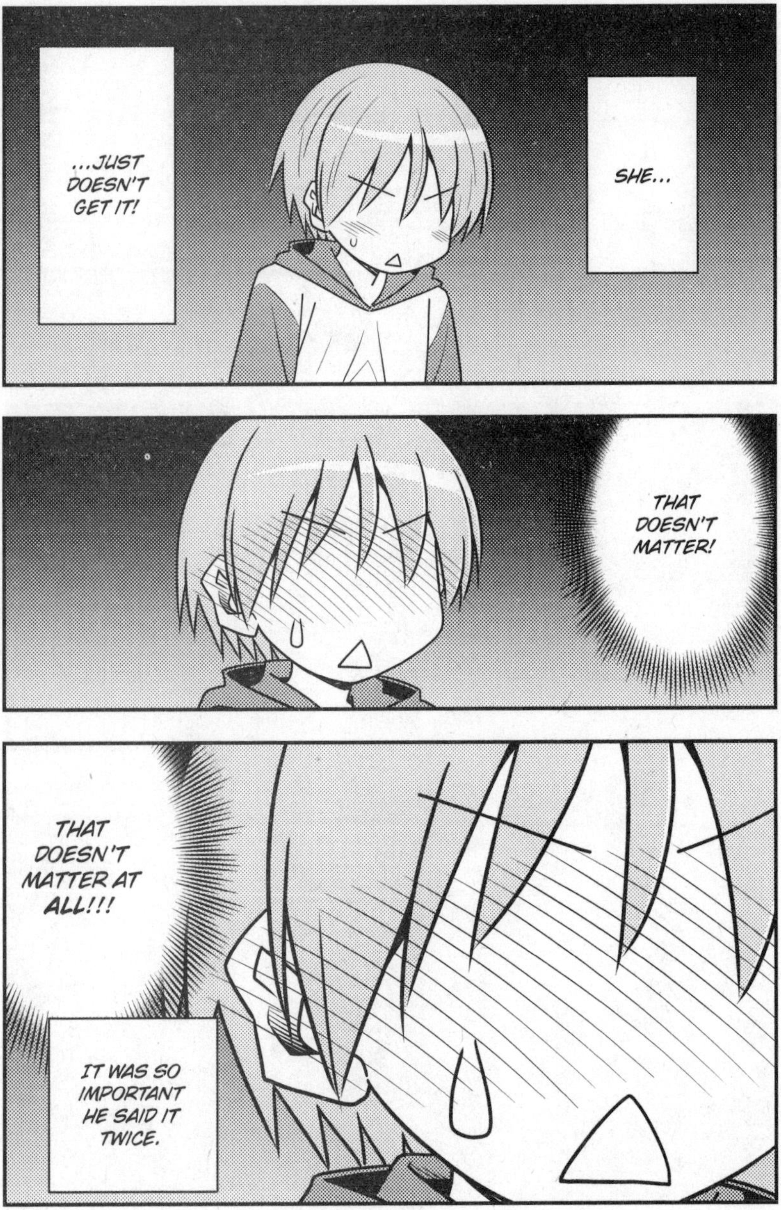

SHE...
...JUST DOESN'T GET IT!
THAT DOESN'T MATTER!
THAT DOESN'T MATTER AT ALL!!!
IT WAS SO IMPORTANT HE SAID IT TWICE.

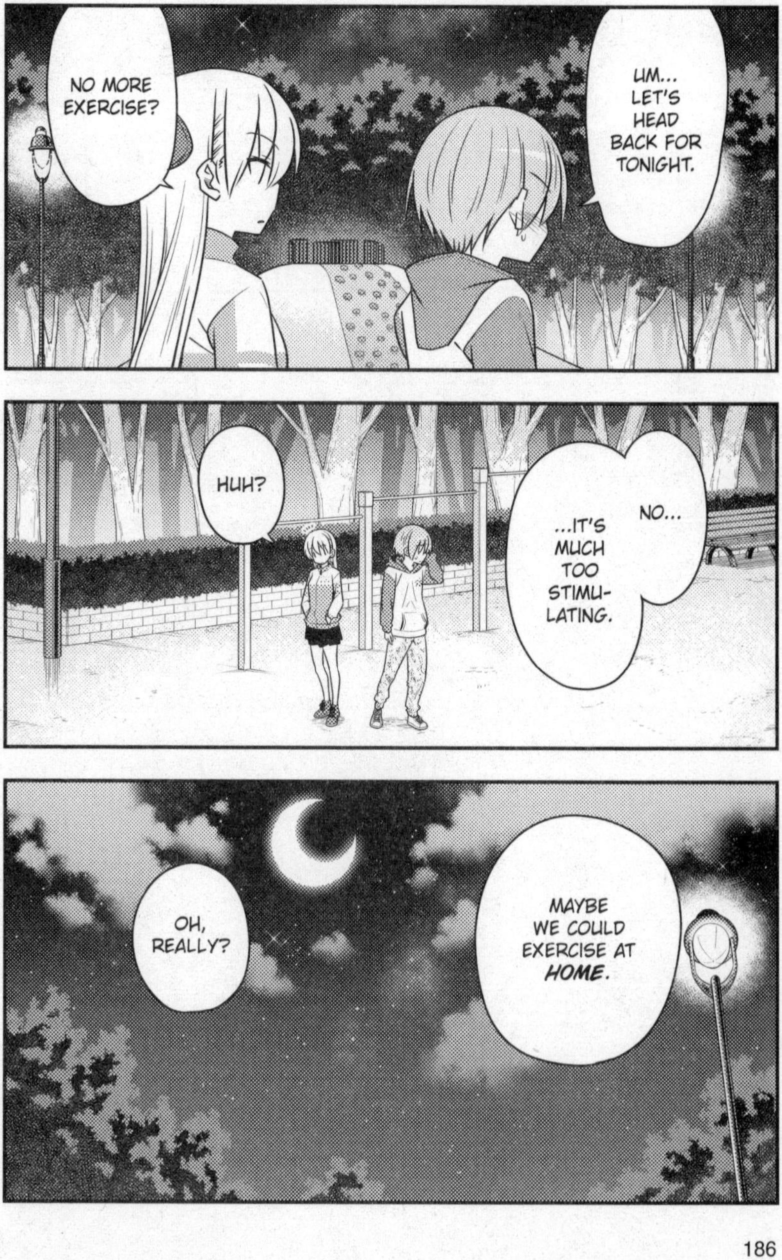
UM... LET'S HEAD BACK FOR TONIGHT.
NO MORE EXERCISE?
NO...
...IT'S MUCH TOO STIMU-LATING.
HUH?
MAYBE WE COULD EXERCISE AT HOME.
OH, REALLY?

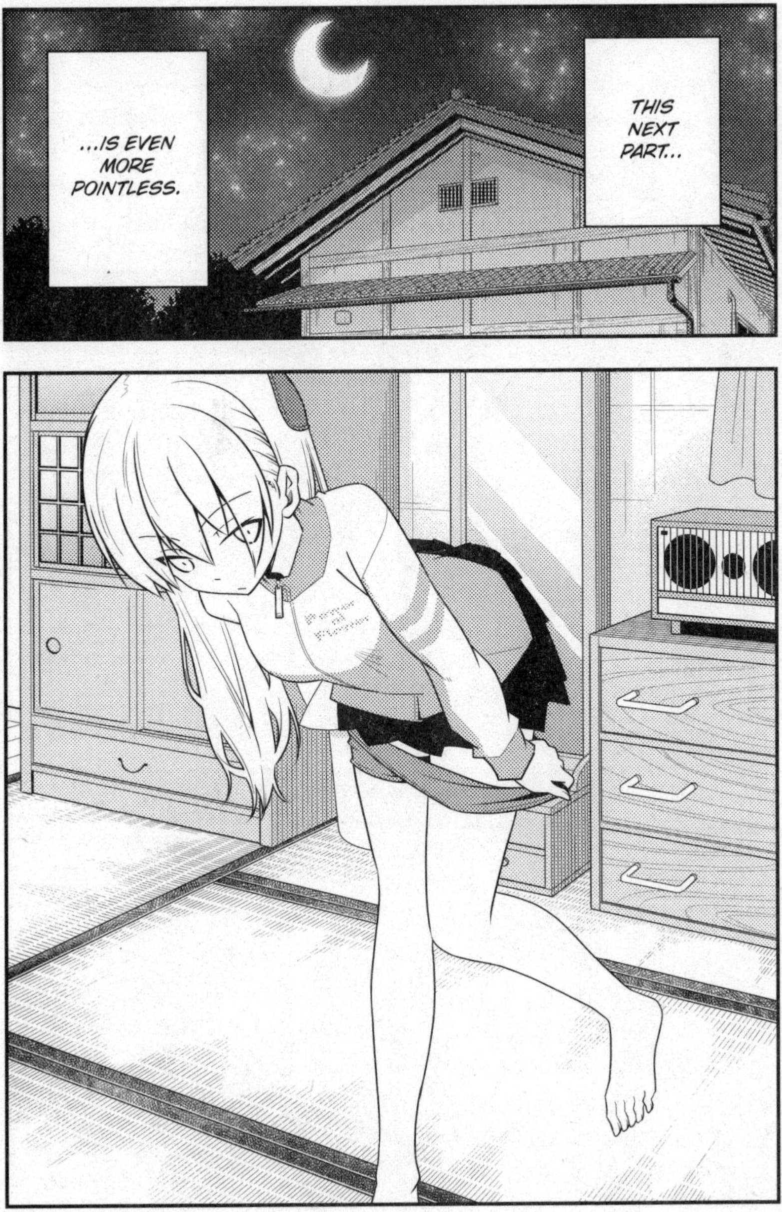
THIS NEXT PART...
...IS EVEN MORE POINTLESS.

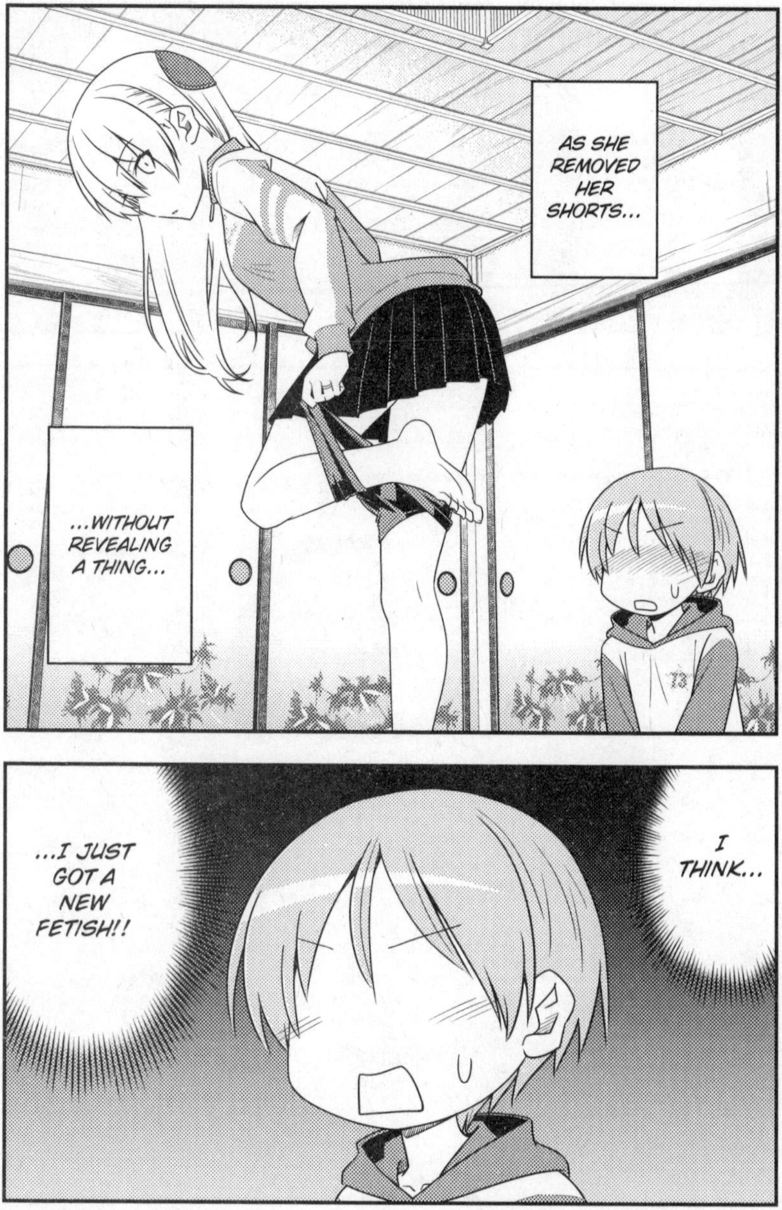
AS SHE REMOVED HER SHORTS...
...WITHOUT REVEALING A THING...
I THINK...
...I JUST GOT A NEW FETISH!!

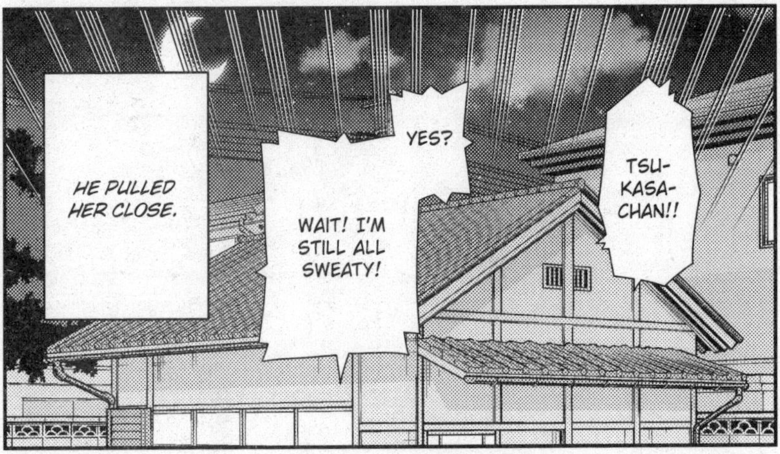
TSU-KASA-CHAN!!
YES?
WAIT! I'M STILL ALL SWEATY!
HE PULLED HER CLOSE.

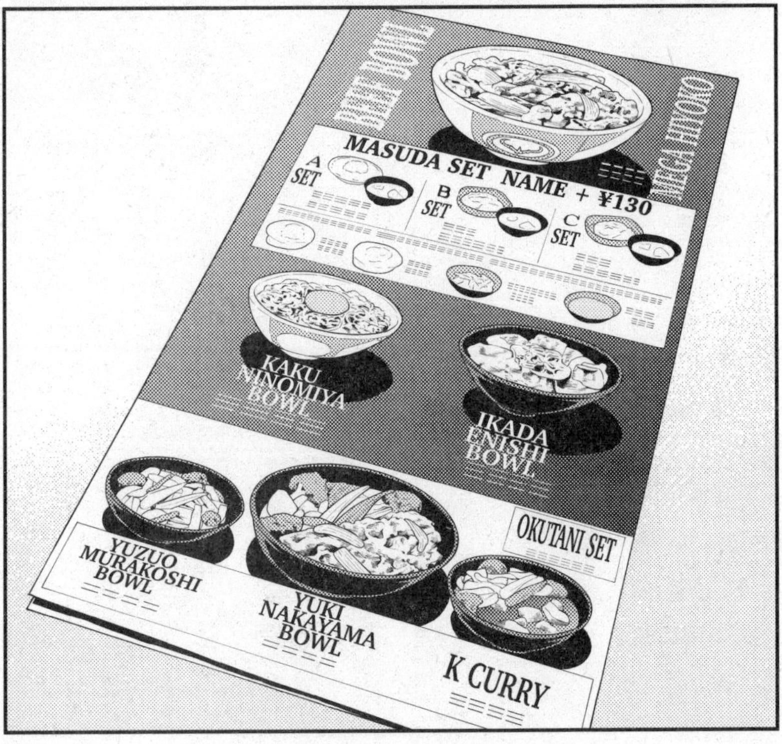
BEEF BOWL
MEGA HITOKO
MASUDA SET NAME + ¥130
A SET
B SET
C SET
KAKU NINOMIYA BOWL
IKADA ENISHI BOWL
OKUTANI SET
YUZUO MURAKOSHI BOWL
YUKI NAKAYAMA BOWL
K CURRY

Chapter 90 ½ / End

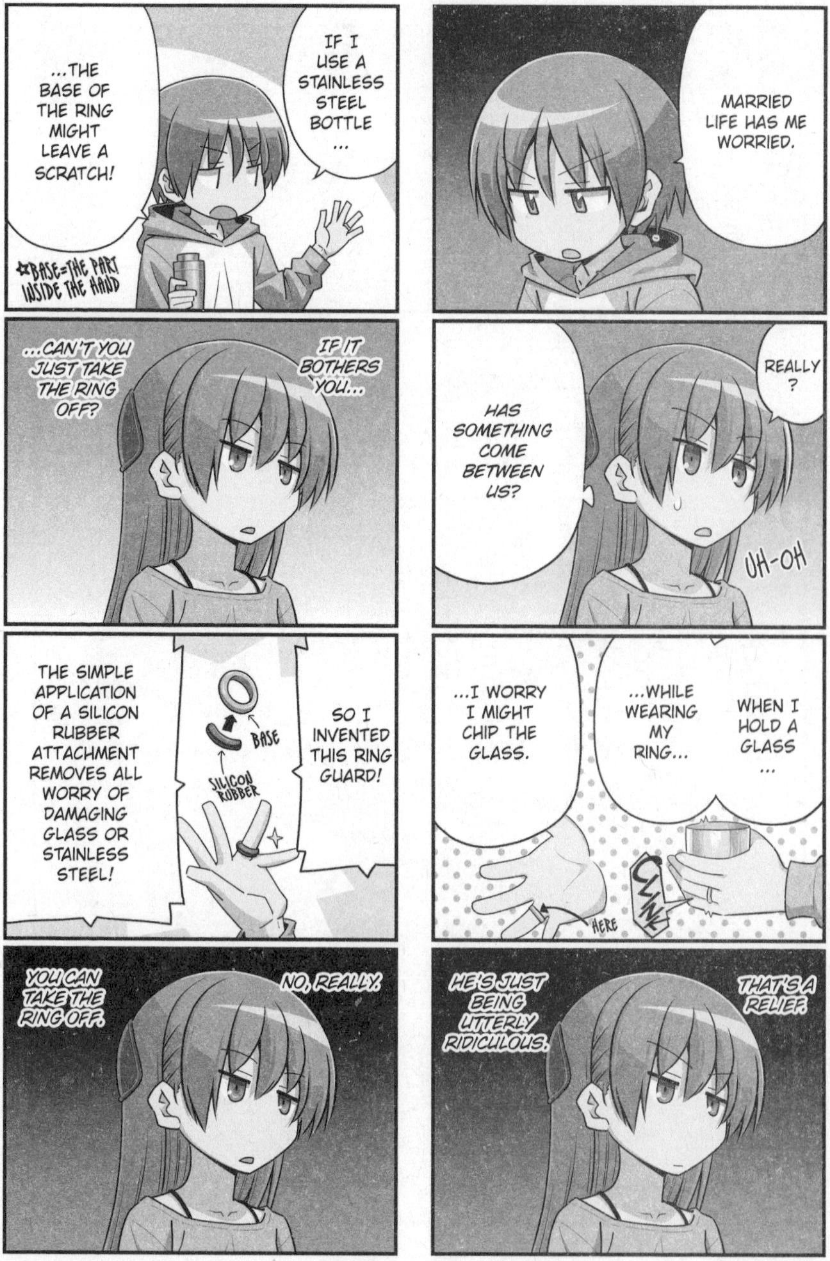
MARRIED LIFE HAS ME WORRIED.
REALLY ?
HAS SOMETHING COME BETWEEN US?
UH-OH
WHEN I HOLD A GLASS ...
...WHILE WEARING MY RING...
...I WORRY I MIGHT CHIP THE GLASS.
CLINK
HERE
THAT'S A RELIEF.
HE'S JUST BEING UTTERLY RIDICULOUS.
IF I USE A STAINLESS STEEL BOTTLE ...
...THE BASE OF THE RING MIGHT LEAVE A SCRATCH!
☆BASE=THE PART INSIDE THE HAND
IF IT BOTHERS YOU...
...CAN'T YOU JUST TAKE THE RING OFF?
SO I INVENTED THIS RING GUARD!
BASE
SILICON RUBBER
THE SIMPLE APPLICATION OF A SILICON RUBBER ATTACHMENT REMOVES ALL WORRY OF DAMAGING GLASS OR STAINLESS STEEL!
NO, REALLY.
YOU CAN TAKE THE RING OFF.

Fly Me to the Moon

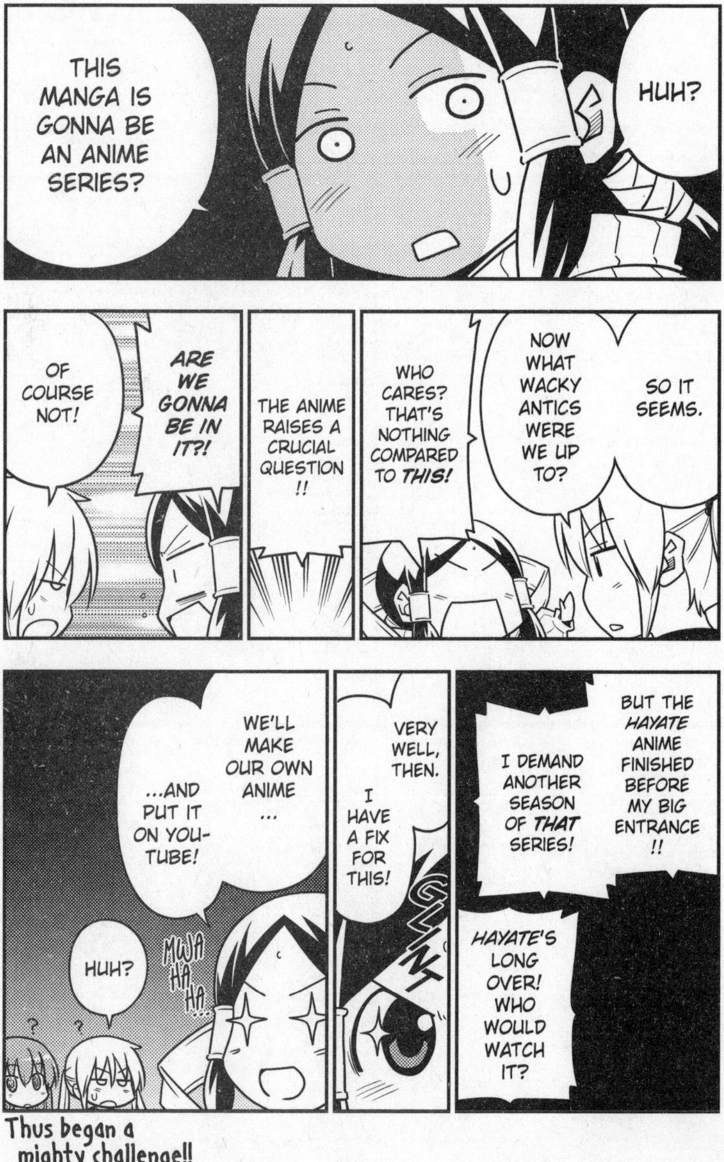
HUH?
THIS MANGA IS GONNA BE AN ANIME SERIES?
SO IT SEEMS.
NOW WHAT WACKY ANTICS WERE WE UP TO?
WHO CARES? THAT'S NOTHING COMPARED TO *THIS!*
THE ANIME RAISES A CRUCIAL QUESTION!!
ARE WE GONNA BE IN IT?!
OF COURSE NOT!
BUT THE *HAYATE* ANIME FINISHED BEFORE MY BIG ENTRANCE!!
I DEMAND ANOTHER SEASON OF *THAT* SERIES!
HAYATE'S LONG OVER! WHO WOULD WATCH IT?
VERY WELL, THEN.
I HAVE A FIX FOR THIS!
GLINT
WE'LL MAKE OUR OWN ANIME...
...AND PUT IT ON YOU-TUBE!
MWA HA HA...
HUH?

Thus began a mighty challenge!!

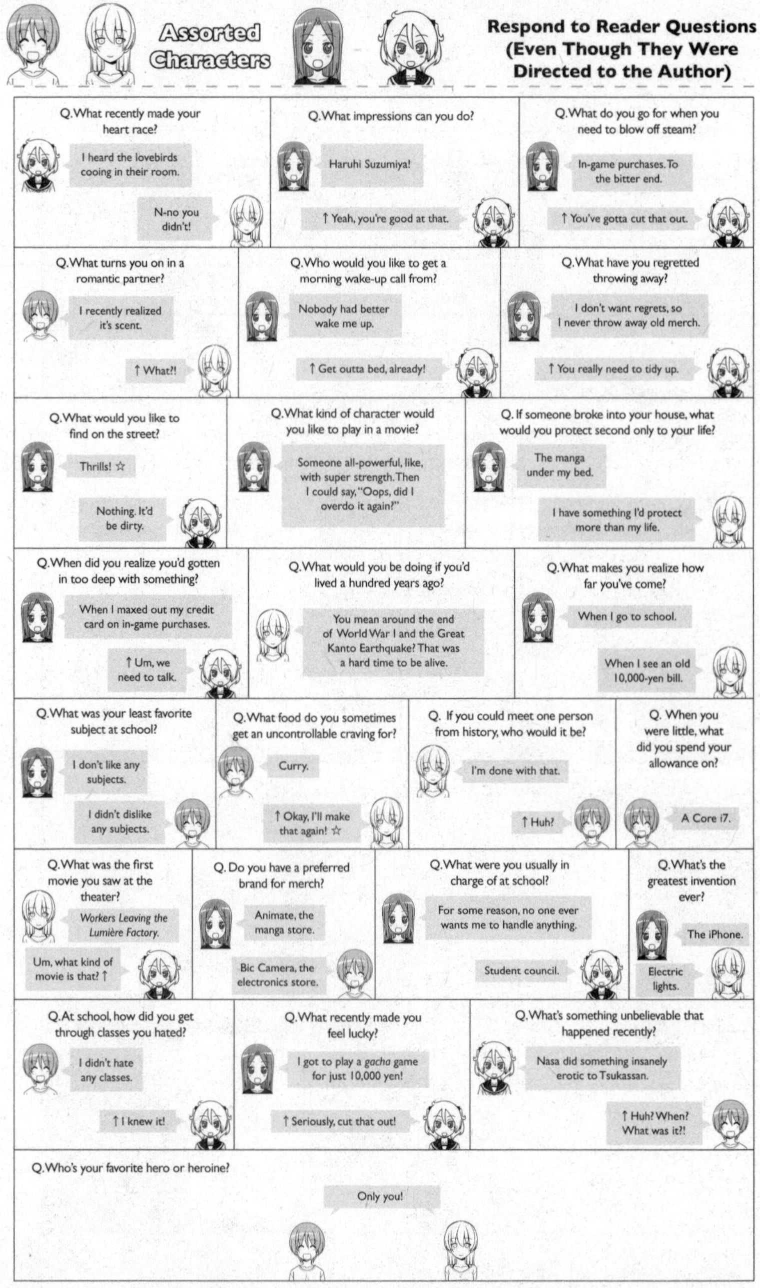
Respond to Reader Questions (Even Though They Were Directed to the Author)
Assorted Characters
Q.What do you go for when you need to blow off steam?
In-game purchases. To the bitter end.
↑ You've gotta cut that out.
Q.What impressions can you do?
Haruhi Suzumiya!
↑ Yeah, you're good at that.
Q.What recently made your heart race?
I heard the lovebirds cooing in their room.
N-no you didn't!
Q.What have you regretted throwing away?
I don't want regrets, so I never throw away old merch.
↑ You really need to tidy up.
Q.Who would you like to get a morning wake-up call from?
Nobody had better wake me up.
↑ Get outta bed, already!
Q.What turns you on in a romantic partner?
I recently realized it's scent.
↑ What?!
Q. If someone broke into your house, what would you protect second only to your life?
The manga under my bed.
I have something I'd protect more than my life.
Q.What kind of character would you like to play in a movie?
Someone all-powerful, like, with super strength. Then I could say, "Oops, did I overdo it again?"
Q.What would you like to find on the street?
Thrills! ☆
Nothing. It'd be dirty.
Q.What makes you realize how far you've come?
When I go to school.
When I see an old 10,000-yen bill.
Q.What would you be doing if you'd lived a hundred years ago?
You mean around the end of World War I and the Great Kanto Earthquake? That was a hard time to be alive.
Q.When did you realize you'd gotten in too deep with something?
When I maxed out my credit card on in-game purchases.
↑ Um, we need to talk.
Q. When you were little, what did you spend your allowance on?
A Core i7.
Q. If you could meet one person from history, who would it be?
I'm done with that.
↑ Huh?
Q.What food do you sometimes get an uncontrollable craving for?
Curry.
↑ Okay, I'll make that again! ☆
Q.What was your least favorite subject at school?
I don't like any subjects.
I didn't dislike any subjects.
Q.What's the greatest invention ever?
The iPhone.
Electric lights.
Q.What were you usually in charge of at school?
For some reason, no one ever wants me to handle anything.
Student council.
Q. Do you have a preferred brand for merch?
Animate, the manga store.
Bic Camera, the electronics store.
Q.What was the first movie you saw at the theater?
Workers Leaving the Lumière Factory.
Um, what kind of movie is that? ↑
Q.What's something unbelievable that happened recently?
Nasa did something insanely erotic to Tsukassan.
↑ Huh? When? What was it?!
Q.What recently made you feel lucky?
I got to play a *gacha* game for just 10,000 yen!
↑ Seriously, cut that out!
Q.At school, how did you get through classes you hated?
I didn't hate any classes.
↑ I knew it!
Q.Who's your favorite hero or heroine?
Only you!

ABOUT THE AUTHOR

Without ever receiving any kind of manga award,
Kenjiro Hata's first series, *Umi no Yuusha Lifesavers*,
was published in *Shonen Sunday Super*. He followed
that up with his smash hit *Hayate the Combat Butler*.
Fly Me to the Moon began serialization in 2018
in *Weekly Shonen Sunday*.

FLY ME TO THE MOON

VOL. 10

Story and Art by **KENJIRO HATA**

SHONEN SUNDAY EDITION

TONIKAKUKAWAII Vol. 10
by Kenjiro HATA
© 2018 Kenjiro HATA
All rights reserved.
Original Japanese edition published by SHOGAKUKAN.
English translation rights in the United States of America,
Canada, the United Kingdom, Ireland, Australia and New
Zealand arranged with SHOGAKUKAN.

Original Cover Design: Emi Nakano (BANANA GROVE STUDIO)

Translation
John Werry

Touch-Up Art & Lettering
Evan Waldinger

Design
Jimmy Presler

Editor
Shaenon K. Garrity

Printed in the U.S.A.

Published by VIZ Media, LLC
P.O. Box 77010
San Francisco, CA 94107

10 9 8 7 6 5 4 3 2 1
First printing, March 2022

viz.com

shonensunday.com

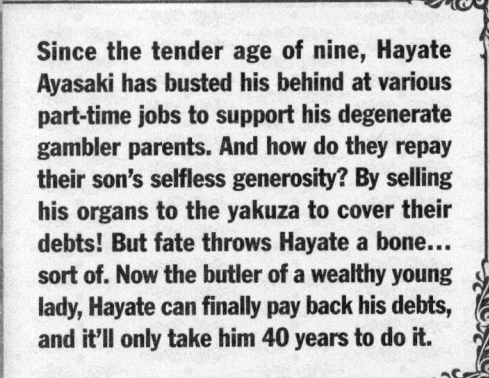

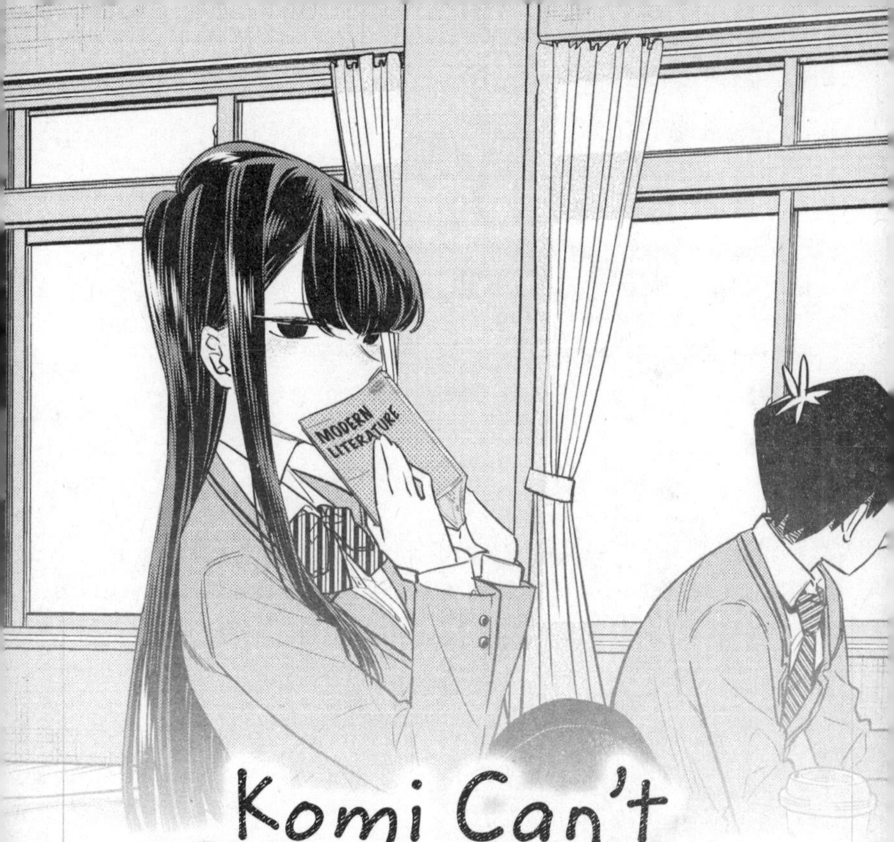
MODERN LITERATURE

Komi Can't Communicate

Story & Art by Tomohito Oda

The journey to a hundred friends begins with a single conversation.

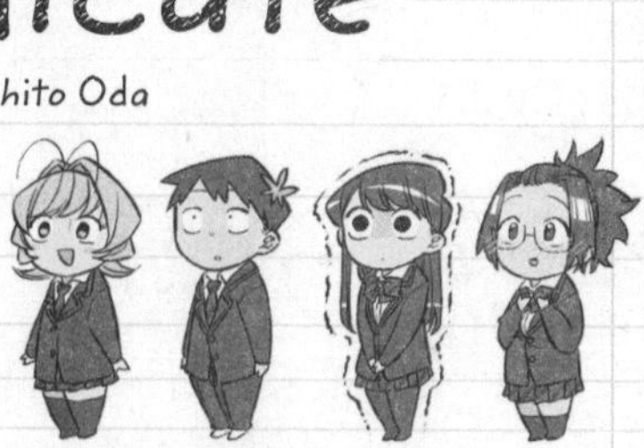

Socially anxious high school student Shoko Komi's greatest dream is to make some friends, but everyone at school mistakes her crippling social anxiety for cool reserve. With the whole student body keeping its distance and Komi unable to utter a single word, friendship might be forever beyond her reach.

Can Detective Conan solve the toughest cases ....while trapped in a kid's body?

CASE CLOSED™

Story and Art by
Gosho Aoyama

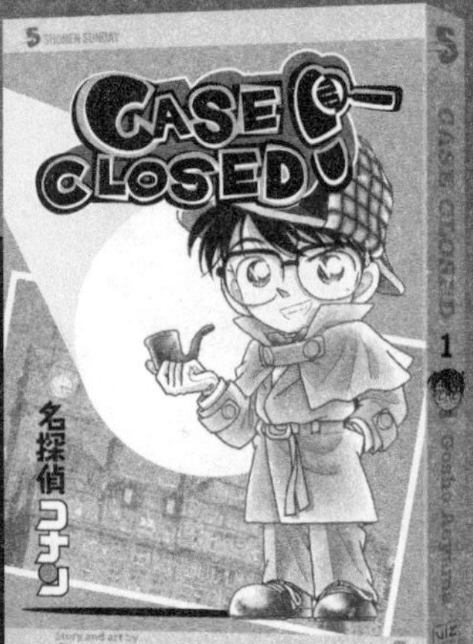
SHONEN SUNDAY
CASE CLOSED
名探偵コナン
Story and art by
Gosho Aoyama
Vol. 1
CASE CLOSED 1 Gosho Aoyama
VIZ

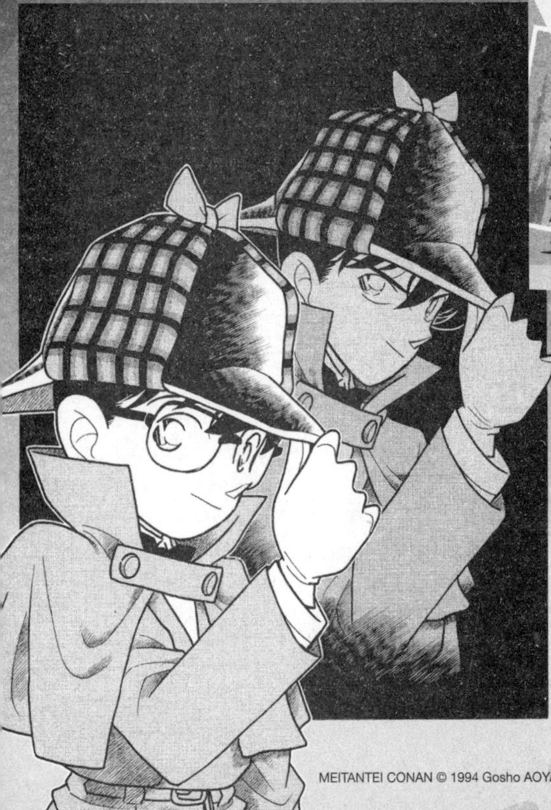

High schooler Jimmy Kudo has had many successes in his young detective career. But what will he do when a pair of shady men feed him a poison that turns him into a little kid?

RATED T+ OLDER TEEN

VIZ

MAO

Exorcise your destiny in an era-spanning supernatural adventure from manga legend Rumiko Takahashi!

Story and Art by
RUMIKO TAKAHASHI

When Nanoka travels back in time to a supernatural early 20th century, she gets recruited by aloof exorcist Mao. What is the thread of fate that connects them? Together, they seek answers...and kick some demon butt along the way!